THE GAME
COOKBOOK

THE GAME COOKBOOK

Geraldine Steindler

Stoeger Publishing Company

Third printing February 1988

Published by Stoeger Publishing Company
55 Ruta Court
South Hackensack, New Jersey 07606

International Standard Book Number (ISBN): 0-88317-111-2
Library of Congress Catalog Card Number: 84-51364
Manufactured in the United States of America

Distributed to the book trade and to the sporting goods trade in the U.S. by Stoeger Industries, 55 Ruta Court, South Hackensack, New Jersey 07606; in Canada, by Stoeger Canada Ltd., Unit 16, 1801 Wentworth St., Whitby, Ontario L1N 5S4

*To a cook's greatest inspiration—
good trenchermen—and most particularly
to those who have graced our table*

SPECIAL THANKS

To:

My Mother and Dad—for suffering through my earliest attempts in the kitchen and teaching me pride in culinary skill.

My Mother-in-law—for introducing me to a whole new world of cooking, the Viennese way.

My husband—who somehow was able to live through all my culinary creations.

Chris Klineburger—although he never did tell me exactly how to make Eskimo ice cream.

That fine old gent, Popowski—for his gems of wisdom during a memorable hunt.

Mrs. G.C.F. Dalziel of Watson Lake, Yukon—for her Northern specialties, and *The Whitehorse Star,* for permission to reprint recipes originally published in *The Whitehorse Star,* Whitehorse, Yukon.

T.F. Stepnowski—for his fine illustrations.

Ray Wells—for his luscious cover photo.

Caryn Seifer—for her crisp book design.

Charlene S. Cruson—for not only helping to revise the book as project editor, but also for some of her own original recipes.

ABOUT THE AUTHOR

Gerry Steindler with prized pronghorn she shot herself.

Once a cook, always a cook. And that's certainly true of Geraldine (Gerry) Steindler. The first edition of her *Game Cookbook* was published in 1965 and, during its 12 reprintings, she continued to experiment, refine and adapt recipes. In this completely revised and expanded *Game Cookbook*, she adds more than 135 new dishes to hundreds of favorites already loved by game aficionados everywhere.

Gerry was raised in a family whose interest in food was more than just "eating three squares a day." Her grandfather was a confectioner, an uncle was a caterer and all members of her clan were hearty eaters, to say the least. Gerry was routinely accustomed to preparing entire dinners before she even graduated high school. When she married avid hunter and gun editor R.A. (Bob) Steindler, she naturally extended her talents to game cookery.

What surprised her in those early years was not the cooking of game so much as the hunting of it. Bob had suggested that she become a shooter—an idea that had horrified her at first. Eventually she became an expert in her own right, enjoying the hunt as enthusiastically as her spouse. The above photo shows her with a pronghorn antelope she bagged herself. All this means she knows not only how to prepare the game once it gets into the kitchen, but also learned first-hand what to do with it before it reached the back porch. And she tells with simplicity and directness how you should field dress game and generally prepare it before you give it to the cook.

Because of her husband's background (his mother brought a collection of Old-World recipes with her from Austria) and her own European ancestry, Gerry calls her compilation of game recipes a "culinary United Nations." (*See* Chapter 4, for example, "All You Can Do With Burger"—it's a virtual smörgasbord of international fixings.) She downplays her numerous hunting trips across the continent, but, as you will see, those experiences have added enormously to her facility at camp cooking, which she details herein. Other travels and her insatiable interest in food sparked ideas for the game adaptations you will find for many native American and Canadian dishes as well.

So you have in this new, completely revised edition of the *Game Cookbook* an extensive and sumptuous selection of game recipes written by a hunter and cook whose expertise is readily evident. And you'll be amused by the personal anecdotes she sprinkles throughout.

We at Stoeger Publishing take pride in presenting this new volume of game cookery and take pleasure in knowing you will enjoy reading—and tasting—the recipes.

—*The Editor*

PREFACE

In the more than 20 years since I wrote the first edition of the *Game Cookbook*, much has changed in the kitchen. The food processor was introduced, the microwave oven, the convection oven and such items as Teflon and Silver Stone coated cookware. All have contributed to revolutionize the way in which—and the speed with which—contemporary cooks approach food. It still amazes me how fast I can whip up a carrot salad by simply pushing the peeled vegetables down the feed tube of my food processor; in literally seconds I have a mound of grated carrots where previously I toiled for 15 minutes grating them by hand. Not only did it take a long time, but occasionally my fingers got scraped along with the carrots. Thank goodness for some modern technology.

Despite these revolutionary kitchen aids, however, some things have remained the same. No matter how I try, I cannot brown a venison roast in a microwave oven to my satisfaction. I must and will continue to use my conventional oven. It's the only way I can seal in those savory juices and roast it to medium-rare as my husband and I like it. And what could replace cooking over a crackling campfire in the deep woods with a cloudless sky overhead? To my mind, nothing.

Perhaps that's one of the reasons more and more people are experiencing a renewed interest in eating game. It's a psychological return to the wilderness, an emotional hiatus from cluttered urbanization, encroaching computerization and, in my opinion, an overly complex society. It's a searching for a simpler age in which, when you put your feet on the ground, you knew where they were and where they were headed. You didn't have to worry or wonder about what tomorrow would bring.

Another reason for the return-to-game trend is that recent nutrition research has revealed that game is lower in fat and cholesterol than domesticated beef or pork. Health-minded moderns are all for that.

In addition, in many circles game is simply becoming fashionable to serve. I read countless food magazines and cookbooks in which I am now commonly seeing recipes for partridge, quail, venison stews and the like. So here we are at almost the 21st century rediscovering a taste preference the Colonists enjoyed (born somewhat out of necessity) back in the 17th century!

Beyond all this, however, and important to those who really love to eat, game has good taste. If you've ever sampled a venison steak properly seared on a grill—well, you'll never go back to beef. No gamy flavor here—if it's done right.

My purpose in revising the *Game Cookbook* is four-fold: to satisfy the growing interest in game cooking; to dispel the misconception that lingers in some minds about the "gamy" taste of game; to assist cooks in choosing and preparing dishes that complement game; and to add, to a book already warmly accepted by game cooks, more than 135 savory recipes I've developed since the first edition was published.

Among the new features of this book are an expanded chapter devoted solely to the preparation of antlered game—the tastiest steaks, stews, ribs and roasts from deer, elk, moose and caribou. A separate chapter of interesting dishes belongs to the other big game—bear, wild boar, pronghorn, mountain goat and sheep—while other chapters emphasize small game, upland birds, waterfowl and fish.

You will find a host of recipes to help you consume all the burger you'll wind up with when you bag your own big game animal, plus instructions for mixing your own sausage. How to disguise game leftovers? You'll discover a number of tricks for turning leftovers into luscious luncheon dishes and Sunday night casseroles. For the daring (and knowing), there is a special section on how best to prepare those delectable variety meats—the liver, heart, kidneys and tongue (moose nose, too!).

Cooks are frequently perplexed at what to serve *with* game and here's where I think my *Game Cookbook* can be particularly useful. I've included dozens of recipes on sauces and garnishes, game and non-game appetizers, soups and stuffings, vegetables and herbs, and breads and desserts—all designed to help the cook create the most elegant Epicurean feast or the simplest campsite supper.

In addition, I've peppered the pages with hints to the cook—tips and shortcuts I've gleaned through the years—and have pinpointed, based on my own experiences cooking on hunting trips, those dishes that are suitable for preparation at camp or on the home grill.

All in all, I hope the *Game Cookbook* will show you how easy it is to prepare, whether you are in your home kitchen or at camp, a delicious game meal—complete with all the trimmings.

Good game eating!

Gerry Steindler
Mapleton, Illinois

CONTENTS

CONTENTS (cont.)

CHAPTER 1
SUCCESSFUL GAME COOKERY

For many of us, hunting has become a delightful—and necessary—escape from the demands of our nuclear era. Every year more people—women as well as men—are taking to the woods and fields with shotgun, rifle, bow and arrow or black powder for relaxation and pleasure, and perhaps a psychological return to a simpler, less technological age. You'd think, therefore, that we would enjoy a keen interest in game on the dining table—and, at last, that seems to be so! To my great delight, more and more do I find game recipes in food magazines and on restaurant menus. Emphasis on good health, low-cholesterol lean meats and dishes with "new" flavor combinations has turned many cooks toward an "old" source: wild game.

It used to be that whenever my husband and I discussed hunting and confessed our preference for game over "store-bought" meats, listeners' expressions ranged from disbelief to ill-concealed sympathy for the poor wife who had to cook the gamy stuff her spouse brought home. We used to receive game from crestfallen hunters whose wives wouldn't—or didn't know how to—cook it. Even our offers of deliciously prepared game to guests used to be refused or, at best, accepted with reservation. Now, however, most of our acquaintances indulge in game dinners with great eagerness, and are always trading recipes or experimenting on their own. Oh, there are still a few reluctant diners, but for the most part, times have changed.

The early settlers of North America depended on the bountiful wild game for their very existence. While it was everyday fare for the backwoodsman, game also graced the most festive tables in Colonial Williamsburg. In Victorian days, the market hunters ravaged the herds and flocks to satisfy the ever-increasing demands of connoisseurs of that elegant—and often overstuffed—era of dining. Today, even if you've never hunted in your life or tasted game, you can find rabbit, pheasant and quail in the freezer compartment of your local supermarket. If you haven't noticed them, take a look—you'll be surprised. The only difference between these animals and the ones you'd take down yourself is that the market-freezer varieties are probably domesticated—and do taste somewhat "tamer" than the true wild animals. It pleases me, though, to see our eating patterns improving and expanding.

Which leads me to the core of the lingering controversy about the taste of wild game, the so-called "gaminess" that pervades some dishes. In my experience, I've found that the gaminess often objected to is simply spoiled or tainted meat, caused by neglect or lack of knowledge on the hunter's part. It is true that an animal's diet does affect the flavor of the meat. A bear feeding on carrion or prowling the garbage dumps certainly cannot be compared with one grown fat on nuts and berries. And there will naturally be a vast difference in flavor between ducks feeding on fish and those feeding on wild celery. The mating season also affects the flavor and texture of the meat of big game animals—unfavorably so! However, these elements of chance are part and parcel of the hunting game. What *is* distressing is the fact that too many pounds of superb meat are wasted each year by conditions over which the hunter *does* have control.

No cook worthy of his or her salt should be expected to work miracles in the kitchen with improperly cared-for game. In fact, it's impossible! Therefore, as a part-time hunter as well as a full-time cook, I shall venture away from the pots and pans long enough for a discussion of those all-important procedures before the chef takes over.

PLAN AHEAD

Caring for game actually begins before you leave home for your hunting trip, whether it be three weeks in a mountain wilderness or a morning's stroll through a nearby shooting preserve. Guns, boots, camping gear, hunter—all set and raring to go! But what about the game you're going to bring home? Oh, sure, your well-sharpened hunting knife is on your belt—but do you have a pocket stone to *keep* it sharp? If you're not going with a guide, what about a hatchet for quartering that bull moose or trophy-sized deer? It may be a long trek back to your hunting vehicle after your noble prize is down, and quartering the beast on the spot may be your only way of getting it out. A few good-sized, heavy-weight plastic sacks take no space at all in a pocket of your hunting coat and are mighty handy for bringing out the treasured heart and liver. Of course, you don't mind a bit of blood on your hunting coat, but it doesn't do the liver much good to be associated with the debris that always collects in hunters' pockets.

Large sacks made of lightweight canvas (or even sturdy muslin bed sheets) are invaluable for keeping dust and flies from the meat. Cheesecloth, frequently suggested for this purpose, is practically useless in rough country; it tears readily and does not really keep out the dust. Our meat sacks are 5 feet long by 3 feet wide, large enough to accommodate a fair-sized critter without struggle. Figure 2 yards of 72-inch lightweight canvas or unbleached cotton duck per sack. Make a double fold of material on each seam, stitch each seam twice with heavy-duty thread, and provide a sturdy drawstring at the top. It doesn't take too long to whip them up on the sewing machine and they can be washed and reused for years.

Even an hour's drive to a shooting preserve calls for a bit of advance preparation. When we were training our young springer pup, we always took along a portable cooler with a few cans of Scotch Ice on our jaunts to the preserve. Early fall days can be mighty warm in most parts of the country, and that cooler prevented many a disastrously parboiled pheasant.

Is this advance preparation "counting your chickens before they're hatched?" Not as far as we are concerned. If we're skunked, so be it. If we connect, we've made sure the game arrives home in edible condition.

THE GUN AND THE SHOT

Far be it from me to add my voice to the ever-raging controversy over gun calibers. But *do* suit your gun to the game you're after and to the country in which you're hunting. A caliber adequate for a clean kill on elk or moose is just too much for a pronghorn. Likewise, a flat shooting rifle capable of downing an antelope at 300 yards in open country is of little use in the heavy brush of the Maine woods.

Use a caliber of rifle and a bullet weight sufficient to kill quickly and cleanly. A wounded and frightened animal that runs is usually so full of adrenalin that you might just as well bury the meat and chew on the hide, once you have tracked him down and ended his suffering. On the other hand, too large a caliber or too heavy a bullet for the job at hand will cause extensive meat damage. Even a well-placed lung shot in this situation may cause so much internal damage that the visceral cavity is punctured by bone fragments.

I think most hunters will agree that a well-placed shot just behind the shoulder will down an animal effectively with little meat damage. A brain or neck shot is not only more difficult because of the small lethal area involved, but it may ruin a lovely head. A spinal shot is certainly a disabling one, but don't plan on too many chops from your animal in this case. A shot in the midsection is to be avoided if at all possible—it may be fatal, but it certainly is messy and the chances are excellent that the meat will be tainted by the spillage from the viscera.

FIELD DRESSING

Big Game. As soon as your animal is down—and do make certain it is actually dead and not just stunned—get the photographs taken in a hurry and then roll up your sleeves. You have a job ahead of you that should be accomplished without delay! Since the body heat of the animal encourages bacterial decay, it is important to remove the innards and allow the carcass to cool as quickly as possible.

Decide now whether or not you wish to have a head mount, as some of your cuts in the field dressing will vary as you proceed. Then, too, greater care must be taken to keep the head and cape hair free from blood if it is to adorn your den wall at some future date.

Exactly how you proceed with the field dressing is a matter of individual preference. Six experienced hunters will give you six slightly different approaches to the matter. The subject has been thoroughly discussed in books and magazines countless times, complete with diagrams. Stoeger has published *Dress 'Em Out,* which does an excellent, detailed job and would serve as a good companion to this book. Several points do bear repetition, however, if you plan to bring home prime meat.

If the animal has scent glands, and you choose to remove these first, be certain that all taint from these areas is *completely* scrubbed from hands as well as knife before you make any further incisions. Captain Jim Smith in *Dress 'Em Out* recommends carrying two knives, one expressly for gland removal.

Although the field dressing should be done with dispatch, especially if the weather is unseasonably warm, do proceed with caution. One hasty slash of the knife can spill the contents of the stomach, bladder or intestines into the body cavity and create just the sort of damage you so carefully avoided with your well-placed shot.

Once the innards have been removed, rescue the heart and liver. Remove the gall bladder from the liver without puncturing it, if one is present, by slicing out a small section of the liver along with it. Antlered game have no gall bladders, but the bovids— goat and sheep—do. Put the heart and liver in the plastic sack you carried along, slosh them around with water to remove the excess blood, then drain and set aside.

One source of spoiled meat has been removed with the innards, but you still have a few minutes' work on the carcass. If the animal is not on an incline with the head uphill, place it so. Spread the cavity wide, and scrub thoroughly with water to remove the blood and any body fluids that remain. Pay particular attention to the wound area. I shall probably be accused of rank heresy over this statement, but water, if at all available, is much preferable to grass or your handkerchief and is more efficient. Wipe the cavity dry and turn the animal upside down over a fence, a bush or downed timber—or hang it from a tree, head up—any method convenient under the circumstances to complete the drainage. To hasten the cooling process, keep the body cavity spread wide to allow for good circulation of air. Insert sticks if feasible.

While you contemplate your next move, let me toss in a suggestion. Although most hunters of our acquaintance don't bother with it, those who live entirely on game would not consider discarding the tongue of the antlered game—it is equally as delicious as beef tongue. Especially if you are not planning on a full head mount, remove the tongue, leaving on the skin and roots. A large moose tongue can be the basis of several delicious camp meals and has the same advantage as liver and heart— you can cook and eat it the same day it was removed from the animal.

Your next move depends entirely on where you are and how warm it is. If it's a long hike back to camp or your hunting vehicle and you have an elk or moose to cope with, skinning the animal on the spot and then quartering it would be most advantageous. This permits more rapid cooling of the meat, so essential with the larger animals. The quarters can then be packed out in the meat sacks you brought along. If you are alone, the sacked quarters should be hung in trees or raised off the ground in some fashion for air circulation until you can return with help.

If a deer must be transported any distance through the woods, the hide is best left on to protect the meat in the dragging or carrying process. Since deer are smaller, they do cool more rapidly than their larger cousins, and removing the hide can safely wait to be done in camp where it's more convenient. In rain or snow, the hide affords protection, especially if circumstances force you to hang your deer for a few days. Hang the deer head up for two reasons: drainage of fluid is better and rain or snow will run off the hide in the same direction as hair growth.

The picture changes drastically, of course, if the weather is warm. Get the hide off as fast as possible, hang in an airy place and then protect the meat from blow flies, dust and magpies with the meat sack drawn over the hanging carcass. No matter when you skin the carcass, trim away, right then and there, all bone splinters and every trace of blood-shot tissue.

Pronghorn, or antelope, are handled in much the same way as deer. Since it is usually warm during pronghorn season, the animal should be skinned just as soon as it has been hog-dressed. It is then hustled into a meat sack to protect it against the clouds of alkali dust and the swarms of flies that seem to appear from nowhere as soon as you start cutting.

Particular care should be taken during the entire operation not to touch the scent patches as you work and thus taint the meat. These patches will come off with the hide. To keep the brittle hairs from breaking off and spreading to the meat, roll the hide hair side under as you skin.

Hanging game to age or season it is another subject of controversy. *If* the weather is dry, *if* the temperature is about 30° to 40° F. (1° to 4° C.) and *if* it can be depended on not to fluctuate too much either way, fine and dandy—hang your game! But be sure it's hung away from predators. Since all these ideal conditions for proper hanging and aging are seldom found outside a butcher's cold room, it has been generally conceded that the sure way to preserve that wonderful meat in its most flavorful condition is to skin it as quickly as possible, cool it rapidly and freeze it without delay. I agree that freezing will not make a prime filet mignon out of a bull elk shoulder roast but then, neither will any amount of hanging. Rapid processing and freezing does, however, insure that the meat will suffer no further deterioration. Some professional butchers have stated in recent years that quick-freezing will accomplish the same tenderizing process as several weeks of hanging.

At the risk of sounding repetitious, I shall state once more what has been said by others thousands of times. It is still unheeded, so obviously needs repeating. DON'T display that unskinned carcass on the top of your car or draped over the radiator. You're only displaying your ignorance, not your prowess as a hunter.

On a trip West one year, we saw numerous animals transported thus. From the license plates, we knew the hunters had at least 12 to 18 hours' drive in 90° to 100° F. (32° to 38° C.) weather before that meat could be processed. Gas station attendants, waitresses in diners, scores of local people talked with us about it. The comment heard over and over was, "We like to see the hunters come, we like to see them get their game, but what a pity to see all that meat ruined! No wonder some folks say they don't like game—that meat is spoiled already!"

Game Birds. The very same principles apply to birds as to large game. Draw—remove crop and intestines—as soon after shooting as possible. The shot pellets can, and very often do, penetrate the internal organs, allowing seepage of the digestive juices and partially digested food into the flesh. In this way, you eliminate to a very large extent the fishy flavor of ducks and geese, and the bitter taste found in some grouse.

Dry-pluck the birds in the field as soon as feasible by pulling the feathers downward in the direction in which they grow. It is much easier to remove the feathers while the birds are still warm and there is also less danger of tearing the skin. (Your wife will also appreciate the lack of feathers in the basement.)

Clean the body cavity and transport the cleaned birds home in a well-iced portable cooler. The final removal of pinfeathers, plus any shot pellets that have penetrated the skin, can be done at home. Store cleaned birds, loosely covered with waxed paper, in the refrigerator for a few days before cooking—or package carefully and freeze. It is a wise idea to mark the packages accordingly if the birds have been badly damaged and would not be attractive for broiling or roasting.

Many of the old recipes call for hanging a bird, either plucked or in plumage, for several days to a week. This, of course, was before the days of central heating and a cool dry spot wasn't too hard to find. The same effect may be obtained by refrigerator storage at 45° F. (7° C.).

One final word: if you have older pheasants in your game bag (indicated by long, sharp claws) save time by skinning them, since they'll not be roasted anyhow. Cut off the feet and the first wing joints and unzip them from their overcoats—the shot pellets which have lodged just under the skin will go along with it.

Small Game. The smaller game animals are drawn, skinned and cleaned, and then stored in the same manner as birds. There are two precautions to be observed, however. Rabbits and opossums are both subject to tularemia. When hunting, beware of the sluggish or the frenzied rabbit, which may be infected with this disease. When cleaning and skinning these animals, either wear gloves or scrub your hands thoroughly *immediately* afterward, lest you become infected by the germ entering the bloodstream through a cut or scratch on your hand. If you discover a spotted liver as you draw a rabbit, proceed no further—just bury the critter then and there.

All of the smaller game animals, except squirrel and porcupine, have scent glands under the skin, along the spine and under the forelegs. The muskrat has an additional pair located in the pelvic region. Care should be taken when skinning not to cut these glands as they are removed.

Strip as much fat as possible from porcupine, opossum, raccoon, woodchuck and beaver before storing in refrigerator or packaging and freezing.

LOCKER PREPARATION AND HOME BUTCHERING

The larger animals—bear, boar and the antlered game—still have to be translated into the more familiar roasts and chops—and here you have several choices.

In many areas, freezer locker plants will do the entire job of cutting to your specifications, packaging and quick freezing at a reasonable cost. If you tell them beforehand when you plan to pick up your processed meat, in many instances they will have dry ice and insulated cartons available to insure your precious cargo on the trip home. Keep in mind, however, the fact that this is an extremely busy season for these people. They may not have the man power or the freezing facilities to do an overnight job for you.

If you have a reliable butcher at home, by all means make use of his speed and skill, as well as his familiarity with your preferences. But be certain *before* you leave on your hunt that he will tackle the job. Many butchers and locker plant owners in urban areas flatly refuse to handle game, or else charge excessive rates for processing to discourage the requests. We have asked quite a number of them why and the answer is an additional reason for the necessity of this chapter. In the past, they have handled game that was tainted or improperly cared for in some fashion and found that the odors permeated domestic meats hanging in the same cooler. There certainly could be no objection, though, if you bring in an animal that has been properly dressed and cooled, and *kept* cool with dry ice on the trip home.

Regardless of who does the butchering, be sure that all possible fat is removed from the meat, as this fat is the final contributor to the objectionable "gaminess" and its "off" flavor permeates the meat even in the freezer. An additional check for blood clots and damaged tissue to be removed should be made during the butchering. If your family is not overly fond of burgers, have the rib sections prepared for barbecuing and enjoy the added bonus of flank steaks. When you do have burgers ground, stress the fact that beef suet or pork be substituted for the game fat in whatever proportion you desire. At least a small amount of fat is essential for juicy burgers. Some old-timers, and they are indeed rare jewels, will even prepare sausage for you with their own jealously guarded herb blends.

Specify the thickness of steaks and chops—there's nothing more disappointing to a lover of rare meat than a paper thin chop or steak. And venison chops *are* most tender and flavorful when cooked rare. If you have a small family, order a few choice roasts cut to serve a larger number of people on gala occasions. One of our favorite stunts is to have the tenderloins removed whole, to be sliced as needed for filet mignons of the desired thickness. You might also consider a crown roast of venison, made of 12 ribs—a truly noble feast in the grand manner, for which I have included a recipe (*see* page 32).

You may get a raised eyebrow from the butcher on this next suggestion, but it is a good one. Ask him to collect all the bones in one or two packages to be used later for soup (*see* Chapter 11). Perhaps you can persuade him to bone and tie some of the roasts. Boned meat takes much less freezer space and there is less danger of the wrapping being punctured. If you have not already eaten all the heart and liver, it, too, can be packaged and frozen, but not as long as the other cuts of meat.

Request that freezer wrapper paper with a plastic coating be used (never butcher paper) and that the packages be double wrapped and clearly marked with the contents.

How to Butcher Game Yourself. You can, of course, do the job yourself. It is not as difficult as some would have you believe—and I speak from experience! I might never have had the courage to volunteer for the job, but circumstances forced me into

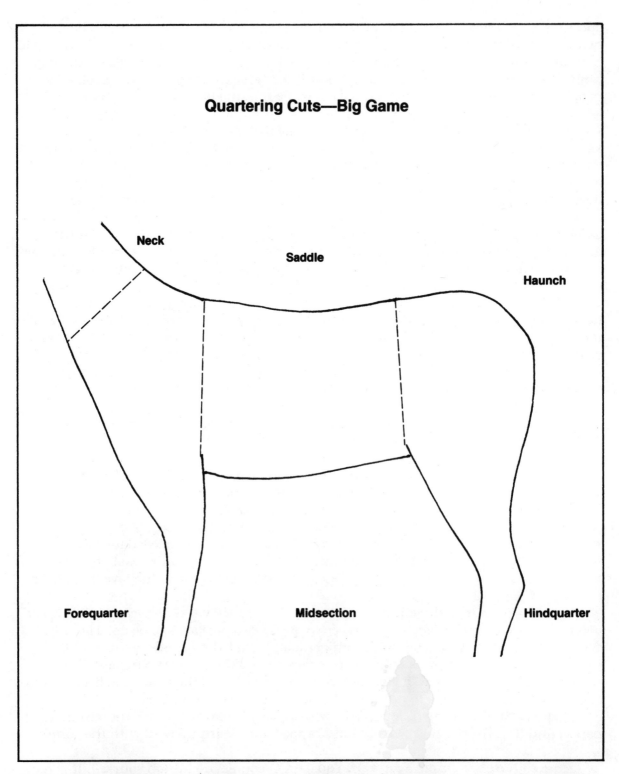

Quartering Cuts—Big Game

Neck

Saddle

Haunch

Forequarter

Midsection

Hindquarter

1. The basic quartering cuts will yield three large sections: the forequarter, the midsection and the hindquarter. First, divide the carcass in half lengthwise by sawing on either side of the spinal column, or directly through it, then quarter each half as indicated.

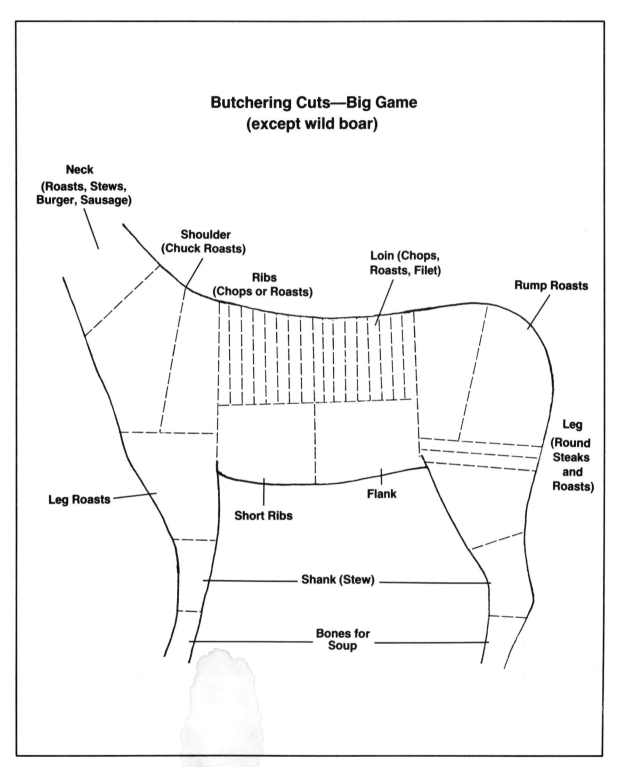

Butchering Cuts—Big Game
(except wild boar)

Neck
(Roasts, Stews,
Burger, Sausage)

Shoulder
(Chuck Roasts)

Ribs
(Chops or Roasts)

Loin (Chops,
Roasts, Filet)

Rump Roasts

Leg
(Round
Steaks
and
Roasts)

Leg Roasts

Short Ribs

Flank

Shank (Stew)

Bones for
Soup

2. Depending on where the animal was shot, butchering it yourself should provide you with any combination of roasts, chops and steaks, in addition to meat to be ground up for burgers and sausage.

it one year and I have never hesitated to tackle it since.

My husband shot a mule deer the last day of our hunt and we brought it home skinned and quartered, along with two pronghorn that had been cut, packaged and frozen at a locker plant in our hunting territory. Knowing that we would be on the road for 36 hours, we packed all the meat in a large wooden box, added 40 pounds of dry ice and insulated the box with our sleeping bags. After my husband left for his office the next morning, I brought a good sturdy table into the kitchen and armed myself with a sharp knife, a meat saw and a cleaver. With a diagram of beef cuts from a cookbook to guide me, and a box of Band-aids within easy reach, I set to work.

Quartering, in my opinion, is strictly man's work, if only to suspend the animal by its hind legs. If you can work in a garage or screened porch, I recommend it. Drive two sturdy spikes in an overhead beam and hang the carcass with meat hooks placed in the slits between the Achilles' tendons and the bones of the hind legs. If you *must* work outside, tie a stout rope through each slit you have made and hoist away over a sturdy tree branch. Be sure the carcass is securely anchored and evenly balanced, for you will be exerting a fair amount of pressure on an already weighty object.

Your first job is to remove the neck by cutting at right angles to the backbone ahead of the shoulder blade (*see* Illustration 1). Then open up the carcass completely by splitting, with hatchet or cleaver, the breastbone and the pelvis right down the midline. The carcass is then divided into two halves, either by splitting with a hatchet along one side of the spinal column, or by sawing through the middle of the spinal column. The second method is slower and a bit more difficult, but does produce a neater finished product.

Remove the halves from the hooks or ropes and place them on a sturdy table to quarter them. You might assume that a whole carcass would give you four quarters, but you are now about to produce three quarters from each half—the forequarter, the hindquarter and the midsection. The forequarter is removed by a cut just behind the shoulder blade, the hindquarter is cut directly in front of the pin bone or front part of the pelvic bone. The remainder is the midsection, comprising the ribs and the loin. Wipe each quarter with a damp cloth to remove any hairs or bone chips.

Now we've arrived at the point where I started operations. It is convenient to have a fairly empty refrigerator so the quarters may be kept cool until processed.

Decide, before you begin cutting, whether you want rib roasts or chops from the *midsection* (*see* Illustration 2). Remove the flank or belly meat from the lower part of the loin end; reserve for stew, burgers or flank steak. Remove the lower portion of the ribs with a saw cut for spareribs. What remains should resemble a whole pork loin. Cut it into chops of desired thickness by slicing between the ribs and then severing the backbone with a good whack of the cleaver. Do the same with the loin chops, only there will be no ribs to guide you.

The *forequarter* will end up as three basic pieces—the shoulder blade section, the leg and the shank. Cut the leg off right below the shoulder joint—with a bit of prodding, you should have no trouble finding it—then cut off the lower portion of the leg where the meat is scanty, the shank. The leg roast can be boned and tied or packaged as is. I prefer to bone the shoulder roast (so I can stuff it), especially if the animal is not too large. However, you may simply cut it in two at right angles to the backbone for blade pot roasts. Your saw will get a good workout here!

Quartering and Butchering Cuts—Wild Boar

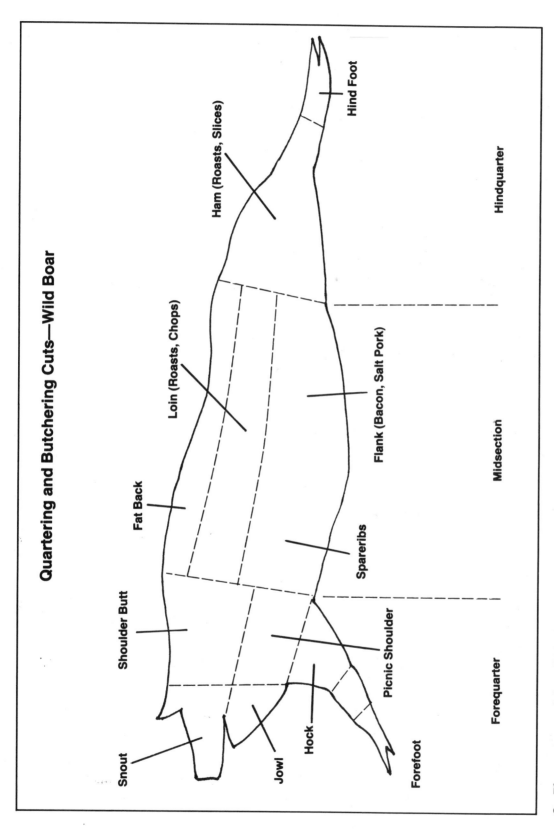

Labels: Hind Foot, Ham (Roasts, Slices), Loin (Roasts, Chops), Fat Back, Shoulder Butt, Snout, Jowl, Hock, Picnic Shoulder, Spareribs, Flank (Bacon, Salt Pork), Forefoot, Forequarter, Midsection, Hindquarter

3. The anatomy of the wild boar (also feral hogs and javelina) varies from the antlered and other big game animals. Therefore, when butchering wild porkers, expect to find more fat (except on the javelina) and major differences in butchering yields. Processing a wild boar closely parallels that of a domestic hog, including the varied and delicious uses for all the parts.

The *hindquarter* is divided in similar fashion. The hip section will provide one or two rump roasts, depending on the size of the animal. A cut made just below the point where the hip and leg bones join will separate the rump from the leg or haunch, which furnishes the steaks and roasts. You may prefer to keep one leg whole and cut the other for steaks. When my sawing arm grows tired, I cut each steak to the desired thickness, cut around the leg bone with a thin boning knife and release the steak from the bone. When the size of the steaks begins to diminish, I bone out the remainder for a leg roast, again cutting off the scanty portion at the bottom, the shank.

All you have left is the neck section, which can be cut into two portions for pot roasts or trimmed from the bones for stew, burgers, mincemeat or homemade sausage, for which I have provided instructions. You won't believe how easy it is. And nothing gets thrown away!

Not being a professional butcher, I found it helpful to take a breather from the cutting and sawing operations and package each quarter as I finished cutting it. I set up wrapping operations on one section of my kitchen counter—with scale, freezer paper (one side plastic-coated), plastic film, freezer tape and marking pencil. Freezer paper heavy enough to prevent air seepage—and thus freezer burn—does make a bulky package when you double wrap. Because of its stiffness, it is also hard to exclude all air from awkwardly shaped pieces. I experimented successfully with a thin inner wrapper of the self-adhering plastic film pressed down to exclude all air, and then an outer wrapping of the heavy freezer paper—"drug store" wrapped with a double fold and sealed with tape. Each package was weighed and marked clearly as to contents.

This method of working also enabled me to "quick" freeze smaller portions of meat at one time. Overloading the freezer with a large quantity of unfrozen meat is not recommended, since it puts a strain on the motor and the meat is not frozen quickly enough to give satisfactory results.

As I worked, the bones were collected in large plastic bags, to be tended to on another less hectic day. The stew meat was set aside in a large pan and cut into one-inch cubes when all else was done. The Band-aids? Yes, I did use one after our beagle jumped too enthusiastically for a scrap of meat and got my finger as well.

In most cases, ⚹ designates recipes that can be prepared at camp using the basic ingredients found in camp kitchens or trail packs. A few recipes are somewhat elaborate and are more suitable for the home grill.

CHAPTER 2

ANTLERED GAME

Cooking game, especially the larger animals, requires no magic incantations or involved recipes. With the meat properly cared for from the time the game was shot, no unpleasant taste needs to be overcome by marinating in a witch's potion, nor does the flavor need to be masked by a great assortment of herbs and spices. The flavor of game is delicious as is—and the simpler the recipe, the better, in most cases.

When people have commented favorably on game served in our home and then said, "But it must be so complicated to cook it right," my answer has always been, "No, it's really quite simple." I have not been trying to sound modest, and I shall probably ruin my reputation as a game cook by stating flatly that it *is* simple. The weird contortions so often recommended are those needed to disguise the flavor of spoiled meat. If you've been with me thus far, you can serve a dinner to please even the most discriminating gourmet without spending hours in the kitchen. The major battle was won before the game ever reached the kitchen—and that's as it should be.

There are a few basic principles involved—and that's all. First, and most important, the animal fat which has already been removed must be replaced in some fashion to prevent dryness. This is done by larding (drawing strips of fat pork through the meat with a larding needle), by wrapping the meat in bacon, and by using beef suet or butter, and the like.

Second: treat each animal individually. Game is not standardized as beef is. It only stands to reason that a large bull elk or moose will require a slightly different approach in the kitchen than a pronghorn doe or a young deer. When I was learning to cook, I was always dreadfully annoyed when Mother said, "Just cook it until it's done"—it seemed to me then a most unscientific attitude. Now I can appreciate her wisdom, for the cooking time "until done"—and even the cooking method—will vary greatly from one animal to the next, even in the same species. So throw away the rule books and the timers and let your intuition take over.

Basically, antlered game—deer, caribou (reindeer), elk and moose—are all cooked in the same manner as beef. *Deer,* including the muley, blacktail and whitetail, is the most widely known to the majority of hunters and certainly ranks high on the scale of good eating. *Caribou,* with its diet of moss and lichens, is juicy and flavorful. *Elk* is considered by some to be the very best of all and is compared to prime beef. *Moose,* the largest member of the deer family, is considered most desirable for the table when shot in late August or early September. During the rut, from the middle of September to November, the meat of the bull is apt to be stringy and to have a very strong flavor.

The basic rule for cooking game is the same as for any meat: roast or broil the tender cuts, braise or stew the tougher ones. The tender cuts are, of course, the saddle and the haunch; the tougher ones, the forequarter and the shank. However, what is tender enough for roasting or broiling on a young animal may require a period of long slow cooking on a really mature beast. Round steak, from the top of the hind leg, is a perfect example. I have had marvelously tender steaks from antelope and 3-year-old deer, broiled over charcoal until they were just pink inside. The same broiling method was *not* successful with the same cut from a patriarch of an Idaho elk herd. It would have been, however, had the round steaks been from a cow or yearling elk.

But how do you decide on the appropriate method for all that meat in the freezer? One test made on a round steak in the privacy of your own family will give you a very good indication of how you should proceed the rest of the winter.

Occasionally it happens to all of us that we are given a piece of game, with no indication of its age or tenderness. When in doubt, use any one of the non-seasoned meat tenderizers as directed on the package or use the long, slow cooking method.

So far I have not mentioned marinating as a means of tenderizing. Some game cooks will recommend it to you for practically everything—not I. I concede that the acid in a marinade (usually wine vinegar) will help somewhat in tenderizing, but I have also noticed that most of these same recipes still require long slow cooking. Many claim that it eliminates the strong gamy flavor, others state equally as vehemently that it enhances the gamy flavor. You pays your money and you takes your choice. As for me, I'll skip the marinade nine times out of ten and stick to the long slow cooking method with a mildly acid ingredient such as lemon, tomato or dry wine, cooked with the meat. These complement and enhance the flavor of the meat, but don't dominate it as a marinade frequently does. The one exception I make in favor of a marinade is in preparation of some of the classic German and Austrian dishes—there the sweet-sour tang is expected and appropriate. This is only one person's opinion, however, so try it both ways and make your own decision.

ROASTS

Every cook has a favorite way of cooking a roast of beef. There are so many new kitchen aids on the market—nylon, self-basting oven cooking bags, automatic microwave ovens that will cook an entire meal, not alone a roast, convection ovens and Heaven knows what else—that there is no longer any hard and fast rule for turning out an excellent roast. Follow any method you prefer, as long as the result is a roast attractively browned on the outside, yet still rare and tender in the middle, with a rich brown gravy. If your family is adamant in their preference for well-done roasts, then you'd better stick to the pot roast versions, since venison roasts are tender and juicy when done only to the medium-rare stage.

Easy Roast Venison

Suitable for any tender leg, loin or rib roast of the antlered game.

Leg, loin or rib roast
Salt pork for larding
Flour
Freshly ground black pepper
Rosemary leaves
1 cup game stock (*see* page 186)
1 cup Cumberland Sauce (*see* page 172)

Preheat oven to 450° F. Insert long thin strips of salt pork into the roast with a larding needle or tie bacon strips over the roast. Sprinkle flour lightly into the bottom of the roasting pan, place the roast on the flour, season with freshly ground black pepper and strew a few rosemary leaves in the pan. Brown at 450° F. for 15 minutes, add 1 cup game stock and roast 12 to 15 minutes per pound at 325° F., basting several times with the pan juices. If the roast is rather small in diameter, reduce the roasting time 2 or 3 minutes per pound.

Gravy may be made in the usual manner (*see* Sauces), substituting game stock for water, or the pan juices may be combined with 1 cup Cumberland Sauce and heated just to the boiling point. Wild rice or chestnut purée would be good companions.

Fruit Glazed Venison Roast

This is a pleasant variation in flavor, suitable for all the antlered game.

1 venison roast
Salt pork
Salt and black pepper
1 cup + 2 tablespoons orange juice
Generous pinch allspice
1 tablespoon lemon juice
2 tablespoons butter, melted
¹/₂ cup tart jelly (crab apple or currant)

Lard roast with salt pork, season with salt and pepper, and sear at 450° F. for 15 minutes. Reduce oven heat to 325° F. and cook covered for 12 minutes per pound, basting frequently with a blend of 1 cup orange juice, allspice and lemon juice. Twenty minutes before the roast is done, brush with a glaze of the melted butter, 2 tablespoons orange juice and jelly.

Serve with glazed orange slices, wild rice and mushrooms.

Loin of Venison with Wild Mushrooms

1 boned venison tenderloin roast
Freshly ground black pepper
3/4 cup butter
1/4 cup Cognac
1 to 2 cups onion, thinly sliced
1 to 2 cups Meadow mushrooms,
    puffballs, thinly sliced *or* 1/2 cup (or
    whatever amount you can scrape
    together) dried wild mushrooms,
    such as chanterelles, porcini, etc.*

Preheat oven to 450° F.

Place roast in a heavy roasting pan and brush it with 1/2 cup melted butter. Season with black pepper and put in the hot oven for 15 minutes. Reduce heat to 350° F. and continue to roast and baste, turning the meat occasionally. Cook 15 minutes per pound for medium-rare.

When the roast is almost done, melt the additional butter in a skillet and lightly sauté the onions and mushrooms together.

When done, remove the roast to a heated platter and pour the Cognac into the bottom of the roaster. On top of the stove, heat the pan on high and scrape up any of the baked-on drippings and stir to blend. Add to the onion/mushroom mixture and serve warm over sliced venison.

* Dried wild mushrooms are becoming commonplace in the specialty sections of many supermarkets, but if you can't find them, at least try a specialty food store; it's worth the effort.

Roast Leg of Moose or Reindeer with Red, Red Game Sauce

1/4 cup butter
4 or 5 sprigs parsley, minced
1/2 teaspoon dried savory, crumbled
1/2 teaspoon dried tarragon, crumbled
10 to 12 juniper berries, crushed
1 6-pound roast from hind leg (haunch)
Freshly ground black pepper
Flour
1 cup red wine or equal parts wine and
    game stock

Red, Red Game Sauce:
1 cup game stock
1/4 cup currant jelly
1/2 cup dry red wine
1 tablespoon brandy
1 1/2 tablespoons roux (*see* page 166)

Preheat oven to 450° F.

In a small saucepan, melt butter without browning, add herbs and cook together several minutes. Let stand. Season roast with black pepper and lightly sprinkle with flour. Place in roasting pan; pour over savory butter and place in preheated oven. After 20 minutes, reduce heat to 325° F., add wine (and stock), cover and roast 25 minutes per pound, basting frequently. When roast is tender, remove to a heated platter and keep warm while you prepare the sauce.

Add game stock to the juices in the roasting pan, set over heat and stir briskly to loosen any crusty bits in the pan. Strain through a sieve into a small saucepan, add currant jelly, red wine, brandy and roux. Stir briskly until sauce is smooth and thickened. Allow to simmer a few minutes and pour into preheated gravy boat.

If juniper berries are difficult to find in your area, write to one of the companies specializing in herbs and spices. In the meantime until your juniper berries arrive, substitute equal parts of gin and stock for the red wine and achieve practically the same results, since the main flavoring ingredient in gin is the juniper berry.

Roast Young Caribou

1 saddle or rump caribou roast
Salt pork
Garlic slivers *or*
Onion, sliced
Freshly ground black pepper
1 bay leaf
2 stalks celery, chopped, including the
    tops
Cider or red wine
1 cup sour cream

Lard roast with salt pork. Either insert slivers of garlic into gashes in the roast or arrange slices of onion in the bottom of the roasting pan. Season with pepper, add the bay leaf and celery, including the tops, to the roaster.

Sear at 450° F. 15 to 20 minutes, then roast covered at 300° F. for 15 minutes per pound, basting every 20 minutes with cider or red wine. Remove roast to a heated platter, keep warm while you make the gravy.

Skim off any excess fat, heat pan juices to boiling point, scraping sides of roaster to loosen any browned particles, adding a bit more wine or cider if necessary. Strain into small saucepan, then slowly add 1 cup sour cream, stirring constantly. Heat just to boiling point, but do not allow gravy to boil once sour cream has been added. Serve over sliced caribou.

Rump Roast—Russian Style

You've heard it over and over—red meat, red wine—but do try this one. Some rules are made to be broken.

1 rump roast
White wine
Salt pork
Freshly ground black pepper
Salt if desired

Russian Game Sauce
    (*see* page 173)

Place a rump roast in a deep glass or earthen-ware dish, cover with dry white wine and bring to room temperature (1½ to 2 hours). Remove the roast and reserve the wine. Lard roast with salt pork, season with freshly ground black pepper and salt.

Roast in preheated oven at 450° F.

15 to 20 minutes, reduce heat to 300° F. to 325° F. and roast 15 minutes per pound, covered, basting frequently with the reserved white wine. Serve with sour creamed Russian Game Sauce.

Crown Roast of Venison

This is truly a noble feast—well worth the use of all the rib chops at once. Your butcher will probably have a hand in the preparation of the roast, but you will still be paying your mighty hunter a fine compliment when you match his skill in the field with yours in the kitchen.

The preparation of a crown roast is really quite simple, but it does require a skilled hand with the saw and butcher knife. The backbone is removed from sufficient of the rib chops to make an attractive crown, usually a part, if not all, of the two racks. The rib bones are left rather long so they curve outwardly as the meat section is turned to the center. The whole is firmly tied or sewed together. Have the butcher trim all fat and return the meat trimmings as well as the backbone to you.

Simmer the bones and meat trimmings as directed in Chapter 11 for stock needed in the balance of the recipe.

2 cups each onions and celery, finely chopped
¼ cup butter plus additional for basting
½ pound ground venison or mildly seasoned sausage
2 cups long-grain rice, uncooked
Freshly ground black pepper to taste
Salt if desired
½ teaspoon dried thyme
½ teaspoon dried marjoram
1 tablespoon parsley, finely chopped
6 to 7 cups game stock or beef bouillon for gravy and stuffing
3 eggs, slightly beaten
Roux

In a large skillet, sauté onion, celery and meat in butter until all is lightly browned, stirring to blend. Add rice,

seasonings and two cups of stock, mixing well. Cover and simmer over low heat until the liquid has been absorbed by the rice, about 25 to 35 minutes, stirring occasionally so it doesn't stick to the pan. Check seasonings and allow stuffing to cool. Add slightly beaten eggs and mix thoroughly. Brush roast liberally with butter.

Preheat oven to 450° F., place roast on rack in the roasting pan, covering the rib ends with foil to prevent charring, and sear for 15 minutes. Place 1 cup stock or water in the bottom of the roaster, fill center of the roast with stuffing, mounding it attractively, and lower oven to 350° F. Roast 12 to 15 minutes per pound or use a meat thermometer inserted carefully between the ribs and roast only to the medium-

Crown Roast of Venison (cont.)

rare stage. Baste the outside of the ribs once in a while and cover the top of the stuffing if it begins to get too brown.

When the roast is done, transfer to your most elegant platter, remove the strings and foil and keep warm while you prepare the gravy. Add 3 cups stock to the roaster, set over heat and bring to a boil. Stir to loosen any browned residue in the pan; strain and return to pan. Thicken with roux, as directed on page 166. Check seasoning of the gravy and allow to simmer 5 minutes. Garnish rib ends with crab apples and decorate the platter with additional apples and sprigs of parsley. Keep the vegetables simple, but elegant. To carve, just slice down between the ribs.

Rack of Venison au Poivrade

1 rack of venison
Salt pork for larding
Freshly ground black pepper
3 to 4 tablespoons butter, melted

Black Pepper Sauce:
1 cup game stock
1 *tablespoon* coarsely ground black
**   pepper**
Bouquet garni of ¼ teaspoon dried
**   thyme, 3 sprigs parsley, ½ bay leaf**
⅓ cup onions, chopped, or 2
**   tablespoons shallots, diced**
¾ cup port wine
3 tablespoons roux (more or less,
**   depending on amount of pan**
**   juices)**
½ cup heavy cream
More black pepper and salt if desired
1 tablespoon butter

Preheat oven to 450° F.

Tie the venison rack as directed in "Crown Roast of Venison," and lard. Place in roasting pan, liberally season with black pepper and brush with melted butter. Place in oven for 15 minutes, lower heat to 350° F. and continue to roast 12 to 15 minutes per pound for medium-rare. Baste occasionally.

While the venison is roasting, begin to prepare the ***Poivrade (Black Pepper) Sauce:***

In a saucepan, combine ½ cup port wine with the stock, black pepper, herbs and onion; bring to a boil, reduce heat and simmer, covered, about 20 minutes; let stand while roast continues to cook. When ready, remove venison rack to a warm platter. Add ¼ cup port wine to roasting pan; raise heat and scrape any particles that may have adhered to bottom of pan.

Strain both the sauce you've prepared to this point and the pan drippings. In a small saucepan, melt your roux and add the sauce and drippings, whisking with a wire whisk until mixture is smooth and medium thick. Add heavy cream and simmer about 10 minutes. Correct seasoning and stir in butter.

You might suspect that this sauce would be hot and spicy, but one of the cooking "miracles" that always amazes me is that the flavors of the sauce meld so beautifully with the game to create a mellow, thoroughly tantalizing dish. This is luscious, incidentally, served with steamed cabbage wedges, German style.

✤ STEAKS, CHOPS AND RIBS

With backyard cooking as well as camp cooking so popular, many men have become excellent chefs, especially when it comes to steaks and chops. Again, use any of the means of broiling that you think produces the best steaks. One of our friends tells of a venerable and highly esteemed camp cook who set a huge kettle of deep fat on the fire until it was bubbling and sputtering. He then drew each steak slowly through the boiling fat with tongs. Our friend admits that he was horrified as he witnessed the whole operation, but delightfully surprised when he tasted the delectable results. I don't necessarily advocate your trying this method; I only mention it to prove that there are many means to the same end.

In preparing your steaks, if you have decided to have the backstrap removed in one piece and frozen solid, as I have mentioned before, then cut your filets across the grain about twice as thick as you like your steaks to be (2 inches). Place each filet between two sheets of waxed paper and whack it with the flat side of your cleaver. This will help to tenderize the meat and will also provide a good-sized filet of the proper thickness (1 inch).

There is only one problem in broiling game steaks and chops. Somehow you must add fat to the meat so it doesn't dry out. Remember there is no thick rim of fat on a properly prepared venison steak. Do salt your steak *after* broiling and use only freshly ground black pepper, even if you've never bothered with it before. You're preparing one of the most delectable meats possible and it deserves only the finest ingredients!

I like to dip chops or steaks in melted butter or the finest olive oil before broiling. You can bone chops, too, and wrap each in a strip of bacon, skewering it neatly in place. A nice addition, but not really necessary, is the use of seasoned butters, added after the steaks are on the platter (*see* Chapter 10).

Have your guests assembled, the rest of the dinner completed and ready to put on the table, the steak platter sizzling hot—then broil your steaks! 6 to 8 minutes total time for a 1-inch steak is about the maximum!

Ribs very seldom last beyond the time spent in camp—this is only fitting and proper. They are at their best cut in sections, propped over a good bed of coals and broiled as is, or basted with a simple sauce, such as Barney's Barbecue Sauce (*see* Chapter 10).

If you are fortunate enough to have the ribs reach home, use them as soon as possible—they do take a fair bit of freezer space.

Marinades for Steaks, Chops and Ribs

Even though I tend to prefer plain steaks and chops, American cooking has come a long way in terms of experimentation with tastes. And, after all, how many times can you serve "plain" steaks to the same guests. Just remember that regardless of which marinade you use, dry the meat before you grill it. My husband likes to dip the steaks in any reserved marinade as they are cooking; they stay juicy that way. Here are a few marinades that I use for special occasions.

Beer. Simply sprinkle the steaks or chops with freshly ground black pepper and place in a ceramic dish; cover with beer and let sit for about 2 hours, turning after the first hour. Dry before you grill.

Green onion. Mix together ¹/₂ to 1 cup white wine with 1 package dry green onion dip mix.

Herb. Add whatever herbs you fancy to a plain vinaigrette dressing (oil/vinegar), salt, pepper and garlic powder and blend together.

Mustard. Smear the steaks or chops with Dijon or country stone-ground mustard with horseradish for a really lively change of pace. The vinegar in the mustard is the tenderizing agent. And don't worry about how it looks as you place it over the coals, it changes as it cooks.

Oriental. This is the one we like best. Mix together 2 tablespoons soy sauce, 2 tablespoons molasses, 1 chopped scallion and ¹/₂ teaspoon dry mustard. Season the meat first with freshly ground black pepper and garlic powder. Marinate for about 2 hours, turning after the first hour. *Or* mix just the soy sauce and the molasses, season as above and add a sprinkling of dried thyme (chops are outstanding this way).

If you enjoy your chops and steaks unembellished but are looking for that occasional extra something for variety, in addition to the seasoned butters I mentioned before, why not try any of the brown or game sauces listed in Chapter 10. Also, here are two excellent recipes prepared with tenderloin cuts of venison (the section where you'd ordinarily obtain your steaks and chops).

 ## Hungarian-Style Cutlets with Peppers

Paprika lard (see below) *or* strained bacon drippings
1¹/₂ to 2 pounds venison cutlets (from the tenderloin)
¹/₄ cup flour seasoned with garlic powder and freshly ground black pepper

Vegetable Garnish:
2 tablespoons paprika lard *or* strained bacon drippings
3 cloves garlic, sliced lengthwise
3 cups frying peppers, sliced lengthwise
1¹/₂ cups ripe tomatoes, peeled and sliced lengthwise
1 teaspoon sweet Hungarian paprika (1 tablespoon if you substitute bacon drippings for lard)

1 teaspoon sugar, if necessary
Freshly ground black pepper

To prepare this dish in true Hungarian fashion, first make your paprika lard. Melt 1 cup of lard in a saucepan (or 3 to 5 minutes in a glass dish on medium heat in a microwave oven). Cool to lukewarm. Add 1 tablespoon sweet Hungarian paprika and ¹/₄ cup water, stir and bring to a boil. Remove from heat and let sit, undisturbed, for about ¹/₂ hour. The mixture will separate so that on the top will rise a clear, red oil-appearing liquid. Skim this off and reserve it—this is the paprika lard. As it cools, it will turn a brilliant orange color and become hard and opaque, like the original lard. You can chill it and wrap it in waxed paper, cutting off amounts as you need them. This also makes it a convenient, carryable camp ingredient.

Now prepare your garnish, the fried peppers. The Magyars call them Hungarian, or banana, peppers; the Italians call them Italian frying peppers; the horticulturalists call them *Capsicum frutescens*. Whatever name you know them by, make sure you do not use the darker green bell peppers. The taste does differ.

In a heavy iron skillet, melt the paprika lard (or bacon drippings if you have no lard, or simply prefer the bacon flavor) and lightly sauté the garlic and onion. Add the peppers, tomatoes, 1 teaspoon paprika if you've used the paprika lard (1 *tablespoon* if you've used the bacon drippings), sugar—if the tomatoes are not at their ripest, and the black pepper. Simmer about 20 minutes, stirring occasionally, until the mixture

blends and the peppers are cooked through.

Before the vegetables are almost finished, you can start doing the cutlets. In another iron skillet, melt 2 tablespoons paprika lard or bacon drippings and sauté the cutlets (which you have dredged in the seasoned flour) on both sides, quickly and evenly. Remove to a platter and continue sautéing until all the cutlets are done. Add more lard as needed.

Arrange the cutlets on a platter and top with the pepper mixture. Serve with rice and cucumber salad with sour cream. Serves 4.

Note: This dish is also wonderful made with venison or wild boar chops or thicker steaks grilled over an open fire, rather than sautéed. If you do this, use the paprika lard as you would a barbecue sauce, dipping the chops or steaks into it, and/or brushing it on as you grill.

Venison with Bean Sprouts

Here is a dish prepared in the traditional Oriental manner, adapted to tenderloin cuts of venison. I have grown to love Oriental cuisine because it stresses three essentials of good cooking: freshness of ingredients, ease of preparation and visually pleasing results. In addition, as you will see, Oriental-style cooking is extremely versatile and makes an excellent marriage with game.

¹/₂ to 1 pound venison tenderloin, sliced into thin 2-inch strips, marinated (see below)
2 tablespoons peanut or vegetable oil
2 large scallions, sliced, including the greens
2 cloves garlic, sliced crosswise
1 cup game stock
2 cups green beans, cut into 2-inch

pieces or sliced broccoli or any combination of other greens you desire
3 tablespoons oyster sauce
2 teaspoons cornstarch dissolved in water
¹/₂ cup oyster mushrooms (or whatever kind you can procure), sliced
³/₄ pound mung bean sprouts

Venison with Bean Sprouts (cont.)

Have all ingredients ready to go and the marinated venison at room temperature. In a wok or large skillet, heat the peanut oil. Lightly sauté the scallions and the garlic. Add the venison strips with the marinade and sauté them next. Add the game stock, then the green beans, cover and cook for about 3 minutes (if you like your vegetables more well-cooked, you can steam them for about 3 minutes before you place them in the wok).

Uncover the wok, stir and add the oyster sauce and the cornstarch if the gravy needs to be thickened. Finally add the mushrooms and the sprouts and stir until heated through. Serve with rice to 3 or 4 people.

Marinade: 1 scallion, chopped; 1/4 teaspoon garlic powder (or 2 cloves garlic, diced); 3 tablespoons soy sauce; 2 tablespoons dry sherry and a sprinkling of freshly ground black pepper. Combine all ingredients with venison strips and let marinate in a ceramic or glass bowl for about 1 hour.

Moose Chop Suey

I am grateful to Mrs. G. C. F. Dalziel of Watson Lake, Yukon, and the publishers of *The Whitehorse Star* for permission to include some of her recipes originally published in *The Whitehorse Star,* Whitehorse, Yukon.

"Slice long thin strips of moose tenderloin, dump in paper bag with a cup of flour, shake in bag till coated with flour, brown till golden in fat. Thoroughly drain tin of whole mushrooms (saving broth till later) and brown mushrooms with meat, add a finely chopped Spanish onion, a cup of finely chopped cabbage, a half cup diced celery and a tin of bean sprouts and let simmer for half hour, using mushroom broth if liquid gets too low in the pan. Mix two tablespoons cornstarch with enough soy sauce to make a paste and add to mixture to thicken.

"To serve, place in large platter, sprinkle with sesame seeds, and surround with white fluffy rice."

(*See* also Mrs. Dalziel's brisket recipe, page 44.)

Baked Ribs with Barbecue Sauce

Ribs
Barbecue Sauce (*see* Chapter 10)

Place ribs in large roasting pan, cover with Barbecue Sauce of your choosing, or your own favorite blend. Cover roaster and bake at 350° F. for 1 1/2 hours, turning and basting several times.

Oriental-Style Venison Ribs

2 to 4 pounds ribs

Marinade:
¼ cup soy sauce
¼ cup dry sherry
¼ cup honey
2 tablespoons prepared ketchup
2 tablespoons chili powder
3 scallions, chopped (incl. the green tops)
3 cloves garlic, minced, or ½ teaspoon garlic powder

Combine all the ingredients for the marinade, place the ribs in a glass or ceramic dish and pour the marinade over the ribs. They will not be submerged in this, but rather should be coated with it. Marinate for at least 2 hours, turning and coating after the first hour.

Preheat oven to 350° F. Place a metal rack in a large shallow roasting pan and set the ribs on top. Add hot water to cover the bottom of the pan; the steam created will keep the ribs moist as they cook. Roast for about a total of 1½ hours, depending on how many pounds you have and how meaty the ribs are; they should be well cooked. Turn them after the first half hour; and for the last half hour, increase the heat to 400° F. so they brown well. Baste frequently during the entire roasting process.

ROUND STEAK AND VARIATIONS

As I have mentioned before, the steaks from the hind leg of a mature animal will frequently require long slow cooking to be tender. Swiss steak always comes to mind in this instance, but one can tire of it. The variations I have included here will, I hope, encourage you to go even further afield and develop your own variations.

Braised Elk or Moose Steak

Thick round steak
Freshly ground black pepper
2 cups dry red wine
2 small onions studded with 2 cloves each
2 parsnips cut into small strips
½ to 1 cup turnips cut into small strips
2 stalks celery cut into small strips

Sear the steak in drippings, season with freshly ground pepper, cover with dry red wine. Add vegetables, cover and simmer until tender and liquid is almost completely evaporated.

 **Forgotten Steak**

2 pounds round steak, cut into serving portions
1 package dried onion soup mix
2 cups water
¼ cup dry red or white wine (optional)

Place all ingredients in a skillet, cover and forget about them for about 1½ hours, or until steak is tender. Thicken gravy with roux, if desired, and serve over rice. Serves 3 to 4.

Oriental Pepper Steak

This is, to a certain extent, a misnomer, since the orientals cook both meat and vegetables only a very short time (*see* "Venison with Bean Sprouts"). This compromise has two advantages—you can save the prime steak the Orientals would use here and have a pleasant variation, not only for the cook, but for the diners as well.

2 pounds round steak
½ cup butter
Dash of garlic salt or 1 small clove of garlic, minced
Dash of powdered ginger
½ cup soy sauce
1 cup beef bouillon or game stock
3 green peppers, sliced into strips
5 or 6 scallions, including the green tops, sliced
Salt and pepper
3 to 4 tablespoons cornstarch
½ cup white wine or water

Remove all tendons and connective tissue and slice steak into thin strips while the meat is still partially frozen. Cook over medium heat in butter with garlic and ginger until well browned. Add soy sauce and bouillon or game stock, cover and simmer until tender. Add green pepper and scallions, cook only a minute or so. Add cornstarch mixed with wine or water and stir over low heat until sauce is clear and thickened. Check seasonings—you may not need any salt and pepper. Serve with rice to 4.

 Swiss Steak

Round steak, at least 1-inch thick
Flour
Salt and pepper
Chopped onion
Canned tomatoes or V-8 juice
Bay leaf
Old-fashioned Chili Sauce (*see* page 177)

Combine flour, salt and pepper and

pound into steak with the back of a cleaver or the edge of a plate. In heavy skillet, brown on both sides in drippings, along with onion. Add tomatoes or V-8 juice and bay leaf. Cover and simmer until tender.

I have, on occasion, substituted for the onion and tomato our old family recipe for Chili Sauce with equally successful results.

❧ Spicy Swiss Steak

If you're tired of the usual Swiss steak, try this one. The flavor is subtle, despite the many ingredients.

Boned round or chuck steak 1-inch thick, cut into serving portions
¼ cup flour
4 whole cloves
Generous pinch marjoram or thyme
4 or 5 juniper berries
2 teaspoons salt
Generous sprinkling coarsely ground black pepper
¼ teaspoon ground ginger
Butter
1 small clove garlic, split
Beef bouillon or game stock

Combine flour, herbs and seasonings (except the garlic) and crush together, using mortar and pestle. Pound seasoned flour into steak on both sides with back of cleaver.

Melt butter in heavy skillet that has a tight fitting lid; add garlic and cook for a minute or so. Remove garlic and brown steak on both sides. Add enough stock to cover bottom of pan. Cover tightly and simmer until tender, adding more stock if necessary.

Stroganoff

Stroganoff, as originally created, requires the choicest cuts from the tenderloin or rib. However, I prefer to save those cuts for broiling or roasting and have evolved this recipe using the less tender cuts.

2½ pounds round steak
½ cup flour combined with 1 teaspoon salt and ½ teaspoon freshly ground black pepper
½ cup butter
1 onion, chopped
2 cups beef bouillon or game stock
½ pound mushrooms, sautéed briefly in ¼ cup butter
1 cup sour cream blended with ¼ cup tomato paste and 1 teaspoon Worcestershire Sauce
Finely chopped parsley

While still partially frozen, remove tendons, bone and connective tissue from steak and cut into thin strips. (This is easier to do when the meat is still firm.) Coat strips of meat with seasoned flour.

Heat butter in large skillet with tight fitting lid. Brown meat slowly, turning with tongs to brown all sides, one half at a time. When meat is nearly all browned, add chopped onion and cook another 2 minutes. Slowly add bouillon, scraping skillet to loosen any browned particles. Cover tightly and simmer over very low heat until meat is tender.

Ten minutes before serving, add sautéed mushrooms and then sour cream mixture in small amounts, stirring till sour cream is completely blended in; continue cooking over low heat 5 minutes, but do not boil. Serve in preheated dish, garnished with chopped parsley.

It is traditional to serve this dish with rice, but noodles may be used. (This is excellent party fare, by the way.)

Stuffed Venison Flank Steak (or Round Steak)

Flank or round steak
Stuffing (*see* Chapter 11)
Hot drippings or butter
Freshly ground black pepper
Salt if desired
Game stock or beef bouillon
Cornstarch dissolved in water
    (optional)

For flank steak, score on both sides in criss-cross fashion diagonally against the grain of the meat. For round steak, pound lightly with back of cleaver.

Spread with any favorite stuffing (Mushroom and Rice, Sage and Onion Bread Stuffing). Roll and tie or skewer firmly.

Brown in hot drippings or butter on all sides. Season with salt and pepper. Decrease heat to lowest possible point, add enough game stock or beef bouillon barely to cover the bottom of the skillet. Cover and simmer slowly until fork tender, adding more stock if necessary. The gravy may be thickened with a cornstarch and water paste.

 Stuffed Venison Rolls

4 round steaks, thinly cut and pounded
    with the flat side of a cleaver
4 slices game or sweet Italian sausage,
    cooked
1 dill pickle, quartered lengthwise
Freshly ground black pepper
Garlic powder
Flour
2 to 3 tablespoons vegetable oil
1 medium-large onion, chopped
1 cup game stock
1 cup dry red wine
1/4 teaspoon dried thyme
1/2 bay leaf
1/4 teaspoon dried basil

Place 1 slice each of cooked sausage and dill pickle atop each steak. Roll up and tie or secure with toothpicks. Season stuffed venison rolls with black pepper and garlic powder and dredge in flour.

In a large skillet with cover, heat the oil and brown rolls on all sides. Remove from pan. Add the onion to the skillet and sauté till golden. Add the remaining ingredients, stir to blend and return the rolls to the pan. Cover and simmer about 1 1/2 hours or so, until tender. Thicken gravy, if desired. Serves 4.

Venison Sauté Chasseur (Hunter's Style)

2 pounds round steak, cut into serving
    portions
1/4 cup butter
1/2 pound mushrooms, sliced
6 or 8 scallions or shallots, sliced,
    including part of the green tops

1 cup dry white wine
1 cup bouillon or stock
Bouquet garni of parsley, thyme and
    bay leaf
Herb croutons (with parsley and
    tarragon)

Venison Sauté Chasseur (cont.)

Brown steak lightly in butter, then mushrooms and scallions. Add wine, stock and bouquet garni. Cover tightly and simmer on low heat until tender—or transfer contents of skillet to a buttered casserole, cover and bake at 325° F. When serving, top with herb croutons.

A slightly different, but equally delicious, flavor may be obtained by substituting dry vermouth for the usual white wine. Since vermouth itself is very aromatic, with at least 16 different herbs, omit the bouquet garni.

Venison Italiano I

2 pounds boned round steak, cut into serving portions
4 tablespoons olive oil
1 clove garlic
3 cups canned tomatoes, sieved, or tomato purée
1 teaspoon oregano
Salt and pepper
1 teaspoon dried parsley
Mozzarella cheese

Brown steak in oil with garlic, add tomato and seasonings. Cover and simmer until fork tender. If desired, a slice of Mozzarella cheese may be placed atop each portion and slid into the oven until cheese is melted. Serves 4.

Venison Italiano II

In this variation, you are in effect using the venison as the base for the tomato-meat sauce.

¼ cup olive oil
5 whole cloves garlic, peeled
1½ pounds venison round steak, cut into 1-inch cubes
1 medium onion, chopped
1 6-ounce can tomato paste
3 to 4 leaves fresh basil, crushed, *or* 1 teaspoon dried basil
1 28-ounce can peeled plum tomatoes (Italian preferably)
1 28-ounce can tomato puree
Pasta of your choosing
Fresh parsley

Freshly ground black pepper
Freshly grated Locatelli or Pecorino (Romano) cheese

In a heavy Dutch oven (or 8-quart pot with cover—not aluminum), heat the oil and slowly brown the garlic in it on all sides; remove and reserve. Add the venison cubes and brown on all sides; remove these and reserve.

Now sauté the onion till golden; add the tomato paste and the basil and cook, stirring, about 5 minutes over low heat.

Venison Italiano II (cont.)

Add the tomatoes, the purée and 1 of the 28-ounce cans filled with water; stir to blend. Return the garlic and the venison to the sauce, raise the heat until the mixture reaches a boil, then lower it again and simmer, partially covered, about 2 to 3 hours, stirring occasionally.

You should have a fairly thick sauce (thin it with additional water as it cooks if that is your preference), which will not be spicy—rather, almost sweet—and very tasty. Don't be tempted to add oregano; try it this way first. The basil is the key to it all.

Serve over your favorite pasta, garnished with fresh parsley, black pepper and Italian cheese.

POT ROASTS

No one need ever hesitate about serving game pot roasts to guests. Well cooked and attractively served, these are the perfect winter meals. The hostess, too, has the advantage of very little fuss in the kitchen at the last minute, since these dishes tend to themselves very nicely over low heat.

 Pot Roast of Big Game

1 large shoulder or rump roast
Flour, seasoned with freshly ground
    black pepper
Bacon drippings
2 carrots, sliced
2 stalks celery, chopped, including the
    leaves
2 onions, sliced
2 cups fresh or canned tomatoes,
    peeled
2 bay leaves
¹/₂ teaspoon dried thyme
¹/₂ teaspoon ground cloves
¹/₄ teaspoon ground allspice

Coat the meat on all sides with seasoned flour; brown in Dutch oven in hot fat, turning to brown all sides. Add carrots, celery and onions during the last of the browning process. Add tomatoes, herbs and spices, cover and simmer *very* slowly, with the liquid barely bubbling, until tender, at *least* 4 hours. After 2 hours of cooking, turn the meat over in the pot and thereafter, check occasionally to be sure there is enough liquid in the pot. Remove the meat to a hot platter, discard bay leaves, and put sauce through food mill or sieve. Return sauce to the pot and reheat to the boiling point.

Serve with broad buttered noodles. Baked carrots and onions are a very good vegetable accompaniment, also stuffed baked acorn squash.

 **Brisket**

Here is another of Mrs. Dalziel's fine recipes, as originally published in *The Whitehorse Star.*

"Most people, if you offer them meat, want a 'Steak'—that is fine with me, but don't give away the brisket: no finer meal comes off the animal than this. Cut the brisket in fist-size hunks, dredge with flour and place in Dutch oven sizzling hot with kidney fat and brown. Fresh ground pepper and salt and cover with water. Cover and simmer all afternoon, add vegetables and dumplings."

Easy Oven Brisket

1 venison brisket, about 3 pounds
1 tablespoon flour
1 self-basting nylon Oven Cooking Bag
Freshly ground black pepper
1 10¹/₂-ounce can onion soup *or* **¹/₂ package dry onion soup mix blended with 2 cups water or equal parts water/wine**
1 cup carrots, sliced
1 cup potatoes, sliced

Preheat oven to 350° F. Put flour in Oven Cooking Bag and turn to coat all sides. Season roast with black pepper.

Place the bag in a roasting pan; put the brisket in it, the soup and the vegetables. Close bag, tie as directed and poke about 12 holes in the top of the bag with a meat fork to allow steam to escape. Meats tend to cook more rapidly this way, but they retain their juices well. Check this roast after about 1 hour; total cooking time may not exceed 1¹/₂ hours. Thicken gravy as desired.

"Down East" Pot Roast

4 pounds boneless rump, round or chuck roast
Drippings
Salt and pepper, flour
2 cups cranberries
1 cup water
Sprinkle of allspice
4 whole cloves
Orange juice
2 tablespoons sugar
¹/₂ cup tart jelly

Coat meat with flour, seasoned with salt and pepper. Brown in hot drippings in Dutch oven. In the meantime, cook cranberries in water until skins pop, about 10 to 15 minutes, then pour over browned meat. Add allspice and cloves. Cover and simmer on low heat. As meat cooks, maintain level of liquid with orange juice rather than water.

When meat is tender, remove meat to hot platter, strain pot liquid into small saucepan, add sugar and tart jelly. Heat thoroughly and thicken if necessary with flour and water paste. Instead of the usual noodles, you might try skillet corn bread or New England Jonny Cake with this one (*see* Journey Cakes, page 252).

Burgundy Venison with Wild Mushrooms

3- to 4-pound rump or round roast or
    brisket
Flour seasoned with freshly ground
    black pepper and garlic powder
4 tablespoons vegetable oil or lard
1 cup onion, chopped
2 cloves garlic, chopped
1 cup red Burgundy wine
1 cup game stock or beef bouillon or
    consommé
1 bay leaf
1/2 teaspoon dried Mélange Provence
    herbs*
Coarsely ground black pepper
1/2 cup dried wild mushrooms
    (chanterelles or porcini, if poss.)

Coat the roast with the seasoned flour. In a Dutch oven, heat the oil and brown the meat on all sides. Move to the rim of the pan, allowing room to sauté the onion and garlic in the pan drippings until golden brown. Add the Burgundy, game stock, herbs and black pepper. Cover pan and simmer slowly for about 3 hours, or until tender.

Meanwhile, reconstitute the mushrooms by placing them in a small saucepan and covering them with water; cover pan and bring to a boil; reduce heat and barely simmer 20 minutes. Remove from heat and let them stay in the water until ready to use.

When the roast is tender, remove to a warm platter. Take out the bay leaf and thicken the gravy with roux, as desired. Add the mushrooms and heat through. Serves 4 to 6 nicely with wild rice and baby peas with pearl onions.

* Obtainable in food specialty stores, or substitute 1/4 teaspoon each dried thyme and dried basil.

Pot Roast with Sour Cream Sauce

Suitable for buffalo as well as antlered game.

Rump or shoulder roast
Drippings
Salt and pepper
1 onion, sliced
2 carrots, sliced
1 small turnip, diced
2 stalks celery, sliced
Pinch thyme
Few juniper berries
1 bay leaf
1 lemon, sliced thin
1 cup red wine
1 cup game stock
1/2 cup sour cream

In a Dutch oven, brown seasoned meat and vegetables together in hot drippings. Add herbs, lemon, wine and game stock. Cover and simmer over very low heat for 2 hours.

Remove meat, strain sauce back into pot, pressing vegetables through the sieve. Add sour cream to the sauce and blend; return meat to the pot and simmer very gently until tender.

Serve with rice, cranberries and a green vegetable.

Caribou Bouilli

The word "bouilli" (pronounced *boo-yee*) means, simply, boiled, and boiled beef, in French and Viennese kitchens, was prepared in many ways with always appetizing results. Here is my adaptation for antlered game, with horseradish-enhanced gravy.

3- to 4-pound rump or round roast or brisket
2 whole cloves garlic, peeled
1 onion studded with 3 whole cloves
1 stalk celery with leaves, chopped
2 small carrots, chopped
2 parsnips, chopped
6 juniper berries
8 whole peppercorns
1 bay leaf
1 tablespoon white vinegar

Gravy:
1 smallish onion, chopped fine
4 tablespoons butter
2 tablespoons flour
2 cups game stock, strained
2 to 4 tablespoons prepared horseradish, to taste

Place the roast in a large, heavy pot. Cover meat with *boiling* water; bring water again to the boil and simmer about 30 minutes. Discard the water.

Start all over again by covering the roast with boiling water, but this time once it boils again, remove any scum (it should be minimal) and add the garlic, cloved-studded onion, celery, carrots, parsnips, juniper berries, peppercorns, bay leaf and vinegar. Cover the pot and simmer 3 to 4 hours, until meat is tender.

Remove roast from pan to a warm platter. Strain the stock through a sieve; reserve. To make the gravy, melt the butter in a small saucepan, sauté the onion in it and make a roux base by blending in the flour. Slowly pour in 2 cups of the game stock, stirring constantly until gravy is thickened. Add the horseradish and sprinkle in some freshly ground black pepper. If you think you'd still like more of a "bite" to the gravy, add a little more vinegar.

Parsley-buttered red potatoes or spaetzle go particularly well with this dish, which should serve 4 to 6 people.

Sauerbraten

Any of the antlered game may be used successfully in this recipe.

Marinade:
3 cups water
1½ cups vinegar
2 bay leaves
12 whole peppercorns
2 or 3 cloves
1 carrot, sliced
1 onion, sliced
2 stalks celery, sliced

4-pound rump or blade pot roast
2 slices bacon, diced

Gravy:
12 gingersnaps, crushed
4 tablespoons roux
3 to 4 tablespoons sour cream

Sauerbraten (cont.)

Place meat in a glass or ceramic bowl—never metal. In a medium saucepan, combine all the ingredients for the marinade and boil for 5 minutes; cool. Pour the cooled marinade over the roast and cover entirely. Keep in a cool place 3 to 4 days, turning meat once a day.

In a Dutch oven, brown diced bacon and then remove the crisp bits and set aside. Drain the meat, pat dry, brown in hot bacon fat. Add half the marinade as well as the vegetables from the marinade and the crisp bacon and bring the liquid to a boil. Reduce the heat to the lowest possible point and simmer, covered, until tender, adding more marinade as necessary. Turn occasionally with spoon and tongs—don't pierce the meat. The cooking time will depend on the age and tenderness of the meat—at least $2\frac{1}{2}$ to 3 hours. When fork tender, remove to hot platter and keep warm.

Bring marinade (including reserved) to a boil, add gingersnaps and roux, stirring together until thickened. Strain through a sieve; add sour cream and reheat over low heat for 3 to 4 minutes; do not boil.

Serve with potato dumplings (Kartoffelknödel) and red cabbage.

Venison à la Mode

This is an adaptation of the French classic, Boeuf à la Mode, which means "in the current fashion" (not with ice cream on top).

4 pounds boneless rump, round or
    chuck roast
Salt pork
$\frac{1}{4}$ cup brandy
$\frac{1}{4}$ cup drippings
Freshly ground black pepper
1 clove garlic, chopped
2 or 3 shallots or $\frac{1}{4}$ cup onion,
    chopped
Bouquet garni (parsley, thyme, bay leaf
    tied together)
1 cup white wine
1 veal knuckle bone
1 bunch carrots, quartered
12 small white onions

Cut larding pork in long thin strips and marinate in brandy for one hour. Lard the roast, reserving the brandy.

In a Dutch oven, brown the meat in drippings, turning so all sides are browned. Season with freshly ground black pepper. Add all remaining ingredients, except carrots and onions, including brandy. Cover and simmer over very low heat until almost completely tender, at least 4 hours. Add carrots and whole onions, continue to simmer until vegetables are tender—about 45 minutes. Remove bouquet garni and knuckle bone, check seasoning and thicken gravy.

Serve roast with vegetables arranged around it. Pour some gravy over the roast, serve remainder in a sauce boat. Crusty French bread, a crisp salad, fruit and cheese for dessert are delicious accompaniments. Serves 6.

Stuffed Shoulder of Venison

1 shoulder roast, boned
Stuffing of your choice
Bacon drippings
2 carrots, sliced
1 medium onion, sliced
Freshly ground black pepper
2 cups game stock

Stuff boned shoulder roast with any savory stuffing of your choice, being sure that the stuffing is not too moist; the steam generated in the braising process will make it soggy if it's moist to begin with. Tie or sew the roast together.

Sear meat on all sides in heavy skillet in hot fat, adding carrot and onion slices if you wish. Season with black pepper and add enough game stock to fill skillet 1/2-inch deep. Cover and simmer over low heat until tender, adding more stock if needed. Remove roast to serving platter, remove string and thicken gravy if desired.

West Texas Pot Roast

3- to 4-pound venison rump or round roast
4 tablespoons bacon drippings
1 1/2 cups onion, chopped
2 to 3 cups Texas-Style B-B-Q Sauce (*see* page 177)
1 1/2 cups green bell peppers, chopped
16 small white onions
Whole mushrooms, if desired

In a heavy Dutch oven or large heavy pot with cover, heat the bacon drippings and brown the meat on all sides. Move to the rim of the pot; add the onion and sauté lightly. Cover the roast with the Texas-style B-B-Q Sauce, add the green pepper and simmer 3 hours or more, until meat is tender. During the last hour of cooking, add the small white onions and mushrooms, if desired. Serves 4 to 6.

STEWS

Stew is just stew, you say disdainfully? Well, perhaps we're just peasants at heart. But in our opinion, a properly prepared stew—with succulent pieces of meat and vegetables still crisply tender, all in a rich and savory sauce—is a meal fit for a king! Biscuits baked separately to soak up that delicious gravy, or dumplings added to the pot the last few minutes—you can't ask for anything better.

Stews are ideal for camp cooking—the browned meat can be left to simmer in the Dutch oven all day (either in a pit of coals or over a carefully banked fire). When you return to camp, dinner is ready in a jiffy—add vegetables to the pot and while they are simmering, whip up a batch of biscuits or dumplings, make coffee—and dig in.

At home, I usually prepare a double amount of meat and sauce. When the meat is tender, I remove half the meat and sauce, cool and freeze it in quart containers. Then I have only to add fresh vegetables for a delectable meal on short notice. Vegetables, completely cooked in a stew and then frozen, tend to become mushy when reheated—one of my pet peeves!

Canadian-Style Moose

2 pounds moose round, cubed
Flour
4 slices bacon, diced
1 cup onion, chopped
3 cloves garlic, chopped
1 cup dry red wine
1 cup water
2 tablespoons Sauce Robert
Pinch of allspice
1/2 bay leaf
1/4 teaspoon thyme
Freshly ground black pepper
Paprika
1 cup cabbage, shredded
1 cup pearl onions (*or* small white)
1 cup petit pois (baby green peas)
1/2 pound mushrooms, sliced
1/2 cup heavy cream
2 teaspoons cornstarch dissolved in a
     little water
Puff pastry shells, baked

In a large Dutch oven, fry out the diced bacon and remove with a slotted spoon. Dredge moose in flour and brown in bacon fat on all sides. Add the onion and garlic and lightly sauté. Add the red wine, water, Sauce Robert, allspice, bay leaf, thyme, and a sprinkling of black pepper and paprika. Return the bacon to the pot and add the cabbage; simmer for 2 to 3 hours, stirring occasionally, until meat is tender.

Add the pearl onions, peas and mushrooms and cook for another 15 minutes (perhaps less, until the vegetables are crisp-tender). Then add the heavy cream and simmer another 10 minutes; thicken with cornstarch if the sauce needs it, before serving in the baked pastry shells.

Hungarian Goulash

Hungarians usually make their national stew with veal—occasionally with beef. However, any stew meat of the deer family is an excellent substitute. This is my Mother-in-law's recipe, one I have enjoyed many times.

3 pounds stew meat
1 1/2 pounds onions, thinly sliced
2 or 3 green banana peppers, cut into
     1-inch pieces
Butter
2 teaspoons sweet Hungarian paprika
Salt and pepper
1 tablespoon roux
1/2 cup sour cream

Melt butter in heavy covered saucepan, put in thinly sliced onions and simmer until they are golden in color. Add paprika (more if you are not using the real Hungarian paprika), add 1 soup ladle of water, cook until the water evaporates, repeat with the soup ladle of water, add meat, green pepper and salt and pepper. Barely cover with water and

Hungarian Goulash (cont.)

simmer on very low heat, covered, until the meat is tender, adding more water if necessary. Thicken gravy with roux (*see* Sauces), stir well, add sour cream and

heat just below boiling point, stirring constantly.

Serve with rice, noodles or dumplings.

 Skillet Stew with Sour Cream

3 pounds stew meat, cubed
1 onion, sliced
Drippings
Salt and pepper
3 cups canned tomatoes
2 cups sour cream *or* 2 cups
**   evaporated milk plus 2¹/₂**
**   tablespoons vinegar or lemon juice**
Generous dash of paprika

In a heavy iron skillet, brown meat and onions in drippings. Season with salt and pepper, add tomatoes and sour cream along with paprika. Cover the skillet and set over lowest possible fire, so the liquid is barely bubbling. Stir once in a while and restrain yourself until the meat is really tender, about 2 or 3 hours.

Plain boiled potatoes, noodles or rice are served with it.

 Venison Stew

All of the seasonings listed may not be available in camp, but proceed without them—hunger is still the best seasoning.

3 pounds game, cut into 2-inch cubes
¹/₄ cup drippings
Boiling water or stock to cover
Juice of ¹/₂ lemon
Dash of Worcestershire Sauce
1 clove of garlic
2 onions, sliced
2 or 3 bay leaves
Salt and pepper
Dash of paprika
Pinch cloves or allspice
Carrots, small whole or quartered
**   lengthwise**
Small white onions (cut an X in top and
**   bottom so they won't separate in**
**   cooking)**
Potatoes, cut into cubes

Brown the meat thoroughly in hot fat in a Dutch oven—don't use all the drippings at once, but add as necessary. I prefer to brown only a part of the meat at a time, then remove it to a plate; this way you can be certain all is browned evenly. Return all the meat to the pot, add water or stock, garlic, sliced onions and seasonings. Cover and simmer over very low heat until the meat is almost completely tender, stirring occasionally to prevent sticking and adding a bit more liquid if necessary.

Add vegetables and continue to simmer 20 to 30 minutes—only until the vegetables are tender—don't let them disintegrate! Check for the need of a bit

Venison Stew (cont.)

more salt during the last 15 minutes—the addition of the vegetables may require it.

If you haven't drowned the meat in liquid, the gravy should not need thickening, but if it does, blend flour and water to a smooth paste and add drop by drop, stirring carefully so as not to break the vegetables.

Venison Stew—French Style

Unless yours is a deluxe camp, this adaptation of Boeuf à la Bourguignonne had best be made at home.

3 pounds stew meat, cubed
Drippings
Salt and pepper
1 large onion, minced
1 cup stock
3 tablespoons roux
4 tablespoons tomato paste
1 cup red Burgundy wine
Parsley, thyme, bay leaf and a few celery leaves tied together
Mushrooms, sautéed in butter
Small whole onions, parboiled for 6 to 8 minutes

Brown meat in drippings, season with salt and pepper, and remove from skillet. Add minced onion to skillet and cook briefly—do not brown. Add stock, roux and tomato paste to onion and stir constantly as you bring the mixture to a boil. When all is smooth, replace meat, add Burgundy and herb bouquet. Cover and simmer over low heat until meat is tender.

Fifteen minutes before serving, add mushrooms and whole onions to contents of skillet and continue to simmer until the flavors are blended.

Serve with broad egg noodles.

Zesty Venison Stew

2 pounds venison, cut into 1-inch cubes
2 tablespoons vegetable oil
1 large green pepper, cored, seeded and cut into 1-inch squares
1 large onion, sliced thin
3 cloves garlic, peeled and cut into large pieces
1/4 cup distilled white vinegar
1/4 cup apple cider vinegar
1 16-ounce can whole tomatoes (or 2 cups fresh tomatoes, cut up)
1/3 cup molasses
1 tablespoon honey
2 teaspoons chili powder
1 teaspoon sweet Hungarian paprika
a.f.g. salt
1 1/2 cups carrots, thinly sliced on an angle
1 1/2 cups green beans, sliced on an angle
Freshly cooked white or wild rice

Heat oil in large Dutch oven or saucepan with cover. Add meat and brown on all sides. Remove meat and reserve. Add green pepper, onion and garlic to pan and sauté lightly; cover and reduce heat, simmering for 10 minutes.

Pour vinegar into pan, raise heat and stir, scraping any browned bits from bottom of pan. Return meat to pan and add tomatoes, molasses, honey, chili powder, paprika and salt. Cover and cook over low heat for about 1 hour, or until meat is fork-tender. Add carrots and green beans and cook a half-hour. Total cooking time for meat from a button buck, for example, should not exceed 1 1/2 hours; older meat will require longer.

Serve over rice. Because of the chili flavor, this dish is especially good served with corn bread or sticks.

CHAPTER 3

BEAR, BOAR AND OTHER BIG GAME

Generally speaking, the big game in this chapter—bear, mountain goats and sheep, pronghorn and the category of wild boar, feral hogs and javelina—require longer cooking time than the antlered game. The one exception is the pronghorn.

Native to North America, the *pronghorn* is often called the American antelope because of its similarity in appearance to true antelope. As far as taste goes, however, it is much more akin to venison and is, in fact, more delicate in flavor. You can substitute it in any of the venison recipes in the preceding chapter, or try the pronghorn dishes in this chapter, which do not call for long cooking requirements.

Bear, on the other hand (and we're talking pretty much black bear here), should be cooked in the same manner as pork—that is, *always* well done because of the possibility of trichinosis. The excess fat must be trimmed off and may be rendered for use as shortening. I've never cooked with it myself, but those who have, prefer it to all other shortenings.

Since our remaining bison herds are protected, most of us will have little chance of cooking *buffalo* meat. However, if you are fortunate enough to participate in the occasional hunt to reduce a herd to proper size for its range, cook the meat as you would for any pot roast, removing the fat first.

Mountain goats are hunted primarily for their trophy heads and the flesh of the billies is considered by many to be tough and strong, although still edible before the rut. The flesh of the nannies is excellent. *Wild sheep*, such as the Bighorn, are prized not only for their trophy heads, but for their meat. Wild mutton ranks high in the gourmet class. As with domestic mutton, the fat is unappetizing and should be removed before cooking.

Wild boar, or the wild hog, which is a cross between the Russian boar and the razorback, is also cooked like domestic pork. The young ones are particularly good, but even the old tuskers are delicious after some tenderizing. After all, long slow cooking is necessary for porkers anyway. *Feral hogs* (literally hogs gone wild) are becoming more abundant these days, if not a menace in some parts of the Southeast, specifically Florida. They tend to have a little more fat on them than the wild boars and, if you're smart, they can even be fattened up before they are killed. The *javelina* (or collared peccary), in contrast, is a small member of the porcine family, found only in Arizona, New Mexico and Texas. It has the least fat of the three types of porkers discussed here and some say the meat can be stringy. Slow cooking in a savory sauce often helps.

BEAR

Backwoods' Bear Ragout

This is a one-pot meal that will accommodate whatever you happen to have; my emphasis is on the old-time and less-familiar vegetables.

3 to 4 pounds black bear, cubed
Bear fat
3 large onions, coarsely chopped
3 to 4 whole cloves garlic, peeled
¼ cup flour
1 bay leaf
12 whole peppercorns
6 whole juniper berries
Pinch of allspice
1 to 2 cups turnips, in large chunks
3 Jerusalem artichokes, in large chunks
3 to 4 parsnips, in large chunks
¼ cup fresh parsley, coarsely chopped
2 small kohlrabi, in large chunks
2 cups dry red wine
1 to 2 cups water
1 tablespoon dark brown sugar
Small whole new potatoes (6 to 12)
Whole baby carrots (12)
Roux to thicken, if desired

In a large Dutch oven (I use a 12-quart stainless steel pot for this one), heat the bear fat and brown the cubed meat on all sides. Add the onion and garlic and sauté lightly. Stir in the flour and add all the remaining ingredients, except the new potatoes, baby carrots and roux, making sure there is enough liquid in the pot to cover the meat and vegetables. Cover and simmer 3 to 4 hours, stirring occasionally, until meat is tender. Add the new potatoes and carrots and cook them until they are fork-tender, another 30 minutes or so. Thicken with roux if desired.

This dish could also be prepared in a slow-cooking crock pot, which you'd leave on all day.

☀ Barbecued Bear Leg

This is where the men take over!

1 bear leg
Barbecue Sauce (*see* Chapter 10)

Spit the bear leg and roast over a deep bed of coals in a pit. Be sure you're on sandy or clay soil, not humus or root-filled soil, especially where shallow-rooted evergreens are present. The fire in your cooking pit could start such roots smoldering and the results are disastrous.

To get back to your bear—baste frequently with your favorite barbecue sauce, made in rather large quantities, for this will be a fairly lengthy procedure. Remember that bear must be well done, the time, of course, depending not only on the bear's size, but on your fire.

Bear Rump Roast

Suitable for a young animal. Saddle or leg could also be used.

1 bear rump roast
2 cloves garlic, sliced thin
Freshly ground black pepper
Salt if desired
Lard, salt pork or bacon
Beef bouillon *or* red wine
Roux
Currant or wild blueberry jelly

Cut garlic into small slivers, insert in gashes in the roast, season with black pepper and salt if desired. Lard or tie with bacon or fat pork (adjust salt if you are using bacon). Roast uncovered at 325° F. for 35 to 45 minutes per pound, with just enough beef bouillon or red wine to cover the bottom of the roasting pan. Baste frequently with the pan juices, adding more liquid if necessary.

Make gravy of the pan juices, thickening with roux as necessary. Serve with noodles and currant or wild blueberry jelly, or make the gravy with the currant jelly added to it.

Roast Saddle of Bear

1 saddle of bear
Freshly ground black pepper
Salt if desired
Salt pork
1 cup cider
2 tablespoons soy sauce
1 teaspoon ginger
1 tablespoon lemon juice
2 tablespoons honey

Season with salt and pepper and then lard a saddle of bear. Combine cider, soy sauce, ginger, lemon juice and honey and pour over the meat. Roast as directed for Bear Rump Roast, basting with the pan juices.

This is also excellent served cold with any of the game sauces in Chapter 10.

Bear Steak

Bear steak
1 onion, thinly sliced
1/2 pound mushrooms, sliced
1 green bell pepper, sliced
2 to 3 tablespoons butter
1 cup dry red wine
1/2 cup water
Bouquet of bay leaf, parsley, celery
    tops
Pinch garlic powder
2 whole cloves
1 teaspoon meat glaze
1 6-ounce glass currant jelly

Cut a thick steak, sear under high flame on both sides. Then broil slowly until well done about 3 inches from flame. About 1/2 hour is required for this operation. Serve with sauce prepared in the following way.

Sauté onion, mushrooms and green pepper in a small amount of butter for 5 minutes; do not brown. Add remaining ingredients and simmer 20 to 25 minutes. Remove herb bouquet, blend in currant jelly and correct seasoning.

Pot Roast of Bear

Use any of the pot roast recipes found in this chapter and the one on Antlered Game. Just remember that to ensure against trichinosis, cook the bear about 45 minutes to the pound, until well done and tender.

MOUNTAIN GOAT AND SHEEP

Goat or Sheep Curry

I must confess it's taken me years to discover that true curry is a wonderful blend of aromatic spices, not just a powder you buy in a jar. If you've never experimented with curry "from scratch," do—you'll love it.

2 pounds goat or sheep round, cubed
3 to 4 tablespoons peanut oil
1 cup onion, chopped
2 cloves garlic, chopped
Freshly ground black pepper
2 tablespoons flour
1 cup chicken stock or bouillon
1 cup cow's milk or *unsweetened*
    coconut milk
1 teaspoon fresh ginger, chopped*
1 bay leaf

Curry:
1 teaspoon coriander seeds, finely
    crushed
1/4 teaspoon ground cumin
1/2 teaspoon ground cinnamon
1/4 teaspoon ground cardamon

* Fresh ginger will keep indefinitely peeled and plopped in a jar of dry sherry; cover the jar and refrigerate.

Goat or Sheep Curry (cont.)

In a large heavy pan or Dutch oven, heat the oil and brown the meat on all sides. Add the onion and garlic and sauté lightly. Sprinkle with black pepper and stir in the flour until well blended.

Pour in the chicken stock and milk (you might try goat's milk, although I have not). Stir until mixture begins to thicken. Add the fresh ginger, bay leaf and the curry spices (wrap coriander in a piece of cheesecloth if you haven't been able to crush it finely enough). Cook for about ½ hour and taste to see if the curry is to your liking. If you like your curry "hotter," simply add more of the spices, going lightly with the cumin, for that is the one that adds the most "zip." Continue cooking over low heat, covered, for another 1½ to 2 hours, until meat is very tender.

Serve this over rice (from 4 to 6 people) garnished with sautéed golden raisins and slivered almonds, and grated coconut. For a beverage, especially if you've prepared a spicy version, try beer.

 ## Grilled Goat or Sheep

2 pounds prime cuts goat or sheep

Marinade:
¼ cup lemon juice
¼ cup butter, melted
2 cloves garlic, minced
1 small onion, finely chopped
1 teaspoon parsley, chopped
Sprinkling of oregano
Freshly ground black pepper

Small white onions
Green peppers

Cube about 2 pounds prime cuts of goat or sheep and marinate a few hours or overnight in a blend of the marinade ingredients.

With this mixture you will be able to coat the meat, rather than soak it. Place cubes on skewers, alternating with small white onions and pieces of green pepper if desired. Grill over medium-hot coals, turning frequently and brushing with any remaining marinade. Cook until well done and serve with rice.

Leg of Sheep—English Style

1 leg of sheep
1 bay leaf
1 onion, sliced
½ lemon, sliced thin
1 teaspoon salt
Water to cover
Caper Sauce (*see* page 167)

To eliminate the possibility of a strong flavor, remove all fat from the leg. In a large kettle, cover joint with boiling water, and boil hard for 10 minutes. Skim any fat that rises; add bay leaf, onion and lemon and simmer, covered, until tender. Add salt halfway through cooking period.

Serve with Caper Sauce.

Excellent for that goat or sheep.

**3 pounds neck or shoulder meat, cubed
   and trimmed of all fat**
Drippings
Salt and black pepper
Water to cover
**Bouquet garni (parsley, thyme and bay
   leaf tied together)**
Turnip, diced (if available)
Carrots
Small whole onions
Potatoes

Brown the meat in drippings, season with salt and pepper, add water to cover and herbs. Cover and simmer on low heat until tender. Add turnip, carrots, onions and potatoes and cook for about ¹/₂ hour longer.

Herb biscuits or parsley dumplings are a tasty accompaniment.

Mountain Sheep Roast

Roast from hind leg or saddle
Lemon juice
Vegetable, peanut or olive oil
Salt and freshly ground black pepper
Garlic, if desired, or rosemary leaves
Water

Remove all fat possible, rub the roast with lemon juice and then brush with oil. Season with salt and freshly ground black pepper, insert slivers of garlic in the roast or sprinkle a few rosemary leaves in the bottom of the roaster.

Sear in preheated oven at 475° F. until browned, about 20 minutes. Add water to cover bottom of pan; reduce heat and roast at 300° F. 25 minutes per pound until tender, basting frequently.

Mint jelly, parsley buttered new potatoes and fresh peas are traditional, but you might also try curried rice, for a change.

Roast Saddle of Goat

Marinade:
**1 cup white wine *or* ¹/₂ cup water and
   ¹/₂ cup wine or cider vinegar**
1 teaspoon salt
1 onion, thinly sliced
8 or 10 peppercorns, crushed
2 bay leaves
4 tablespoons salad oil

Flour
Freshly ground black pepper
Salt if desired

Savory leaves, crumbled
¹/₄ cup melted butter
¹/₂ cup water
2 teaspoons lemon juice

Combine all the ingredients for the marinade in a glass or ceramic bowl and marinate the roast for two days.
Cover and set in a cool place, turning the meat at least once or twice a day. Remove from marinade, drain and pat dry.

Sprinkle lightly with flour, black

Roast Saddle of Goat (cont.)

pepper and salt and crumbled savory leaves. Preheat oven to 475° F., roast for 15 to 20 minutes, then lower oven temperature to 325° F. and roast ½ hour per pound, basting with a blend of melted butter, water and lemon juice.

Scandinavian-Style Sheep or Goat with Dill

The basic method is the same as the English-style leg of sheep; the difference is in the seasoning. If you have only a tiny plot of land, by all means plant some dill next year. It has dozens of uses in the kitchen—in breads, fish dishes, vegetables and salads, as well as dill pickles. The feathery leaves freeze well in plastic bags for year-round use.

Shoulder or leg roast
Water to cover
1 tablespoon salt for each 2 quarts of water
6 sprigs fresh dill *or* a generous pinch of dill seed
1 cup medium white sauce (*see* page 166)
2 tablespoons lemon juice or vinegar
2 teaspoons sugar
3 tablespoons dill, finely snipped

Place meat in a large kettle, add water to cover, measuring as you do so. Add proportionate amounts of salt and dill. Bring to a boil uncovered; skim foam. Cover and simmer slowly until tender. Remove to a warm serving platter and keep warm until the meat has a chance to firm up (about 20 minutes).

Prepare White Sauce, add vinegar or lemon juice, sugar and snipped dill. Carve the meat in thin slices, arrange on platter, pour over some of the sauce and serve the rest in a sauce boat.

Red cabbage or beets are good here.

Wild Sheep with Greek-Style Vegetables

A unique blending of herbs gives this dish a wonderful aroma while it is cooking and a delicious flavor when it is done.

2 pounds sheep or goat round, cubed
Flour
Olive oil (3 to 4 tablespoons + ½ cup)
Freshly ground black pepper
1 medium onion, chopped
3 cloves garlic, chopped
½ cup wine vinegar
1½ cups water
Large bouquet garni of 1 teaspoon *each*: coriander seeds, dill weed, caraway seeds, thyme, rosemary

1 large eggplant, peeled and cubed
2 large green bell peppers, seeded and cubed
2 cups ripe tomatoes, peeled, seeded and chopped
1 teaspoon sugar
1 tablespoon fresh lemon juice

In a large Dutch oven, heat 3 to 4 tablespoons olive oil and brown on all sides the cubed meat that you have dredged in flour. Add the onion and garlic and sauté briefly. Season with black pepper and add the vinegar and water and simmer the meat, covered, about 2 hours.

Then add the additional ½ cup olive oil, the bouquet garni, eggplant, green pepper, tomatoes, sugar and lemon juice; cook for another 30 to 45 minutes, until the vegetables and meat are very tender. Serve with rice.

PRONGHORN (American Antelope)

 ## All-American Kabobs

2 pounds pronghorn, cubed
2 cups B-B-Q Sauce, Texas Style (*see* page 177)
1 pound small white onions, peeled
3 to 4 green bell peppers, cubed
1 pound large button mushrooms, wiped clean and left whole

Marinate cubed pronghorn overnight in Texas Style B-B-Q Sauce; use a glass or ceramic bowl with lid. When ready to start grilling, spear onto your skewers in any order you wish: a cube of pronghorn, a small onion, a piece of green pepper and a mushroom. Alternate until you fill up each skewer. Grill over hot coals, brushing with B-B-Q Sauce as you turn the kabobs.

Serve with rice, cold potatoe salad, corn-on-the-cob, or your favorite B-B-Q fixings.

Colorado Fondue

Pronghorn has such a good flavor that we particularly enjoy its steaks and, for parties, this festive dish that guests cook themselves.

2 pounds pronghorn, cubed (use a good cut, as from the tenderloin)
Vegetable or peanut oil
Sauces for dipping, such as Curry Mayonnaise, Garlic Mayonnaise, Mustard Mayonnaise, Horseradish Sauce or your own favorites

Have cubed pronghorn at room temperature and your sauces already prepared. Assemble your guests around the table and set up your fondue pot in the center, heating the oil and passing samples of sauce and pronghorn to each diner. Spear a piece or two of meat onto the end of a small skewer (each person gets his own, usually with a marking to distinguish it from the others'), put the skewer in the hot oil, leaving it there till meat is medium-rare, about a minute or so. Then dip cooked pronghorn in the sauce of your choice—and enjoy.

Colorado Fondue (cont.)

This way of eating fosters great conviviality and is a special treat among good friends.

Curry Mayonnaise. Blend well 2 teaspoons curry powder with ¹/₂ cup prepared mayonnaise; let stand about ¹/₂ hour.

Garlic Mayonnaise. Stir 2 teaspoons minced garlic into 1 cup prepared mayonnaise; let stand before serving.

Horseradish Sauce. Mix well 1 tablespoon prepared horseradish, ¹/₂ teaspoon Worcestershire Sauce, ¹/₂ cup mayonnaise, 2 tablespoons sour cream.

Mustard Mayonnaise. Combine well 2 teaspoons country stone-ground mustard with ¹/₂ cup mayonnaise; let flavors blend.

 ## Panhandler Pronghorn

2 pounds pronghorn, cubed
¹/₄ to ¹/₂ cup flour, seasoned with freshly ground black pepper
2 to 3 tablespoons vegetable oil or bacon drippings
2 cups onion, chopped
3 cups Old-fashioned Chili Sauce (*see* page 177)
1 teaspoon chili powder
¹/₄ teaspoon cumin

Dredge the meat in the seasoned flour. In a large, heavy skillet heat the oil and brown the pronghorn on all sides. Remove from pan; reserve. Add the onion and cook until golden. Return the meat to the pan and add the remaining ingredients; simmer about 1¹/₂ hours, or until meat is tender.

Serve over rice.

Pronghorn in Beer

2¹/₂ to 3 pounds pronghorn round cut into 1-inch cubes
Flour seasoned with freshly ground black pepper
Bacon drippings or blanched salt pork drippings
2 cups onion, thinly sliced
2 cloves garlic, chopped
2 tablespoons flour
1 teaspoon paprika
1 12-ounce can beer
1 cup game stock or beef consommé
1 bay leaf
1 tablespoon fresh parsley
¹/₂ teaspoon dried thyme
1 tablespoon apple cider vinegar
1 tablespoon light brown sugar

Dredge the meat cubes in flour. In a heavy Dutch oven, heat the bacon or salt pork drippings and brown the meat on all sides. Remove with a slotted spoon and reserve. Add the onion and garlic to the pan and sauté lightly, adding more drippings as needed. Stir in the flour until well blended, and add the beer and game stock, stirring until smooth and

Pronghorn in Beer (cont.)

slightly thickened. Add the herbs, vinegar and brown sugar and return the meat to the pan. Cover and simmer over low heat for about 2 to 3 hours, or until tender. Before serving, check the gravy for seasoning and sprinkle in a little freshly ground black pepper and salt, if desired.

If it is convenient, this dish may be baked in a 350° F. oven in a covered casserole for 2 to 3 hours, rather than the stove-top cooking.

❧ Pronghorn Goulash

2 pounds pronghorn round, cubed
4 tablespoons vegetable oil
2 medium onions, chopped
2 cloves garlic, chopped
4 tablespoons flour
1 tablespoon sweet Hungarian paprika
¼ teaspoon freshly ground black
  pepper
¼ teaspoon dried thyme
1 28-ounce can peeled tomatoes
1 cup sour cream

In a Dutch oven, heat the oil and brown the pronghorn cubes on all sides. Add the onion and garlic and cook till onion is translucent. In a separate cup, blend together the flour, paprika, black pepper and thyme. Add to meat/onion mixture and blend in well.

Stir in the tomatoes, breaking them up a bit so they cook more evenly. Cover and simmer, stirring from time to time so the meat does not stick; cook a total of 1½ hours.

When meat is tender, blend in the sour cream, heat through but do not boil. Serve over rice or buttered egg noodles. Serves 4 to 6.

Pronghorn Pot Roast

3- to 4-pound rump or round roast
Freshly ground black pepper
Flour
Bacon drippings or lard
1 cup onion, chopped
2 cloves garlic, chopped
2 cups fresh plum tomatoes, peeled and
  chopped *or* 1 12-ounce can V-8
  juice plus ½ cup water
1 tablespoon brown sugar
1 bay leaf
1 teaspoon caraway seeds

Season the roast with black pepper and coat with flour. In a Dutch oven, heat the bacon drippings or lard and brown the meat on all sides. Move to the rim of the pan and add the onion and garlic and sauté these lightly. Add the remaining ingredients and simmer 2½ to 3 hours, or until meat is tender.

Before I thicken and season the gravy, I like to strain it to remove the caraway seeds. Often my guests will not know what the unique flavor of the gravy is and I simply tell them it is my "secret" ingredient. Thicken the gravy with roux as needed and check the seasoning; add black pepper and salt, if desired.

This is delicious with plain old mashed potatoes and a mixed vegetable. Serves 4 to 6.

WILD BOAR, FERAL HOGS AND JAVELINA

Baked Boar Chops

6 to 8 boar chops
Freshly ground black pepper
Salt if desired
Raw Cranberry Relish (*see* page 179)
Orange juice

Brown chops slowly in skillet, season with pepper and salt. Place in buttered casserole, cover each chop with raw cranberry relish, cover casserole and bake at 350° F. at least 1 1/2 hours or until tender. Add a bit of orange juice if needed near the end of the baking time. Serves 3 to 4.

Baked Boar Ribs with Sauerkraut

Wild boar ribs
Sauerkraut
3 strips bacon, diced
2 apples, sliced
Caraway seeds
4 to 6 juniper berries
1/2 cup dry white wine
Freshly ground black pepper
Salt if desired
Idaho baking potatoes

In a roaster, place sauerkraut, diced bacon, apple slices, a liberal sprinkle of caraway seeds, the juniper berries and the wine. Place boar ribs on top and sprinkle with pepper and salt. Bake at 350° F. for 1 1/2 hours. Scrub a few Idaho potatoes and toss those in the oven next to the roaster the last 45 minutes. Serve with your favorite mustard.

Braised Wild Boar—Hungarian Style

1 wild boar roast, 4 to 6 pounds
Flour seasoned with garlic powder and
    freshly ground black pepper
2 tablespoons strained bacon drippings
2 plum tomatoes, chopped
2 frying or banana peppers, sliced
2 parsnips, sliced
2 carrots, sliced
1/2 bay leaf
8 juniper berries
1/4 cup water
2 tablespoons fresh lemon juice
1 cup red Hungarian wine
2 teaspoons sweet Hungarian paprika

Have the roast at room temperature. Dredge in flour. Preheat oven to 350° F. In a Dutch oven, heat the bacon drippings on top of the stove (or whatever heat source), and brown the roast on all sides.

Add the remaining ingredients in order, stir and cover; place in the oven and braise the roast about 40 minutes to the pound, turning occasionally, until thoroughly cooked and tender. Be sure to use the Hungarian ingredients as stated—the banana peppers, paprika and wine. I have used the popular

Braised Wild Boar—Hungarian Style (cont.)

Hungarian wine "Egri Bikavér," or "Bulls Blood of Eger," with delicious results, although I have also sampled the Soproni "Kékfrankos," a little lighter red wine, which would do equally nicely.

When the meat is done, place it on a platter. Remove the bay leaf from the "gravy" and strain the juice directly into a blender, reserving the vegetables. Take half the mushy vegetables and puree them in the blender with the juice; this will become your final gravy. Add more vegetables as necessary, depending on how thick you like your gravy.

You will love this dish with its remarkably subtle flavor. Serve it with Hungarian red wine and some warm homemade bread or popovers. Serves 8.

Boned Boar Ham Epicure

1 whole boar ham
Prune and Apple Stuffing or Sage and Onion Stuffing (*see* Chapter 11)
Freshly ground black pepper
Salt if desired

With a thin, sharp boning knife, remove the bone from the whole ham, working from the underside where the bone is closest to the surface. Stuff the pocket lightly with Prune and Apple Stuffing or Sage and Onion Stuffing, allowing for expansion of the stuffing. With a curved needle, such as is used for upholstery work, sew up the opening, catching sufficient flesh in the sewing process so that the stitching won't pull out as the ham is cooked. Season ham with salt and pepper (plus poultry seasoning if sage dressing was used).

Roast at 350° F. for 30 minutes per pound, basting with pan drippings. Any additional stuffing may be baked in the roasting pan or in a separate tin the last hour. Make gravy in the usual fashion.

Garnish the platter with glazed apple slices, glazed oranges or rosy spiced crab apples. (Remove all evidence of your surgery—the string—before serving, of course.) Your husband will be delighted not to have to carve around the bone, and I believe your guests will be impressed with the stuffing-centered slices.

Carolina Boar Chops 'n Pecan Gravy

These cornbread-pecan stuffed chops are not for calorie counters. They are very rich, very tasty and probably should be saved for some special occasion.

1 cup dry cornbread stuffing crumbs
¹/₃ cup milk *or* light cream
1 egg, slightly beaten
4 tablespoons butter, melted, plus 2 tablespoons
2 tablespoons + ¹/₂ cup pecans, finely ground
4 large double-thick boar or hog chops

Freshly ground black pepper
Flour
2 tablespoons vegetable oil
¹/₂ cup + 2 teaspoons Southern Comfort
1 cup chicken stock
1 cup heavy cream
2 teaspoons cornstarch

Cornbread-Pecan Stuffing. Combine cornbread crumbs, milk (or half and half or light cream), the beaten egg plus a little water, the melted butter and 2 tablespoons ground pecans. Mix well so all the crumbs absorb the liquids, and let stand for about ½ hour; this should not be a mushy stuffing, however.

Meanwhile, slice each chop horizontally to allow for stuffing. Season with black pepper and dredge in flour. In a large skillet, heat the remaining butter and oil and brown on all sides. Cool, then stuff with the cornbread stuffing. Place the chops in a buttered casserole large enough to accommodate them. Preheat your oven to 350° F.

In the skillet in which you browned the chops, pour the ½ cup Southern Comfort, turn up the heat and reduce the liquor by half, scraping any bits that adhered to the bottom. Add the chicken stock and stir. Pour some of this blend into the casserole, just enough to cover the bottom. Don't add too much, because you don't want the stuffing to get soggy. Reserve the rest for the gravy, but should the liquid level get too low in the casserole, add more. Bake the chops about ¾ hour on one side, gently turn over and bake another ¾ hour.

When chops are tender, carefully remove them to a platter and keep them warm. In a small saucepan, strain in the pan juices from the casserole; add the remaining chicken stock and the heavy cream. Stir to blend and simmer about 5 minutes. Add the cornstarch which you have dissolved in a little water, ½ cup ground pecans and 2 teaspoons Southern Comfort. Simmer another 10 minutes, stirring constantly until the gravy thickens and the flavors mellow. Serve over boar chops.

Because this dish is so rich, I would recommend serving with it only plain green vegetables and a simple salad. Peach pie would be a nice touch for dessert, though, if you've got room.

Javelina Chops with Apple

4 to 6 javelina chops
Flour
Vegetable oil
Freshly ground black pepper
4 to 6 whole cloves
4 to 6 slices onion
**4 to 6 slices *red* apple, unpeeled but
    cored**
Water, white wine *or* apple cider

In a large skillet, heat the oil and brown on all sides the chops which you have dredged in flour. Season with black pepper and into the center of each, place 1 whole clove, then top with one slice each of onion and apple. Pour a little water, white wine or cider into the bottom of the pan, cover and simmer for about an hour or so, until the meat is tender.

Buttered egg noodles go well with this dish.

Javelina Spanish Rice

2 pounds javelina, cubed, *or*
    6 steaks or chops
Vegetable oil
1 cup onion, chopped
2 cloves garlic, chopped
1 to 2 large green bell peppers, seeded
    and coarsely chopped
Freshly ground black pepper
2 teaspoons chili powder
1/2 teaspoon ground cumin
3/4 cup long-grain rice, uncooked
3 1/2 cups peeled tomatoes, coarsely
    chopped, with juice (1 28-ounce
    can)
1/2 cup cheddar cheese, shredded

In a large skillet or Dutch oven, heat the oil and brown the javelina on all sides. Add the onion, garlic and green pepper and sauté briefly. Season with black pepper, the chili powder and ground cumin. If you are using meat from the round, for example, cover it and cook it in the skillet for about an hour with the tomatoes, then add the rice the last hour. If you're preparing steaks or chops, add the tomatoes and rice together and cook, covered, for only an hour or so, until the meat is tender. Add the cheddar cheese and heat through till cheese is melted.

Roast Saddle of Boar

1 saddle of boar
Freshly ground black pepper
Salt if desired
Poultry seasoning *or* dried savory
    leaves

Season the saddle of a young boar with salt and freshly ground black pepper, sprinkle on some poultry seasoning (the type you normally use for turkey

stuffing) or crumble a few dried savory leaves in the bottom of the roasting pan. Roast uncovered in a slow oven 325° F. for 35 minutes per pound, basting with the pan drippings. If desired, a small amount of water may be placed in the bottom of the pan; make gravy with the pan juices.

    Serve with sweet potatoes and Gooseberry Sauce.

Skillet Hog Steaks

4 to 6 thick hog steaks or chops
Flour
Vegetable oil
Freshly ground black pepper
Garlic powder
1 onion, chopped
1/4 teaspoon dried thyme
1/4 teaspoon dried basil
1/4 cup dry white wine
Water

Dredge steaks or chops in flour. In a large skillet (with cover), heat oil and brown steaks on both sides; season with black pepper and garlic powder. Add onion and sauté lightly. Add remaining ingredients—the water to keep the steaks moist during cooking—and simmer for 1 to 1 1/2 hours, until meat is tender.

Wild Boar—Austrian Style

Boar shoulder joint
Salted water to cover
1 cup vinegar
2 cups water
2 cups red wine
2 onions, sliced
Soup greens: carrot, celery, parsnip,
    parsley
1 bay leaf
10 to 12 whole peppercorns
10 to 12 juniper berries
Roux
1 cup cranberry sauce

Simmer shoulder joint in salted water to cover for 1½ hours. Drain and return to kettle with the remaining ingredients, except the roux and the cranberry sauce. Cover and simmer until tender. Slice meat and arrange on hot platter, keep warm. Make gravy from 2 cups of the cooking liquid, enough roux to thicken, then add the cranberry sauce.

CHAPTER 4

ALL YOU CAN DO WITH BURGER

"What am I going to do with all that burger?" I've heard that lament from many a hunter's wife. Unfortunately, some butchers think only in terms of steaks and hamburgers. They may be rushed or completely indifferent and take the easiest way out by putting as much as possible through the meat grinder. The butchers are not wholly to blame, however. I have heard hunters say, "I don't care—just cut it up and freeze it for me!" Serves 'em right for not being more specific!

On the other hand, there *are* times when it is wise to have a good quantity of meat ground. If you have a venerable trophy animal on your hands, grinding the less tender cuts may be the ideal solution. And that includes not only the buck that got in the way of your gun, but the boar, mountain goat or sheep, too.

The only trouble is that ground meat has a storage life of about 4 to 6 months in the freezer, and the cook may be hard pressed for new and different ways to get rid of it all before the family rebels.

The answer is simple: be a United Nations cook and invite your friends to share the feasts with you. The lowly burger can be prepared in hundreds of delicious ways, as you will see from the following recipes, including casseroles, meat loaves and one-dish meals that will help you in menu preparation—not to mention mixing it into sausage (*see* Chapter 8).

Despite the ease with which a butcher can grind and package game, you can do your own—with equal ease. All you really need is a good meat grinder (which can be borrowed usually from a hunting buddy). Do not use your food processor, though, for if you use its basic metal blade, you'll wind up with mush, not ground meat. Remember also that regardless of whether you or your butcher prepares the burger, it should be mixed with ground pork—to replace the natural fat that needs to be removed before freezing and cooking. The proportions? Some people prefer 60 percent game to 40 percent pork; others like it 75:25. Suit yourself.

EASTERN EUROPEAN DISHES

There are countless variations of these old European dishes and their original origins have become lost as each cook adds or substitutes ingredients at hand. You may have different ways of preparing them, but the end result is hearty and delicious on a cold winter evening.

Cabbage Casserole

1 head cabbage, shredded
1 pound ground game
2 or 3 stalks celery, chopped
1 green pepper, chopped
3 tart apples, pared, cored and sliced
3 cups canned tomatoes
1 bay leaf
Pinch of cloves (or garlic powder)
Salt and pepper to taste

Preheat oven to 275° F. to 300° F.

Remove outer leaves from cabbage, wash and shred. Let the cabbage drain while you brown the meat in a Dutch oven or deep skillet with the celery and green pepper in a small amount of hot fat. Remove from heat; add cabbage, apple slices, tomatoes and seasonings. Mix together thoroughly and turn into a casserole dish. Cover and bake in a slow oven for 1 1/2 hours.

Stuffed Cabbage Leaves

The Armenians use grape leaves for another variation of this dish.

1 large head of cabbage
1 1/2 pounds ground venison
1 onion, chopped
1 egg, beaten
1 tablespoon salt
1 teaspoon pepper
1 tablespoon paprika
1 cup raw rice

4 cups canned tomatoes, cut into pieces
1 onion, sliced
1 bay leaf
1 cup sour cream

Remove the core and any wilted outer leaves from the cabbage. Place in boiling salted water for 5 to 10 minutes to soften the leaves. Remove each leaf whole and set aside to drain. Combine meat, onion, beaten egg, seasonings, and rice; mix well.

On each cabbage leaf, place about 2 or 3 tablespoons filling, fold the sides of the leaf over and roll up. It may be necessary to remove part of the heavy rib on some of the larger leaves so they will roll more easily; do this by carefully slicing the rib *horizontally* so that it is level with the outlying leaf. Tie each roll with white string and set aside.

Grease a large casserole, place in the bottom the remainder of the cabbage, shredded, onion and bay leaf. Set the cabbage rolls on top and pour over the canned tomatoes. Cover the casserole and bake at 350° F. until the cabbage rolls are very tender allowing 1 to 1½ hours. Add the sour cream, scalded, and serve with dark bread.

In the Near East, this same recipe is used with lamb or mutton. If you have goat or sheep meat available, try it in this recipe instead of the ground venison.

ITALIAN DISHES

The basis of many, although far from all, Italian dishes is "fresh" tomato sauce, which I prepare in huge quantities and freeze in quart containers. One point to consider however: if you use plastic freezer containers for tomato sauce, you will find it almost impossible to reuse them for anything else—the tomato not only stains them, but the pungency of the sauce seems to permeate the plastic. Waxed tubs are the answer to this problem.

Italian Tomato Sauce

3 onions, chopped
4 cloves garlic, chopped (optional)
½ cup olive oil
3 28-ounce cans Italian plum tomatoes, peeled
2 28-ounce cans tomato pureé
6 6-ounce cans Italian tomato paste
4 cups water
1 to 2 tablespoons salt
2 teaspoons ground black pepper
2 tablespoons sugar
3 to 4 bay leaves *or*

Generous sprinkling of dried basil and oregano (fresh preferred)

Brown onions and garlic in olive oil, add remaining ingredients to large kettle, using water to rinse out the tomato paste cans. Cook over very low heat for about 2½ hours, stirring occasionally, as it may tend to scorch. Cool, package and freeze. This will make 4 quarts of sauce.

Italian Meatballs

6 eggs
1¹/₂ cups milk
2¹/₂ cups fine dry bread crumbs
1¹/₂ cups grated Parmesan or Romano cheese
2 cloves garlic, finely minced
8 to 10 sprigs fresh parsley, chopped, or 3 tablespoons dried parsley flakes
Salt and freshly ground black pepper to taste
3 pounds ground game meat
³/₄ pound ground pork
Olive or vegetable oil

In large mixing bowl, beat eggs with milk, add bread crumbs, cheese, garlic, parsley, salt and pepper. Place meats in the bowl, roll up your sleeves and start mixing with your hands. It's the only way I've found to be certain the ingredients will all be thoroughly mixed, especially working with such large quantities.

Set out a large skillet, form balls about the size of golf balls and brown on all sides in hot oil. As the balls are browned, set aside on a large platter to cool, if not to be used the same day. When cool, place on wax paper-covered cookie sheets and freeze. The individually frozen meatballs may be packaged in plastic sacks or containers. The advantage, of course, is that you can always remove just the quantity needed for a twosome or a crowd.

The meatballs will need further cooking in the sauce before they are served, however: 20 minutes for thawed or unfrozen ones; at least ¹/₂ hour if frozen ones are dropped into a simmering sauce.

A 1-pound package of spaghetti, 2 quarts of the sauce and half the meatballs in this recipe will serve 8 to 12 people, depending on how much the aroma stimulates their appetites.

Variations.

Meat Sauce. For each quart of sauce, brown ¹/₂ to 1 pound ground game in small amount of oil, breaking it into little pieces with a wooden spoon as it browns. Add thawed sauce and simmer until very hot.

Meat-Mushroom Sauce. Add ¹/₂ pound sautéed mushrooms to 1 quart of sauce, along with ¹/₂ pound browned burger.

Sausage Sauce. Combine equal amounts of hot Italian sausage, browned and then cut into 1¹/₂-inch pieces, and meatballs, and heat 30 minutes in the sauce.

French Bread Pizza

So you have a few meatballs and sauce left over and you don't think it's worthwhile to freeze them? Try this.

1 to 2 loaves French bread
Leftover meatballs and Italian tomato sauce
Freshly ground black pepper
Dried oregano

Garlic powder (optional)
Mozzarella cheese, grated
Locatelli or Pecorino (Romano) cheese
Olive oil

French Bread Pizza (cont.)

Preheat oven to 425° F.

Slice the loaves of bread in half lengthwise and take out some of the bread filling. In a bowl or saucepan (you really don't have to heat this first, though), combine the meatballs, breaking them up with a wooden spoon, and moisten thoroughly with the tomato sauce. Pour over the bread halves and place on a baking tray. Season with black pepper and oregano, perhaps a little garlic powder and sprinkle on some grated Mozzarella, Romano cheese and a light drizzling of olive oil.

Bake for about 20 minutes in a hot oven until heated through and the cheese melts.

Hunter's Glop

This is not the most sophisticated name for a tasty, wholesome dish such as this, but this is the name and we love the dish.

1 to 1½ pounds game burger
1 cup onion, chopped
3 to 4 cloves garlic, chopped
2 cups Italian tomato sauce
Freshly ground black pepper
¼ cup Locatelli or Pecorino (Romano) cheese, or to taste
½ pound small pasta noodles or elbow macaroni, cooked according to package directions

In a large skillet, brown the meat, breaking it up with a wooden spoon. Add the onion and garlic and cook until soft. Add the sauce and simmer, covered, about 1 hour until the meat is thoroughly cooked. Season with black pepper, stir in the cheese and the cooked pasta, and, voilà, you have a one-dish meal that's delicious with Italian bread and a fresh green salad. Serves 3 to 4.

Stuffed Canneloni with White Sauce

1 recipe Hunter's Glop, without small pasta noodles (*see* preceding recipe)
2 cups medium white sauce (*see* page 166)
1 bay leaf
½ cup Romano cheese (preferably Locatelli or Pecorino)
1½ to 2 dozen canneloni shells, cooked al dente

Preheat oven to 350° F.

In a medium saucepan, prepare medium white sauce and when thick, add the bay leaf; remove from heat and let stand about ½ hour.

In the meantime, cook canneloni shells (if you can't find them, you could roll up cooked lasagne noodles, but it's not as efficient). Fill each shell with 2 to 3 tablespoons prepared Hunter's Glop recipe. After the white sauce has stood for ½ hour, remove the bay leaf and stir in the cheese. Pour over canneloni shells and bake about 30 to 40 minutes until heated through.

Stuffed Pasta Shells

Italian meatball recipe, decreased by
    half (*see* page 72)
Italian tomato sauce recipe, decreased
    by half (*see* page 71)
2 to 3 dozen jumbo pasta shells,
    cooked al dente
Freshly ground black pepper
Locatelli or Pecorino (Romano) cheese,
    freshly grated
Olive oil

Preheat oven to 325° F.

Cook pasta shells, but be sure not to overcook them. Stuff with meatball mixture (1 to 2 tablespoons per shell) and carefully arrange them in a shallow casserole (you will need more than one dish) in which you have swirled a little tomato sauce. Pour some sauce over each shell, then sprinkle on a fresh grating of black pepper and cheese. Drizzle olive oil over all and bake about 1 hour, until meat is thoroughly cooked. This will easily serve 4 to 6 people.

Stuffed Vegetables

With this recipe you may stuff green peppers, onions, zucchini squash or eggplant.

1 pound ground game burger
1 onion, chopped
2 tablespoons drippings
1/2 cup cooked rice
Salt and pepper to taste
Garlic powder
Dried basil
1 1/2 cups tomato sauce
1/4 cup water
Mozzarella cheese

Brown ground meat and onion in drippings for 5 minutes. Combine with the rice and seasonings, stuff blanched vegetables, and place in greased casserole. Pour over and around the vegetables the tomato sauce thinned with water. Top the vegetables with slices of Mozzarella cheese. Bake at 325° F. for 20 to 25 minutes. Sufficient stuffing for 4 to 5 peppers, 6 to 8 onions, or 3 medium squash or eggplant.

Peppers. Cut off stem end, remove seeds and white membrane, blanch in salted water 5 minutes, rinse in cold water, drain.

Onions. Peel, cut off root end, as well as a slice from the top, boil in salted water 10 minutes, scoop out centers, leaving only the 3 outer layers.

Zucchini squash. Cut off each end, scrape out seeds after splitting squash lengthwise; carefully scoop out some of the pulp and sauté with the other stuffing ingredients; blanch in salted water 5 minutes. It is not necessary to peel or blanch squash if they are young.

Eggplant. Cut off the ends, but do not peel or blanch eggplant. Cut in half lengthwise and remove any seeds; carefully scoop out the pulp to be blended and cooked with the other stuffing ingredients.

Lasagne

I usually double this recipe and make an extra casserole to freeze. To keep my casserole dishes in circulation, I line the casserole to be frozen with aluminum foil, freeze the lasagne and then remove the contents from the casserole and place it in a plastic bag. When I am ready to bake it, I peel the foil from the frozen lasagne, replace it in the casserole and bake it, allowing extra time in the oven if the food is not completely thawed.

1 quart tomato sauce
1½ pounds game burger, seasoned with garlic powder and black pepper and browned in small amount of olive oil
1 pound broad lasagne noodles, cooked until barely tender
½ cup Romano or Parmesan cheese, freshly grated
Freshly ground black pepper
¾ pound Mozzarella cheese, sliced
½ pound Ricotta cheese (cottage cheese, drained, may be substituted)

In a deep casserole about 10″ by 6″, layer the ingredients as follows: enough tomato sauce to cover the bottom of the casserole, 1 layer of noodles, ½ the total of Mozzarella cheese, ½ the ground meat, 3 tablespoons Romano cheese, sprinkled evenly over the meat, generous sprinkling pepper and ½ the Ricotta.

Repeat the layering, adding a final layer of noodles on top and covering the noodles with additional sauce, 2 tablespoons grated Romano and black pepper. Bake at 350° F. until bubbling, about ½ hour. Serve cut into squares with any heated sauce not used in the casserole.

MEXICAN DISHES

Arroz con Carne

It is doubtful whether the Mexicans or Spaniards had anything to do with this one—but we enjoy it nevertheless.

4 tablespoons oil or drippings
1 cup raw long-grain rice
1 onion, chopped
1 to 1½ pounds game burger
1 green pepper, chopped
Pinch of garlic powder
1 tablespoon chili powder
1 quart canned tomatoes
½ cup sliced olives, black or green

In a large skillet, brown rice, onion and meat in hot oil. Add remaining ingredients, stir well, cover tightly and simmer over very low heat until rice is tender (about 45 minutes). If mixture appears to be getting dry, add a few spoons of tomato liquid or water, but do not stir.

Chili con Carne con Frijoles

**2 pounds frijoles or garbanzo beans
    (chick peas)**
¹/₄ pound bacon, diced
4 to 5 onions, sliced
**3 pounds burger or chuck cut in 1-inch
    cubes**
**1 quart canned or fresh peeled
    tomatoes, chopped**
1 8-ounce can tomato sauce
3 cloves garlic, finely chopped
Salt and pepper
**Chili powder to taste—start with 2 or 3
    tablespoons and work your way up**
¹/₂ teaspoon ground cumin (optional)

Soak the beans overnight in cold water,
then drain and cook in water or stock
until tender. Drain and set aside.

Cook bacon in large kettle until
crisp; remove and reserve. Brown meat
and onions with 2 tablespoons chili
powder in the bacon fat. Add tomatoes
and sauce, garlic, salt and pepper and
additional chili powder to taste, plus
cumin, if you like your Chili with a
"kick." Simmer at least ¹/₂ hour, allowing
flavors to blend (if using cubed chuck,
until meat is tender). Add cooked beans,
simmer 20 minutes longer.

This makes enough for a large
group—15 to 20 people—but since it
does freeze well, it's just as easy to make
a large amount. When reheating frozen
chili, check the seasoning again; I have
sometimes found it necessary to add
more.

Chili—Quick Version

The Mexicans would not approve of this at all, but it does make a good camp dish. I
have used it at home in emergencies, too, for it takes only ¹/₂ hour from freezer to
table.

1 pound game burger
2 onions, sliced
4 tablespoons butter or drippings
1 green pepper, shredded (if desired)
**2 15-ounce cans Mexican beans in chili
    gravy**
Chili powder to taste
Ground cumin

Brown meat and onions in butter (start
with frozen meat if necessary), breaking
the meat into small pieces as it browns.
Add green pepper and chili beans. Cover
and simmer 10 minutes; check
seasoning, adding more chili powder
and cumin, if desired, and simmer 10
minutes more.

Mexican Meatballs in Sauce

Meatballs:
1¹/₂ pounds game burger
6 tablespoons corn meal
1 egg plus 1 egg yolk, beaten

1 onion, finely chopped
1 garlic clove, minced
2 teaspoons curry powder *or* cumin
Salt and pepper

Mexican Meatballs in Sauce (cont.)

Tomato Sauce:
2 tablespoons butter
1 onion, chopped
1 green pepper, chopped
1 quart V-8 or tomato juice
Chili powder
Freshly ground black pepper

Combine all meatball ingredients and shape into small balls.

In a large saucepan, melt butter and cook onion and green pepper until lightly browned; add juice and season to taste with chili powder and black pepper. Simmer for 10 minutes, then add meat balls, cooking until tender, about ½ hour.

 ## Mexicali Burger Stew

1 recipe Hunter's Glop, without Romano cheese or noodles (*see* page 73)
1 tablespoon chili powder
½ teaspoon ground cumin
½ cup sharp cheddar cheese, grated
2 cups rice, cooked

Prepare Hunter's Glop and season with chili powder and cumin (freshly ground black pepper, too); when cooked, stir in the cheddar cheese and the rice.

Tamale Pie

Very few of us have the time or the ingredients, such as corn husks and the freshly ground Mexican cornmeal, to make real tamales. This recipe might be called a Gringo adaptation.

Crust:
2 large eggs
¼ cup water
1 cup yellow cornmeal
Salt and pepper

Filling:
1 pound ground game meat
2 onions, thinly sliced
1 green pepper, chopped
Butter or oil
2 cups tomato puree
1 cup canned or frozen corn niblets
1 tablespoon chili powder
Pinch of garlic powder

Beat eggs with water, vigorously stir in cornmeal and season to taste. Let the mixture stand while preparing the filling.

Brown meat, onions and green pepper in hot oil. Add remaining ingredients and simmer for 10 minutes, stirring once or twice. Grease a 2-quart casserole and while the filling is simmering, pat out crust on a sheet of waxed paper to conform to the shape of the casserole. Pour in the hot filling, flip the crust on top and bake in a preheated 425° F. oven until the crust is browned.

Tex-Mex Tacos

1 pound game burger
1 cup onion, chopped
2 cloves garlic, chopped
$^1/_2$ cup green pepper, chopped
2 cups Texas-Style B-B-Q Sauce (*see* page 177)
Freshly ground black pepper
1 tablespoon chili powder or to taste
$^1/_2$ teaspoon ground cumin
$^1/_4$ to $^1/_2$ pound sharp cheddar cheese, grated
Lettuce, shredded
Prepared hot taco sauce
2 packages taco shells (or taco chips of your choosing)

In a large skillet, brown the game burger. Add the onion, garlic and green pepper and cook until soft. Add the Texas-Style B-B-Q Sauce and season to taste with black pepper, chili powder and ground cumin; cover and simmer about 1 hour, until meat is thoroughly cooked and the flavors have blended to your liking.

Meanwhile, grate the cheddar cheese and shred the lettuce. Freshen up the taco shells by heating them in the oven briefly (follow package directions).

When the taco mixture is done, you can serve the tacos in the "traditional" manner by filling the shells, then topping with shredded lettuce, cheddar cheese and some hot taco sauce. We like them served another way, however, which we find easier to eat. Break up the taco shells (or use taco chips) and arrange them on a plate, place a layer of shredded lettuce over them, then spoon on the taco meat mixture; top with cheese and then hot taco sauce. This way you can eat the tacos with a knife and fork, not having to worry about dripping sauce. Serves 4.

SCANDINAVIAN DISHES

Scandinavian Meatballs

1 egg
$^1/_2$ cup milk
$^1/_2$ cup dry bread crumbs
1 teaspoon salt
1 teaspoon sugar
$^1/_4$ teaspoon each nutmeg, cloves, ginger
$^1/_2$ teaspoon allspice
1 pound ground game
$^1/_2$ pound ground pork
1 onion, chopped (optional)
2 tablespoons butter

Sauce:
3 tablespoons flour
Salt and pepper to taste
1 cup bouillon
1 cup cream

Beat egg in milk; add crumbs and seasonings and blend well. Add meats and onion, if desired; mix thoroughly and shape into balls. If the meatballs are to be served at a buffet dinner, make them small; if they are to be used as a

Scandinavian Meatballs (cont.)

main dish, make them larger.

Melt butter in large skillet, brown meatballs on all sides and cook thoroughly. Remove to a hot platter while you make the sauce.

Blend flour into fat in the skillet, slowly stir in liquid, blending on low heat until mixture thickens; do not boil.

Check seasonings and pour sauce over meatballs.

For a flavor variation, equally Scandinavian, omit sugar, allspice, cloves and ginger from meatballs and substitute pepper to taste. Serve with sauce made as above, adding 2 tablespoons finely chopped fresh dill.

Game Patties à la Lindstrom

1½ pounds game burger
1 egg, well beaten
1 tablespoon onion, minced
2 tablespoons capers, minced
Salt & pepper to taste
1 pound potatoes, boiled, peeled and finely diced
¾ cup pickled beets, finely diced
Beet juice, if necessary to moisten

Combine meat, egg, onion, capers and seasonings; mix well. Add diced potatoes and beets. If mixture seems too dry, add 1 to 2 tablespoons beet juice. Set in refrigerator for an hour before cooking to permit flavors to blend.

Shape into thick patties and brown thoroughly on each side in butter in a large skillet.

JUST BURGERS

Hamburgers are so much a part of the American diet that we forget that their origin was in Hamburg, Germany. The original Hamburger steak was quite different from the ground meat patty we know today. However, thick or thin, broiled or pan fried, rare or well done, they can still be varied considerably with a bit of imagination.

 Mixed Grill

Our antelope burger was so superb one year that it deserved rather special treatment. It definitely took burgers out of the prosaic class. For each serving, here's how we prepared them.

1 medium-sized burger, wrapped around with bacon and skewered
1 large pork sausage
½ beefsteak tomato, sprinkled with buttered crumbs and oregano
1 or 2 large stuffed mushroom caps (*see* Chapter 13)

Start burger and sausage first, about 3 inches from the broiler flame. After 5 to 8 minutes, add tomato and mushroom; turn the meats and broil an additional 5 to 8 minutes.

1. Instead of the usual fried onions, blend equal amounts of blue cheese and butter, place 2 teaspoons on each patty when they are done. Turn off broiler and leave in the oven just long enough to melt the topping—while you serve up the vegetables.

2. If burgers are pan-fried, remove them to a hot platter. Blend into pan juices a small amount of any canned or dehydrated soup you prefer (mushroom, celery, onion, etc.). Stir in water or milk and allow to come to a boil, stirring and scraping pan. Simmer for several minutes until gravy is smooth and pour over the meat patties.

3. Blend ¹/₂ cup sour cream with 1 tablespoon flour; stir into pan juices with 1 tablespoon capers and a pinch of dried minced onion. Stir until thick and smooth, but do not boil.

4. Heat a cup or so of Creole Sauce while burgers are broiling. Pour over and serve.

5. For nice, juicy grilled burgers, mix ground meat with garlic powder, ketchup, soy sauce and bread crumbs; grill to desired doneness.

MEAT LOAF

The possibilities for variation are endless on meat loaf, too. These are our favorites, which I could make blindfolded by now. However, the following are the ingredients as Mother wrote them down for me years ago.

Beef Loaf

1¹/₂ pounds ground beef (these days I use venison burger) *or* 1 pound ground beef and ¹/₂ pound sausage meat
2 eggs
1 cup milk
²/₃ cup dry bread crumbs
¹/₂ onion, chopped
1 green pepper, chopped
1 teaspoon salt
Generous grinding of black pepper
1 teaspoon poultry seasoning, if sausage meat is not used
Old-fashioned Chili Sauce (*see* page 177)

Preheat oven to 350° F.

Beat eggs with milk; add bread crumbs, onion, green pepper, and seasonings. Blend thoroughly with meat and place in greased loaf pan, pressing down thoroughly with fork. Place in preheated oven for 10 minutes; spoon over Chili Sauce and bake for an additional 35 to 40 minutes, adding additional sauce if necessary.

If there is any left over, it can be wrapped in foil and frozen, to be reheated another day. It is equally good sliced cold for sandwiches.

Or you can try these variations.

Beef Loaf (cont.)

1. Add leftover cooked vegetables to the basic recipe.

2. When reheating beef loaf, frost with leftover mashed potatoes, beaten fluffy again with an egg and a bit of milk. Grated sharp cheese makes a nice addition to the potatoes also.

3. Bake in loaf shape in an open flat pan. After 10 or 15 minutes, long enough for the crust to set, baste with canned soup of your choice, or criss-cross with bacon slices.

Ham Loaf

A good place to use some of the less tender portions of that wild boar.

1¼ pounds ground fresh boar (pork)
¾ pound ground smoked ham
2 eggs
1 cup milk
1 cup fine dry bread crumbs
Generous sprinkling of freshly ground black pepper
6 tablespoons brown sugar, firmly packed
2 to 3 teaspoons dry mustard

Preheat oven to 350° F.

Beat eggs with milk; add bread crumbs and black pepper, mix well with ground meats and pack firmly into greased loaf pan. Mix brown sugar and dry mustard together, add a few drops of water or fruit juice, just enough to form a thick paste. Spread on top of the ham loaf and bake until well done, about 1 hour. (When I have had more ham than pork on hand, I have altered the proportions of meat with no disastrous results.)

For variety, you can bake ham loaf mixture in greased muffin cups 45 minutes, then turn out onto broiled pineapple slices. This is attractive for a buffet supper.

Stuffed Meat Loaf

Any preferred meat loaf recipe
Game sausage, cooked *or*
1 or 2 whole boiled eggs
Bacon slices

Line a loaf pan with half of any preferred meat loaf recipe. Make a well in the center and place a link of cooked game sausage in the center or 1 or 2 whole hard-boiled eggs; cover with remaining meat loaf mixture and seal well. Top with bacon slices and bake an hour or so at 350° F. until done.

Children always like it when I tell them there's a surprise in the middle.

Venison Wellington

Whoever said, "Necessity is the mother of invention," really knew what he was talking about (maybe it was a she who did a lot of cooking!). One afternoon good friends of ours dropped by unexpectedly and, of course, I insisted they stay for supper (!). All I had in my reserve cache was ground venison and some leftover pâté. Here's what resulted.

1 pound ground venison (already blended with pork and/or veal)
1¼ cups soft rye bread crumbs with caraway seeds
⅔ cup light cream
1 egg, beaten
Dash each garlic powder, nutmeg, ginger
Freshly ground black pepper
3 to 4 tablespoons fresh parsley, chopped
1 teaspoon dried minced onion
4 to 6 tablespoons liver pâté
2 bacon slices
1 pastry shell
Pan gravy

Preheat oven to 350° F.

Pour light cream over bread crumbs (you could use any kind, really) in a small bowl; let soak about 5 minutes. Then in a large mixing bowl, combine meat, soaked crumbs, egg (reserve 1 tablespoon beaten egg for the pastry), garlic powder, nutmeg, ginger, black pepper, chopped parsley and minced onion; blend well. Shape into a loaf, place bacon slices on top and put in loaf pan; bake about 1 hour, until done. Cool and remove from pan, reserving drippings.

When the meat loaf is cool, spread the pâté over the top. Roll out the pastry dough, large enough to accommodate the meat loaf, and place the loaf in the center; lift up the sides of the pastry to cover the loaf entirely. Trim and seal the sides with a little water, if necessary. Brush with the remaining tablespoon of egg, place on greased baking sheet and bake in a hot (425° F.) oven for about 20 minutes until golden brown.

Make pan gravy from the drippings in the previous pan and serve over thin slices of this rich, dressed-up meat loaf.

OTHER MAIN-DISH CASSEROLES

Grand Lamb Casserole

2 pounds ground lamb or sheep
2 tablespoons butter
¼ cup onion, minced
1 green pepper, chopped
1 egg
1 cup sour cream
Salt and freshly ground black pepper to taste
Generous sprinkling of marjoram
3 tablespoons parsley, chopped
1 cup carrot, coarsely shredded
½ cup celery, finely minced
Sesame Seed Pastry, baked (*see* page 231)

Grand Lamb Casserole (cont.)

Preheat oven to 350° F.

Brown lamb or sheep in butter, breaking into small pieces. Add onion and green pepper and continue cooking for another 2 to 3 minutes; remove from heat. Add egg beaten with sour cream, seasonings and parsley. Mix well and pour half of mixture into a greased 2-quart casserole. Blend carrot and celery together and sprinkle evenly over meat. Add remaining meat mixture and bake for 30 minutes; top with baked wedges of sesame seed pastry and continue baking for an additional 15 minutes. Serves 6.

Bryn Mawr Casserole

I was introduced to this delectable one at a Chicago Bryn Mawr Club luncheon. It is an Americanized version of lasagne—one well worth remembering when serving a large group of people.

2 pounds ground chuck (any member of the deer family)
4 tablespoons butter
4 8-ounce cans tomato sauce
1 teaspoon salt
Dash of Worcestershire Sauce
2 8-ounce packages cream cheese at room temperature
1 pound cottage cheese
¹/₂ cup sour cream
2 tablespoons green pepper, chopped
¹/₂ cup minced scallions
³/₄ pound noodles, cooked, drained and rinsed

Preheat oven to 350° F.

Brown meat in 2 tablespoons butter, drain off any excess fat. Stir in tomato sauce, salt and Worcestershire Sauce. Blend the cream cheese and cottage cheese with sour cream; add green pepper and *half* the minced scallions. Mix the noodles and cheese blend together and place in the bottom of a large, flat, well-buttered casserole. Spread the meat and tomato mixture on top of the noodles and sprinkle with the reserved scallions which have been tossed with the remaining 2 tablespoons butter, melted.

Bake for 30 to 45 minutes, depending on the depth of the casserole. This amount serves 8 people generously.

Porcupine Casserole

I recall being fascinated with this dish as a child. We've had fun with it through the years at informal suppers. Bob would ask casually in front of our guests, "Say, what's for supper?" When I answered, just as casually, "Oh, I thought we'd try the porcupines tonight," you can imagine the reactions we'd get, especially among the uninitiated!

Porcupine Casserole (cont.)

1 egg
1/4 cup milk
1/2 cup bread crumbs
2/3 cup raw long-grain rice
1 onion, chopped
1 1/2 pounds game burger
Salt and pepper to taste
1 cup V-8 juice
1/2 cup chili sauce

Preheat oven to 350° F.

Beat egg with milk; add bread crumbs, rice, onion and meat. Season to taste and form into good-sized meatballs. Place in a buttered casserole, pour over combined V-8 and chili sauce, and bake, uncovered, for 1 to 1 1/2 hours, depending on the size of the meatballs. Baste occasionally with the liquid, adding more if it seems necessary.

CHAPTER 5

UPLAND BIRDS

Bird shooting was my introduction to hunting. Our constant hunting companion in those days was deadly with his Browning over/under and his springer, the sire of our dog, was equally fabulous. We were training a new hunter as well as a young pup, so nearly every weekend was spent afield from the time the shooting preserves opened in early fall. We valiantly tried not to be outdone by this pair of "hunting fools," who would rather hunt than eat. As a consequence, the portable cooler was always pretty well filled when we returned home.

Until we acquired a freezer, birds were practically everyday fare in our house. I soon learned to present them in different ways to avoid a clamor for hot dogs as a change of pace.

Wild birds, in contrast to their domestic cousins, are lean and need to be covered with bacon or larding pork and basted frequently to prevent drying of their delectable meat. As with any meat or fowl, the young are broiled or roasted, the elders are braised or fricasseed. The best indication of age is the breastbone: if the tip is soft and pliable, you have a young one. If the breastbone is rigid, you have to use a different culinary approach. When roasting or broiling, be certain that the oven is thoroughly preheated. This is particularly important with the tiny birds which require only a brief cooking period under intense heat. These luscious morsels should always be served with croutons or crisp trenchers of bread to soak up every last drop of goodness.

The various combinations of flavors in the recipes I have given are not necessarily limited to one particular species of bird. They may be used successfully with a variety of birds—only the amounts given and the cooking time will vary with the size and age of bird. To ensure a tasty bird every time, please review my field dressing suggestions, page 20. The upland birds included in this chapter are crow, doves and pigeons, grouse, partridge, pheasant, quail, wild turkey and woodcock.

CROW

The less said about these pesky birds the better, including the worn-out phrase "to eat crow"! These black robbers are fine targets for the gunner during the off-season and I approve of them being shot—they cause so much damage. I do *not* approve of them in my kitchen, although I understand the young ones are quite edible, if parboiled. Even if I were in dire straits, I'd certainly look for a more tasty target for my last shell.

DOVES AND PIGEONS

Dove and pigeon shooting can be a most humbling experience, so if your mighty hunter brings home doves or pigeons, treat them with all due respect—and *don't* ask about the shotshell consumption! The mourning dove is protected in some states as a song bird, but where it is legal game, it is considered excellent for the table, along with the white-winged dove and the band-tailed pigeon. Their diet consists mainly of grains and the various legumes—occasionally the flesh may be bitter if the birds have been feeding extensively on acorns.

The young, known as squab, are recognized by their light red breast meat and plump legs. They are best roasted, with one bird per serving. Darker breast meat and scrawny legs indicates a bird for stew or casserole.

Baked Breast of Dove

Figure on 1 to 2 whole breasts per person, depending on size of bird. With a boning knife, carefully remove the meat from the breastbone; skin and follow breading and baking instructions for "Baked Squirrel," page 132.

Breast of Pigeon with Wine Sauce

This is suitable for larger pigeons. Allow the two filets from each bird for one serving. Reserve the remainder of the carcass for soup, pâté or perhaps a Brunswick Stew.

Marinade:
Red or white wine
1 teaspoon lemon juice

Butter
¼ cup currant jelly
1 tablespoon orange juice concentrate
Orange peel, finely shredded
Crisp croutons

Lift and cut away the skin from the breast. With a sharp boning knife, remove the breast filets by cutting down each side of the breastbone.

Marinate the breasts for 1 hour in red or white wine to cover and lemon juice. Drain filets and reserve marinade. Season the filets and gently sauté in butter until tender.

Breast of Pigeon with Wine Sauce (cont.)

Meanwhile, in a small saucepan, reduce the marinade by half and add the currant jelly, orange juice concentrate and some finely shredded orange peel.

Simmer for several minutes and serve the breasts on crisp croutons cut to the same size, with the sauce poured over.

Braised celery is delicious with this.

Braised Pigeons in Italian Sauce

In a flame-proof casserole, brown older birds in butter, being sure all sides are attractively browned. Season lightly, add Italian Game Bird Sauce (*see* page 172), cover casserole tightly and simmer over low heat until tender.

Doves en Casserole

4 older doves
¹/₄ cup butter
¹/₂ onion, minced
Several sprigs parsley and thyme, chopped
1 ounce dried porcini (Italian) mushrooms, broken into small pieces
1 tablespoon flour
2 cups game bird stock
¹/₂ cup dry sherry
¹/₂ cup stuffed olives, sliced
Salt and pepper to taste

Brown birds on all sides in skillet in hot butter; season lightly and remove to a casserole. In the same butter, brown onion, herbs and mushrooms for 5 minutes; add flour and stir until it is slightly brown and bubbly. Lower heat, add stock and stir until sauce is smooth. Add sherry and olives, simmer an additional minute or so and check seasoning. Pour sauce into casserole, cover and bake at 350° F. until tender, about 45 minutes.

Roast Squab

Squab, 1 per person
Lemon juice
Rice and Raisin Stuffing (*see* Chapter 11)
Salt and black pepper
Softened butter
Water
Bacon slices (optional)

Rub the birds with lemon juice. Stuff with Rice and Raisin Stuffing, truss and season lightly with salt and pepper. Spread the birds liberally with softened (not melted) butter and roast covered for 1 hour in a preheated 300° F. oven. Baste the birds frequently with hot water and additional butter. Garnish with sprigs of watercress.

An alternate method of roasting squab is to wrap the seasoned and stuffed birds in bacon slices (but go easy on the salt) and roast at 425° F. for 25 to 30 minutes. Remove the bacon slices when the birds are almost done, allowing the breasts to brown. Be sure to baste with the pan juices during this time, so the meat does not dry out.

GROUSE

With all the common names that vary and overlap from one section of the country to another, the matter of terminology can be rather confusing, especially when you get into the subspecies. There are six main varieties of grouse found in North America:

1. Ruffed grouse—the white fleshed boomer of the woodlands and slashings. One of our most delicious game birds that weighs up to 2 pounds.

2. Spruce grouse—as its name implies, a dweller of the northern spruce forests.

3. Blue or dusky grouse—found in the western pine forests and weighs up to 3¹⁄₂ pounds.

4. Pinnated grouse—larger and heavier than the ruffed grouse, a lover of the wide open spaces; hence, his common name of prairie chicken.

5. Sharp-tailed grouse—a bit larger than the pinnated grouse. Also prefers the prairies, but ranges farther north than the pinnated variety.

6. Sage grouse—largest of all the grouse, weighing up to 8 pounds. As implied by its name, its diet consists primarily of sage tips; only the young birds are to be considered palatable since they depend less on the sage and more on insects and grains.

I have also included under this heading the willow and rock ptarmigan, a close relative of the Scottish red grouse, found in the northernmost parts of the continent.

Braised Grouse—Central European Style

Suitable for any older upland bird.

Stuffing:
Bird liver
Celery leaves
1 juniper berry
Small sprig of thyme
Small strip of orange or lemon peel
1 allspice berry
Chunk of butter

Freshly ground black pepper
Salt if desired
Bacon slices *or* larding pork
Celery, carrots, onion, chopped
Game bird stock plus white or red
     wine—in equal amounts
¹⁄₂ cup heavy cream

Braised Grouse—Central European Style (cont.)

Season the birds with salt and pepper and stuff with stuffing ingredients. Cover with bacon slices or larding pork. In a covered casserole, place a layer of chopped vegetables, including celery, carrot and onion. Barely cover the vegetables with equal portions of stock and wine (white or red).

Place the larded birds atop the vegetables, cover and braise in 400° F. oven until tender. The time, of course, will depend on the size and age of the birds. Add additional wine and stock if necessary.

When birds are tender, remove to a heated platter and keep warm; also take out stuffing from cavities. Strain the sauce from the casserole into a saucepan, bring to a boil, add heavy cream and heat just to the boiling point.

Broiled Grouse

Grouse
Melted butter
Freshly ground black pepper
Salt if desired
Rouennaise (*see* page 222)
Croutons

Depending on their size, the birds may be split in half or you can remove the backbone and breastbone and flatten them for broiling whole. Brush liberally with melted butter, season with salt and pepper. Broil over hot coals or in a preheated broiler for 10 minutes per side.

Remove the birds to a heated platter and keep warm while you prepare Rouennaise from the grouse livers and the pan drippings from the broiled grouse. Spread Rouennaise on toasted buttery croutons and serve.

Grouse alla Milano

"It's different and delicious. What is it?" If you've never used fennel seed in cooking before, do try it. Fennel seed is faintly reminiscent of anise and is used not only in Italian cooking, but in Scandinavian dishes as well.

2 or 3 grouse, depending on size
Flour seasoned with salt and pepper
4 tablespoons butter or olive oil
2 or 3 scallions, finely sliced, including part of the green tops
1 cup game bird or chicken stock
1¹/₂ packages frozen green peas or the equivalent in fresh ones
¹/₂ teaspoon fennel seeds
1 tablespoon lemon juice
Roux, if necessary

Cut grouse into serving portions, coat with seasoned flour; brown in hot fat along with scallions. Lower heat, add stock, cover and simmer until tender. Add peas, fennel seed and lemon juice, continue to simmer 10 minutes more. Check seasonings. If gravy does not seem thick enough, add small amount of roux and blend well.

Serve with fluffy rice and a green toss salad.

Grouse Español

2 to 4 grouse, depending on size, cut
    into serving pieces
Seasoned flour
4 tablespoons olive oil
1 cup onion, chopped
4 cloves garlic, chopped
1/2 cup green pepper, chopped
2 stalks celery, chopped
1/4 cup white wine
1/2 cup game bird stock
Pinch saffron
Mushrooms, sliced
1/3 cup pimiento-stuffed green olives,
    sliced

In a Dutch oven, brown floured grouse in olive oil; remove from pan. Add onion, garlic, green pepper and celery and lightly sauté. Pour in the white wine, game bird stock and add a pinch of saffron, stirring to blend. Return grouse to pan, cover and simmer over low heat until meat is tender. Add mushrooms and sliced olives and heat through.

Serve with rice.

Roast Grouse

Depending on its size, the average grouse will serve 1 to 2 people. Other recipes suitable for grouse may be found under quail, partridge and pheasant.

Grouse
Rice Stuffing (*see* page 205)
Larding pork
Butter
Flour
Roux *or* currant jelly and English Bread
    Sauce (*see* Chapter 10)

Preheat oven to 450° F.

Using the grouse livers, prepare Rice Stuffing. Stuff the birds lightly and truss. Cover the breasts with larding pork and roast on a rack with enough game bird stock just to cover the bottom of the roasting pan.

Roast in hot oven for 15 minutes; reduce heat to 300° F. and continue to roast, covered, for 25 to 30 minutes, basting at least twice with the pan juices. Remove the larding strips, rub with butter and dust very lightly with flour. Then return to 400° F. oven to brown the skin (no more than a few minutes).

Make gravy from the pan juices with roux and additional stock if necessary, *or* serve with currant jelly and the traditional English Bread Sauce.

Roast Grouse with Port Wine

Wild grouse
Salt if desired
Freshly ground black pepper
1 teaspoon butter per bird

Bacon slices *or* larding pork
1 glass port wine

Sprinkle lightly inside and out with salt

Roast Grouse with Port Wine (cont.)

and pepper. Insert 1 teaspoon butter inside each bird, wrap in bacon slices or larding pork. Place in open pan in preheated 400° F. oven for 30 minutes, basting twice with additional butter.

During the last 10 minutes of roasting time, add port wine and baste again.

Serve with wild rice and gravy made from the pan juices.

Roast Grouse or Partridge with Orange Slices

Wild grouse or partridge
Orange slices, 1 per bird
Salt if desired
Freshly ground black pepper
Bacon slices

Orange Sauce:
Shredded orange peel
1 tablespoon orange juice concentrate
1 teaspoon lemon juice
2 tablespoons water
4 tablespoons butter

Preheat oven to 350° F.

Season the birds with salt and pepper, place an orange slice in the cavity of each bird. Wrap in bacon slices and roast in oven for 20 to 30 minutes, basting several times with the Orange Sauce. To prepare sauce, combine all ingredients in a small saucepan and simmer a minute or two to blend.

When birds are done, remove bacon from birds and orange slices from the cavities. Serve on platter garnished with parsley and glazed orange slices (*see* Chapter 10).

Smothered Grouse or Ptarmigan

Wild grouse *or* ptarmigan
Flour, seasoned with salt, pepper and thyme
Melted butter
Mushroom caps
Heated heavy cream *or* dehydrated cream of mushroom soup

At home. Split the grouse or ptarmigan in half and roll in seasoned flour. Brown in hot butter, along with mushroom caps. When all is delicately browned, pour over enough heated heavy cream to half cover the birds. Cover tightly and bake at 350° F. until the birds are tender, about an hour for older birds.

At camp. The above recipe is not limited to the kitchen, as any good "substitute" cook will know. When the birds are browned, add a foil package of dehydrated cream of mushroom soup which has been thinned to the consistency of cream with water and/or evaporated milk. Cover and set over a slow fire in your trusty Dutch oven.

PARTRIDGE

All nicknames to the contrary, there are only two true partridges in this country, both fairly recent imports. One is the Chukar from the region around the Himalayas, closely related to the red-legged or French partridge. The other is the Hun or European grey partridge. The grey is found in the British Isles as well as on the Continent; however, since most of the birds transplanted here came from Hungary, the name Hun has stuck. Partridge is considered a great delicacy by gourmets everywhere and each 10- to 14-ounce bird is sufficient for one serving.

 ## Broiled Partridge

If you are fortunate enough to bag a few of these birds as an added bonus on a big game trip, they are most delicious broiled over the coals of an open fire.

Partridge
Freshly ground black pepper
Salt if desired
Chunk of butter per bird
Partridge liver
Thyme
Dried onion flakes
Bacon strips

Season inside and out with a light sprinkling of salt and pepper; add a small chunk of butter to the cavity along with the bird's own liver with a pinch of thyme or dried onion flakes. Wrap the birds well in bacon strips and skewer. Truss securely on a spit and broil slowly over coals, turning to brown evenly.

It's worth a bit of extra effort to construct a drip pan of heavy foil and place it directly under the birds to catch all the succulent juices that fall from them as they broil. Prepare crisp slices of toast, soak in the pan juices, add the livers which have been cooking inside the birds, put the birds on top—and who needs Escoffier?

 ## Braised Partridge Chasseur

This old European classic, although designated as "hunter's style," seemed destined to be prepared at home exclusively, until the advent of dehydrated and freeze-dried foods. Now those older birds can be prepared just as well in camp as in the kitchen. I'll list the original recipe first and then detail the adaptations.

Allow 1 bird per serving
1 large head cabbage
Butter or bacon fat
1 strip bacon per bird
2 sliced carrots per bird
1 juniper berry per bird
2 cups game bird stock
Shredded lemon peel

Camp Ingredients:
Bacon fat
2 chicken bouillon cubes
2 cups water
Dehydrated cabbage, carrots, minced
    onion
Bacon strips, diced

Braised Partridge Chasseur (cont.)

At home. Core and remove any wilted outer leaves from the cabbage. Parboil in salted water for 8 to 10 minutes, drain and remove 4 whole leaves for each bird to be braised. Shred the remainder of the cabbage and place in the bottom of an earthenware casserole. Brown the seasoned birds in butter or bacon fat, turning so all sides are evenly browned, then wrap each bird in the reserved cabbage leaves and tie securely.

Place in the casserole along with 1 strip of diced bacon, 2 sliced carrots and 1 juniper berry *per bird.* Boil up 2 cups of game bird stock in the pan the birds were browned in, add shredded lemon peel and scrape the pan, loosening any browned bits that adhere. Pour over the birds and vegetables, cover and place in 325° F. oven until birds are tender, about 45 minutes.

Remove strings and serve birds in nests of cabbage with noodles and any tart or spicy jelly.

At camp. Brown the birds in bacon fat in a Dutch oven. Set the birds aside while you add 2 chicken bouillon cubes and 2 cups water to the pan. Let the water come to a boil while you stir until the bouillon cubes are dissolved. Add part of a package of dehydrated shredded cabbage, the same of carrots, a bit of dried minced onion and let it simmer for a couple of minutes. You may need to add more chicken broth at this time, plus a bit of salt. Toss in a few diced bacon strips, the browned birds, cover and set over a slow fire until the birds are tender.

Check occasionally to see that there is enough liquid so the vegetables don't scorch—but don't drown them in liquid. The whole idea in this dish is that the vegetables steam along with the birds and add their savory goodness to the meat.

Partridge en Casserole

This recipe is particularly suited to older birds—grouse and quail as well as partridge.

**Allow 1 bird per serving, depending on
    size**
Juniper berries
Butter
Salt and freshly ground black pepper
Carrots, chopped
Celery, chopped
Onion, chopped
1 pony brandy
1 bay leaf
Pinch thyme
1 tablespoon parsley, chopped
1/2 pound mushrooms, sliced

Insert 1 juniper berry into the cavity of each bird. In a heavy skillet, brown the birds in butter, season lightly with salt and pepper.

Place in a casserole atop braising vegetables (equal amounts of chopped carrots, celery and onions). Add sufficient stock to cover the vegetables almost completely; pour in the brandy, add the bay leaf, thyme and parsley; and arrange fresh mushrooms around the birds.

Cover the casserole and bake in 400° F. oven until birds are tender. The time will vary, naturally, with the age and size of the birds.

PHEASANT

Although epicures insist that some of the smaller birds are superior in flavor, my favorite is still the majestic ringneck. Perhaps it's because his plumage is so beautiful to look at as he cackles indignantly when flushed from the hedgerow. But "handsome is as handsome does" and he is equally enjoyable at the dinner table. The cocks weigh an average of 2½ to 4 pounds, hens about 2 to 3 pounds, so 2 or 3 servings per bird may be planned on.

Breast of Pheasant alla Mama Leone

The inspiration for this dish came from Mama Leone's famous Italian restaurant in New York. One evening while dining there with friends, I tried Saltimbocca alla Romano, veal with Mozzarella cheese and Prosciutto ham. The combination of flavors was most delicious, so the next time we had an abundance of young pheasants I began experimenting. The result is this recipe, which I'm certain you will enjoy.

Pheasant breasts, 1 per person
Freshly ground black pepper
Pinch thyme
Mozzarella or Gruyère cheese, sliced
Prosciutto, sliced
Butter
2 to 3 tablespoons flour
1 cup game bird stock
1 cup heavy cream
2 to 3 tablespoons dry sherry or white
**   wine**

Remove breasts whole, reserving legs and carcass for a game pie. Bone each breast, starting at the lower edge of the ribs and cutting as close as possible to the bone. Be careful not to cut through the skin at the top of the breastbone. Place each boned breast on a sheet of waxed paper, cover with another and flatten slightly with the broad flat side of a cleaver.

Season with pepper and a pinch of thyme (no salt is necessary). Place on each breast a slice of Mozzarella or Gruyère cheese, a slice of Prosciutto or other thinly sliced ham, another slice of cheese, all slightly smaller in size than the breast when folded in half. Fold each breast in half and skewer or sew together.

Preheat oven to 350° F. Brown in butter over moderate heat, then transfer to a buttered baking dish. Bake until tender, about ½ hour.

Meanwhile, prepare the sauce by stirring flour into the butter in which the breasts were browned, using low heat so the roux will remain a delicate color. Slowly blend in game bird stock, stirring constantly. Add 1 cup cream and simmer, stirring constantly, until the sauce is thickened and smooth.

When the pheasant breasts are tender, place on a heated platter, blend into the sauce any juices from the baking dish and several tablespoons dry sherry or white wine. Check seasoning of the sauce and serve over the pheasant breasts.

Hungarian-Style Pheasant

This adaptation of Paprika Huhn is equally good for young or old birds. The length of time for cooking will vary, that's all.

Pheasants, cut into serving pieces
Seasoned flour
Butter
1/4 cup onion, minced
1 tablespoon sweet Hungarian paprika
1 1/2 cups game bird stock
2 tablespoons flour
1 cup sour cream
Lemon rind, grated
1 tablespoon lemon juice

Dredge pheasant pieces in seasoned flour. Brown in melted butter in skillet which has a tight fitting lid. When the browning is nearly completed, add minced onion and sprinkle the birds with Hungarian paprika. (If you are unable to obtain the real McCoy, be as liberal as you wish with what we call pulverized brick). Add 1/2 cup stock or water, cover tightly and simmer until tender, adding more liquid as necessary. Remove birds to heated platter.

Blend 2 tablespoons flour into pan juices, slowly add 1 cup game bird stock, stirring constantly until smooth and thickened. Add sour cream, some grated lemon rind and the lemon juice; continue to heat until almost at the boiling point. Pour a bit of sauce over pheasant and sprinkle with paprika.

Serve with balance of sauce in a preheated bowl accompanied by noodles and cabbage.

Pheasant Amandine

A recipe suitable for young birds.

Wild pheasants
Freshly ground black pepper
Salt
Bacon slices
1/4 cup butter, melted

Almond Lemon Butter:
1/4 cup butter, melted
1 tablespoon lemon juice
1/4 cup blanched, slivered almonds

Preheat oven to 350° F.

Split each pheasant in half lengthwise as you would a broiling chicken. Season with pepper and a scant sprinkling of salt. Place bone side down in a roasting pan, cover with bacon slices, held in place with skewers. Roast in oven until tender, about 1 hour, basting frequently with 1/4 cup melted butter and pan juices. (When the age of the birds is in doubt, cover them with aluminum foil at mid-point in the roasting.)

When the birds are tender, add 1/4 cup melted butter, blended with the lemon juice and blanched, slivered almonds. Return to oven for 10 minutes, basting once more.

Serve with wild rice and spiced cranberry sauce.

♦🔥 Pheasant Amandine—Camp Style

This is the preceding recipe adapted to the campfire or at-home grill.

Wild pheasants
Butter
Bacon slices
Almond Lemon Butter (*see* preceding recipe)

Split birds in half lengthwise. Place a square of butter in the rib section of each half, season and wrap in bacon. Cover each portion with a double thickness of heavy aluminum foil and seal with the drugstore wrap fold, so none of the juices will escape. Place over the coals and turn the packages carefully from time to time to permit the birds to cook evenly. I use very heavy mitts for this job, to prevent puncturing the foil.

Open the packages the last few minutes to permit the bacon to crisp and, using a basting syringe, draw off the excess juices to add to the pan of Almond Lemon Butter, which has been waiting at the side of the grill.

The wild rice has also been steaming, covered, on a slow part of the fire. Serve a green salad and reserve the cranberries for dessert, where they may appear as a frosty cranberry sherbet or Cranberry Bavarian (*see* Chapter 16).

Pheasant Herb Bake

1 large pheasant, cut into serving pieces, *or* several smaller ones split lengthwise
1 cup herb vinaigrette salad dressing
Freshly ground black pepper
Garlic powder
Flour
3 to 4 fresh basil leaves, crushed
Sprinkling of oregano, fresh or dried
2 tablespoons fresh parsley, chopped
Mushrooms (optional)
Black olives (optional)

Preheat oven to 375° F. Place cut-up birds fleshy side down in a good-size casserole in which you have swirled some of the salad dressing. (If you can't find this type of dressing, or don't feel like making your own, just use olive oil and vinegar; it works equally well.)

Sprinkle the birds with black pepper and garlic powder; then half of the fresh herbs, then some more salad dressing. Place in the oven and bake about 30 minutes, depending upon the size and type of birds.

Turn birds over in casserole. *Lightly* sprinkle with flour, then another seasoning with black pepper, garlic powder, fresh herbs and salad dressing. Bake for about another 30 minutes, basting frequently to brown, until meat is tender. To add a little flair to the dish, you may garnish it with fresh whole mushrooms and black olives about 10 minutes before done.

Another variation would be to include browned game sausage to the dish when you first put it in the oven.

Pheasant in Cream

Equally good for partridge or grouse.

Wild pheasants
Butter
1½ tablespoons roux
1 cup heavy cream
Nutmeg, freshly grated
Rouennaise (*see* Chapter 13)
Croutons
Celery (optional)

Brown seasoned birds in a liberal amount of butter in a casserole or skillet over moderate heat; turn to brown all sides. Cover and let the birds simmer in their own juices over low heat until tender. Combine roux with heavy cream, add a fresh grating of nutmeg; stir until smooth and pour over birds. Cook for an additional few minutes, basting the birds with the cream. Remove birds to Rouennaise-covered croutons, blend sauce and pour over the birds.

If you enjoy a bit of crunch in the sauce, add celery which has been sliced on the diagonal and steamed in a small amount of water for 5 minutes—no longer!

Pheasant-Wild Rice Casserole

1 stewing pheasant, or 2 to 3 grouse of
    comparable age
⅔ cup wild rice
Game bird stock (or chicken)
½ pound mushrooms, sautéed
½ onion, minced
2 stalks celery, finely diced
1 green pepper, diced

Cut up birds and cover with game bird or chicken stock; simmer until tender. Remove meat and cut into large dice. Boil wild rice in stock birds were cooked in until rice is half done, about 20 minutes. In buttered casserole, combine rice, fowl, vegetables, adding small amount of stock to finish cooking rice. Cover casserole and bake at 350° F. for ½ hour. Garnish casserole with pimiento strips and parsley sprigs.

Roast Pheasant

Wild pheasant
Freshly ground black pepper
Salt if desired
Liver and giblets, reserved
Bacon strips
Pheasant stock
White wine (optional)
Roux

Stuffing:
Bay leaf
Slice of lemon
Celery leaves
Parsley sprigs
Slice of onion

Roast Pheasant (cont.)

Season with freshly ground black pepper and salt inside and out. Stuff the cavity with any preferred stuffing or the above stuffing ingredients.

Cook the liver and giblets in stock until tender and chop. Reserve stock and giblets for gravy. Cover the pheasant with bacon strips and place in roaster. Add sufficient stock and white wine (if desired) to cover the bottom of the roasting pan. Cover and cook 1 hour at 350° F. or until tender. Remove larding strips, return to oven uncovered to permit skin to brown, basting every few minutes with pan juices. Remove pheasant to heated platter (and remove celery and parsley sprigs) while you prepare the gravy.

Add roux to pan juices, stir until well blended, then add giblets and giblet broth. Stir and scrape sides of roaster, cook slowly until thickened, and pour into preheated sauce boat.

Spanish-Style Pheasant with Saffron Rice

2 young pheasants
1/4 cup butter
Salt and pepper
2 tablespoons flour
Dash of cloves
1 1/4 cups game bird stock or chicken bouillon
6 tablespoons frozen orange juice concentrate
Dash of Tabasco
1 piece of stick cinnamon
2/3 cup golden raisins
2/3 cup shredded toasted almonds
Saffron rice (*see* page 244, no. 4)

Cut birds into serving pieces. Brown on all sides in melted butter in a large skillet with cover. Season with salt and pepper and remove to a plate when they are nicely browned. In the skillet, blend the flour and cloves into the butter. Stir until bubbly, then add the stock, orange juice concentrate and Tabasco and continue to stir until thickened and boiling. Add the cinnamon and raisins and return the pheasant pieces to the sauce. Cover and simmer over low heat until tender, 45 minutes or so.

Just before serving, remove the piece of stick cinnamon and stir the almonds into the sauce. Serve the pheasant on a platter mounded with saffron rice. Pour some of the sauce on the birds, pass the rest in a sauce boat.

Viennese-Style Pheasant

1 pheasant

Pheasant Stock:
1 quart water (approx.)
1 bay leaf
1 teaspoon salt
6 to 8 peppercorns
1 medium onion, sliced
2 carrots, sliced
2 stalks celery, sliced

½ **cup butter**
½ **cup flour**
2 cups pheasant broth
1 cup light cream
½ **teaspoon freshly grated nutmeg**
Pheasant, cut into large dice
½ **pound white asparagus tips**
1 cup mushrooms, sliced
½ **lemon, *very* thinly sliced**

Place pheasant in a large kettle, barely cover with water and add the seasonings and vegetables to the stock. Cover and simmer until pheasant is tender, about 2½ hours.

Remove pheasant from stock; skin and strip meat from bones. Return bones to broth and reduce liquid by half; strain.

In the top of a double boiler over low heat, melt butter and blend in flour; stir until bubbly, but not browned. Slowly add 2 cups of the pheasant broth, stirring constantly until thick; then stir in the light cream.

Place over boiling water and add to the sauce the nutmeg, diced pheasant, asparagus tips, mushrooms and lemon slices; heat thoroughly. Serve over puff pastry rounds or shells.

QUAIL

This little bird, beloved by sportsman and gourmet alike, is one most often hunted and bagged in North America. The best known, of course, is the Bobwhite, often called a partridge; others include the Desert (scaled and Gambel's varieties), Mountain, Valley and Montezuma or harlequin. These delicate, white-fleshed morsels (only 5 to 6 ounces each) are best done in simple fashion with no potent seasonings to mask their delicious flavor.

Appalachian Quail

Quail
Flour
Freshly ground black pepper
Bacon drippings
Wild mushrooms
Onions, sliced
Butter
Applejack or other "spirits"
Fresh parsley, chopped

If the quail are small, leave them whole. If they are good-sized (you're lucky), split them in half lengthwise. Flour and season with black pepper. Brown them on all sides in the bacon drippings, until tender. In another skillet, melt butter and sauté mushrooms and onions; flavor with a little Applejack or whatever other kind of spirits is handy; blend in chopped parsley.

Serve the quail smothered with the mushrooms and onions, along with fried hominy and sweet potato pie.

Roast Quail with Grapes

Quail
Salt
Freshly ground black pepper
Grape leaves
Bacon slices
Melted butter
Trenchers (*see* page 101)
¼ cup water
3 to 4 tablespoons dry sherry or white
    wine
½ cup seedless green grapes
¼ cup filberts, toasted and chopped

Preheat over to 450° F.

Season quail with salt and pepper, place a grape leaf on the breast of each bird, then wrap in bacon strips and tie. Roast in shallow pan in preheated oven for 15 to 20 minutes, basting frequently with melted butter. When quail are done, place on trenchers and keep warm.

Pour water into roasting pan, bring to boil, scraping pan. Lower heat, add dry sherry or white wine, green grapes and simmer several minutes.

Just before serving, add chopped, toasted filberts if desired. (Filberts are not always available in our area, and since I use them quite often, I buy a good supply at holiday time and then keep them in the freezer.)

Quail with Sour Cherry Sauce

This is another treasure from old Vienna, adaptable to a variety of small birds.

Quail
Butter
Freshly ground black pepper
Salt if desired
Sour Cherry Sauce (*see* page 173)

In a flameproof casserole, brown the quail in butter on all sides; season lightly with salt and pepper, cover and place in oven preheated to 400° F. for 15 to 20 minutes. Place the birds on a heated platter and keep warm while you prepare the Sour Cherry Sauce in the casserole where the birds were cooked.

Quail Esterhazy

1 quail per serving
Salt and black pepper
1 hard roll, slightly larger than quail,
    per serving
Butter
Onion, finely minced
Thyme
Ground clove, (optional)
Bay leaf, crushed

White wine
Milk
Bacon slices

Preheat oven to 325° F.

Sprinkle quail inside and out with salt and pepper. With a sharp knife, cut each hard roll in half, gently pull out soft crumbs inside. Make a stuffing of roll

Quail Esterhazy (cont.)

crumbs, melted butter, onion gently sautéed in butter, thyme and bay leaf (plus a sprinkle of clove, if desired). Moisten with a bit of white wine and toss lightly to blend. Stuff the quail lightly, do not pack.

Place each bird between two roll halves, moisten tops of the rolls with milk, and place a slice of bacon atop each roll. Tie or skewer together and place in a shallow pan. Roast in a slow oven until tender for about 35 to 40 minutes.

Serve with red cabbage and boiled potatoes.

Sautéed Quail with Mushrooms

Quail, 1 per person
Lemon
Salt if desired
Freshly ground black pepper
Mushrooms, sliced
Butter
¹/₂ cup white wine
Fresh parsley
Trenchers, 1 per bird

Rub quail with the cut side of a lemon; season inside and out with salt and pepper. Brown quail along with sliced mushrooms in skillet in melted butter. Add white wine when birds are nicely browned on all sides, toss in a few parsley sprigs; cover and simmer 10 to 15 minutes until birds are tender.

Dish each bird into a trencher, discard wilted parsley, pour over mushrooms and sauce and garnish with fresh parsley.

Trenchers for Quail and Other Small Birds

Take large rolls or small loaves of bread, just slightly larger than the birds you are using. Cut off the tops and scoop out the soft crumbs, leaving only a shell. Dry and grind the crumbs for other uses. Butter the bread shells liberally and toast in a slow oven until they are very crisp and lightly browned. This way they will retain their crunchiness even when they have absorbed the juices from the birds.

WILD TURKEY

Wild turkey is truly the king of the game birds—not only in size, but in the skill with which he eludes the craftiest hunter. In the 14th and 15th centuries, the kingdom of this regal bird extended from Canada and New England south to Mexico. As civilization marched across the continent, the domain of this bird of the forest diminished. Today the wild turkey is a rarity in the northern and central states, although the turkey population has seen a recent rise. But even in some of the southern states where he is found in abundance, it takes a skilled hunter to bag this wary and alert bird. Male wild turkeys average 15 pounds and are stuffed, trussed and cooked in the same manner as the domesticated birds. However, allowance must be made for their lack of fat.

Roast Wild Turkey

Prepare your favorite stuffing, allowing about 1 cup per pound of bird, dressed weight. Perhaps, since this is a rare treat, you might like to try something a bit special—browse through Chapter 11 and decide.

   I would suggest cooking a larger (and therefore older) bird in foil. This method has several advantages: the most important in this case is that the meat does not have an opportunity to dry out, basting is almost completely eliminated and the steam within the foil helps to tenderize even the hardiest old gobbler. Here's how to proceed.

Cover entire stuffed and trussed bird with a liberal coating of softened shortening or butter. If you have some capon fat (as I occasionally do in the freezer) place this on top. Pad wing tips, tail and leg ends with double folds of foil to prevent puncturing of the foil wrapper. Tear off sufficient foil of the heavy-duty variety to cover the entire bird loosely. You may have to use two pieces, double-folded together. Place the foil on a large shallow pan, set the bird in the center and bring the long ends of the foil over the breast of the bird, folding together loosely. Turn up the foil at each end in a single fold at least 4 inches from the outer edge of the foil. The wrapping should not be completely airtight, but should prevent the drippings from running out. Roast in a hot oven, preheated to 450° F., according to the following table:

Oven-ready weight (in pounds)	Cooking time (in hours)
8	2½
10	2¾
12	3¼
15	3½
20	3¾ to 4

About 45 minutes before you expect the bird to be done, carefully open the wrapper and fold the foil back in pan fashion. Check for tenderness of the thigh by pressing the meat (protect your hand with a paper towel). Return bird to oven to finish browning, basting frequently from this point on. When bird is done, remove pan juices with a basting syringe to a saucepan, lift bird to a heated platter and remove strings or skewers. Set the bird in a warming oven for 20 minutes while you prepare gravy.

Wild Turkey with Bacon-Swiss Chard Stuffing

This recipe is tasty with other game birds also.

1 wild turkey, dressed
Bacon-Swiss Chard Stuffing (*see* page 201)
Bacon slices
1 tablespoon shallots, chopped
1 turkey liver
2 cups game bird stock (or chicken stock)
¼ cup white wine
3 to 4 tablespoons roux
Freshly ground black pepper
Salt if desired
2 teaspoons Cognac

Follow instructions above for stuffing and roasting wild turkey, but use Bacon-Swiss chard stuffing and top bird with bacon slices. Then prepare liver-enhanced gravy as follows.

While turkey is roasting, fry 1 slice bacon in a small skillet and remove (eat it if you want to). In the bacon grease, lightly sauté the shallots and the turkey liver. Place game or chicken stock in a blender and add the cooked shallots and the liver; purée.

When the bird is done, remove to a warm platter. In a separate saucepan, melt the roux and stir in the white wine, cooking for a few minutes. Add the liver-enhanced stock and any pan juices; cook until mixture boils, stirring constantly until thick and smooth. Check seasoning and stir in the Cognac; serve over sliced turkey.

WOODCOCK

Although the woodcock is included among the upland birds, both he and the snipe are members of the same clan of shore birds. He has deserted the shore line habitat of his brethren and seems to prosper well near cultivated land. As a matter of fact, we have seen woodcock not 50 feet from our house, boring for worms and grubs in the soft earth beside the stream. It takes a bit of looking to see woodcock, since they are masters of camouflage and usually begin feeding only at twilight. Hunting the mysterious little birds is a sporty but strenuous affair and is becoming more popular every year.

Hunters who are successful in their quest of the woodcock have a rare treat in store, for the dark meat of these birds is considered the best of all game birds. The English consider the tail of the woodcock a great delicacy and do not draw the birds, but merely wipe them with a soft cloth. However, this is a matter of personal taste and I don't feel it necessary to follow this tradition. I prefer them cleaned in the same manner as any other game bird. Any of the recipes for quail may also be used for woodcock, allowing 1 bird per serving.

⚜ Broiled Woodcock

Woodcock
Salt if desired
Freshly ground black pepper
Bacon strips *or* larding pork

Season with salt and pepper, wrap in bacon or larding pork and broil over moderate coals for a *total* of 15 to 18 minutes. Arrange a drip pan of foil to catch the juices as the bird broils. It is generally cooked only to the pink stage and not well done.

Serve with crisp croutons or toast, as with quail.

Casserole of Woodcock

Stuffing per bird:
¼ cup raw diced chicken livers
¼ cup Madeira
1 teaspoon lemon juice

Bacon slices
2 tablespoons butter
¼ cup game bird stock
¼ cup Madeira
Salt and pepper

Preheat oven to 400° F.

Stuff each bird with the diced livers that have cooked for 5 minutes in the Madeira and lemon juice. Wrap each bird in bacon slices and brown in butter in a flameproof casserole. Add the stock and another ¼ cup Madeira and season to taste with salt and pepper. Cover casserole tightly and bake in preheated oven 15 to 20 minutes.

Serve from the casserole, garnished with croutons and fresh parsley.

Woodcock in Caper Sauce

4 woodcock, split in half lengthwise
2 tablespoons butter
2 tablespoons flour *or* 1½ tablespoons prepared roux
Freshly ground black pepper
Game bird stock
1 tablespoon white vinegar
1 egg yolk
2 tablespoons sour cream
2 teaspoons cornstarch
2 teaspoons lemon juice
1 tablespoon capers
Sprinkling of dried tarragon

In a large skillet or Dutch oven, melt the butter and stir in the flour until well blended *or* simply melt down your prepared roux. Add the woodcock pieces and coat them well with the roux; season with black pepper and pour in enough game bird stock to cover the pieces about halfway; pour on the tablespoon of vinegar.

Simmer until birds are tender, then stir in a binding of the egg yolk, sour cream, cornstarch and lemon juice. Stir until gravy thickens and is smooth; then blend in capers and tarragon.

Serve with wild or brown rice.

Roast Woodcock

Woodcock
Freshly ground black pepper
Salt if desired
Croutons

Stuffing per bird:
1 bird liver
¹/₂ tablespoon butter

Basting per bird:
1 tablespoon butter
¹/₂ cup heavy cream

Season each bird with salt and pepper; place the bird's liver and a piece of butter in the cavity. Roast in an oven preheated to 375° F. After 10 minutes, baste with butter and cream. Continue roasting for another 15 minutes, basting at least once more. Serve on croutons with the sauce poured over. The livers may be mashed on the croutons or served inside the bird, as you wish.

Roast woodcock are also delicious stuffed with a veal forcemeat (*see* Chapter 11).

CHAPTER 6

SHORE BIRDS, WILD DUCKS AND GEESE

The shore birds, which include the coot, gallinule, rail and snipe, are often seen in the company of wild ducks and geese. The shore birds consume a great deal of protein in the form of worms, bugs, etc., but when found near inland waters where their diets consist of marsh grasses, rice, wild celery and the like, all the species are good eating. Beware the water birds, the ducks such as the canvasback and redhead, however, that dive for fish and crustaceans, for they tend to retain their "fishiness." Draw and clean them immediately after you land them, and use a marinade, if possible, when preparing them to help minimize unsavory flavors.

Except for mature ducks and geese and the elusive king rail, the birds in this chapter tend to be rather small. Most are under a pound and the younger ones may not weigh even 5 ounces. So plan your cooking accordingly.

COOT

Although the coot is frequently observed swimming among ducks, this small marsh hen is a member of the rail family. A dweller of the shallow ponds and muddy bogs of the U.S. and southern Canada, the coot consumes a diet of primarily vegetable matter, but occasionally you will find a fish eater. The average size coot weighs in at about 1¼ pounds and should be skinned as soon as possible after shooting. Prompt drawing and cleaning is a must. If you suspect that you have a few fish eaters in your bag, then a marinade might also be advisable.

Braised Coot

Coot breasts and legs
Butter
Freshly ground black pepper
Salt if desired
Bird stock and white wine—in equal
    amounts
Roux
Tart jelly (optional)

Use only the breasts and legs, the meatiest parts of the bird. Brown the coot pieces in butter; season with salt and pepper. Reduce heat and add stock and white wine to cover, or use a part of the marinade for coot (below) as liquid. Cover and simmer until tender. Thicken the gravy with roux (plus tart jelly, if desired) and serve.

Marinade for Coot

1 cup water
1 cup wine vinegar or lemon juice
1 teaspoon salt
½ teaspoon black pepper
1 bay leaf
1 onion, sliced

1 carrot, sliced
1 stalk celery, sliced

Combine all ingredients and boil for 5 minutes. Cool and marinate the coots for a few hours in a cool place.

Sautéed Coot

Coot breasts and legs
Marinade for Coot (above)
Butter
Salt if desired
Freshly ground black pepper
½ glass tart jelly
1 teaspoon lemon juice

Remove the breast meat in two filets and

cut off the legs at the thigh joint. Marinate as directed above, then drain. Sauté in butter, season with salt and freshly ground black pepper; cover and simmer for 20 minutes, or until tender.

Remove the coot to a hot platter and blend the tart jelly and lemon juice into the pan drippings. Pour over the birds and serve.

GALLINULE

The Florida and purple gallinules, like their English cousin the moorhen, can best be described as chickens who deserted the barnyard for the bogs and marshes. They do not rank among the highest as table food, but can be delicious when skinned and braised. The average size is about 12 to 14 ounces, so plan your meal accordingly.

Braised Gallinule

Gallinule, split in half
Butter *or* drippings
Salt
Cayenne
Italian Game Bird Sauce (*see* page 172)

Brown the split birds in butter or drippings; season rather highly with salt and cayenne, cover and simmer slowly for 1/2 hour. Pour over Italian Game Bird Sauce and simmer for an additional 1/2 hour or until tender.

RAIL

Four subspecies of rails are sought after by confirmed rail hunters: the Virginia (the smallest—5 ounces), the sora (7 ounces), the clapper (14 ounces) and the king rail (weighing up to about 18 ounces). These birds used to be found in teeming numbers, but urban development (what else!) has seriously constricted their fresh and saltwater marsh habitats. Despite the difficulty in hunting them—the heat and mosquitoes can be fierce at the time of the rail migrations—they are still hunted by what I will call "elitist" gunners who happen to know of them and their whereabouts—not to mention that the plump little birds, which to some extent feed on wild grasses, do provide a delectable meal.

Unlike snipe, always pluck these birds, never skin them. Recipes for quail and snipe may be substituted, allowing at least 1 bird per serving, depending on the variety.

Roast Rail

Rail
Freshly ground black pepper
Salt if desired
Veal Forcemeat (*see* page 206)
Bacon slices
Melted butter

Preheat oven to 400° F.

Season with salt and pepper, stuff with veal forcemeat and wrap in bacon slices. Roast in oven preheated to 400° F. for 30 minutes, basting frequently with melted butter. Serve on toast or trenchers.

Breaded Rail

Rail
Freshly ground black pepper
Salt if desired
Flour
1 or 2 eggs, beaten

Fine dry bread or cereal crumbs
Pinch marjoram
Butter
Lemon wedges

Breaded Rail (cont.)

Split the birds in half lengthwise as you would a broiling chicken and season with salt and pepper. Dredge in flour, then dip in beaten egg and last in fine dry bread or cereal crumbs which have been seasoned with a pinch of marjoram. Gently sauté in butter, allowing 15 minutes per side. Serve with lemon wedges.

Try also baked breaded rail, using the recipe for "Baked Squirrel," allowing for difference in baking time.

Rail Curry

2 or 3 rail
¹/₄ cup butter
¹/₂ cup minced onions
1 tablespoon curry powder*
1 tablespoon flour
2 cups chicken or game bird stock
Salt and freshly ground black pepper to taste

Split the rail in half lengthwise, brown in butter and set aside. In the same pan, brown the onion. Blend in the curry powder, flour and the stock, stirring until all is thickened and smooth; add salt and pepper to taste.

Return the birds to the sauce, cover and simmer for ¹/₂ hour or until tender. Rice, chutney and the usual curry accompaniments should be provided.

*Or try mixing your own blend, *see* page 56.

SNIPE

Snipe, like woodcock, are considered a great delicacy. These little long-billed creatures are protected in many areas, but even where snipe shooting is legal, hunters will pass up the opportunity in favor of the larger birds. It's a pity, for the snipe not only provides good shooting, but also good eating. Any of the recipes given for woodcock are appropriate; the only difference is that the snipe is skinned before cooking. Allow 1 bird per person.

Broiled Snipe

Snipe
Salt and freshly ground black pepper
Bacon slices
Liver, heart and snipe gizzards
Parsley
Nutmeg

Optional:
¹/₂ cup white wine
¹/₂ cup sour cream
1 tablespoon bread crumbs
Grated lemon peel

Broiled Snipe (cont.)

Season lightly with salt and pepper, wrap birds in bacon slices and skewer. Broil over moderate coals with a drip pan to catch the juices, about 15 minutes.

Meanwhile, chop the liver, heart and gizzard and gently cook in butter with parsley, nutmeg and salt. Make golden brown toast, spread the liver, etc., on it, place the cooked birds on the toast and pour the pan drippings over all.

An alternate sauce may be made from the giblets in this way: cook the giblets as described above, then add 1/2 cup white wine and 1/2 cup sour cream. Blend in 1 tablespoon fine dry bread crumbs and a small amount of grated lemon peel. Pour the sauce over the birds and garnish the platter with croutons.

Barnegat Stew

Any combination of shore birds (including woodcock perhaps, enough to feed 4 people)
Seasoned flour (use paprika, garlic powder and black pepper)
4 tablespoons olive oil
1 cup onion, chopped
2 stalks celery, chopped
1 28-ounce can peeled tomatoes, drained and diced
1/4 cup white wine
Juice of 1/2 lemon
Freshly ground black pepper
2 tablespoons fresh parsley, chopped
3 to 4 leaves fresh basil, crushed, or 1/2 teaspoon dried basil
1/4 teaspoon coriander seeds, crushed
1/4 teaspoon dried thyme

Cut the birds into serving pieces, or use a combination of bird halves, breasts and legs. Dredge in seasoned flour.

In a large Dutch oven, heat the oil and brown the pieces on all sides; remove from pan. Add the onion and celery and lightly sauté; pour in the diced tomatoes, white wine and lemon juice. Season with black pepper and the herbs and stir to blend. Simmer this about 20 minutes, covered, then return the birds to the pot to cook until tender. Since these birds do not require long cooking, don't simmer them until the meat falls off.

Snipe Creole

Snipe
Butter
Freshly ground black pepper
Creole Sauce (*see* page 174)

Cut the snipe into serving pieces. Sauté on all sides in butter; cover with Creole Sauce and simmer until pieces are tender. Serve with rice.

Snipe with Sherry

Snipe
Butter
Parsley, minced
Shallots or scallion, finely minced
Salt
Freshly ground black pepper
Nutmeg, freshly grated
¹/₄ cup sherry per bird
1 teaspoon lemon juice per bird

Brown the snipe in butter; season with minced parsley, a bit of finely minced shallot or scallion, salt and pepper and a fresh grating of nutmeg. Add ¹/₄ cup sherry plus 1 teaspoon lemon juice per bird. Reduce heat, cover and simmer for 20 minutes. Serve on buttered toast or trenchers.

WILD DUCKS

Among the puddle ducks most desirable for the table are the mallard, black, widgeon, pintail, ring-necked and teal; among the divers, the canvasback and redhead. For the most part, these birds are vegetarians and their dark flesh is considered a delicacy the world over. However, each duck is only as good as its diet and some of the vegetarians do resort occasionally to a diet of fish and crustaceans. Prompt drawing and cleaning of ducks will eliminate the possibility of the "fishy" taste to a great extent.

Ducks should be dry plucked and not skinned. To remove the down which remains, *don't* plunge them into hot water into which paraffin has been melted. If the water is hot enough to melt the paraffin, it's hot enough to parboil the skin of the duck. Instead, melt paraffin in the top part of a double boiler over hot water (never over a direct flame) and allow the wax to cool slightly. Paint the wax on the ducks and let it harden, then zip off wax and down together.

Most purists insist that ducks should not be washed, but merely wiped clean with a soft cloth. In contrast, others advocate soaking for hours in buttermilk or salt water. A quick rinse in cold water as part of the cleaning process is not detrimental, especially if the flesh has been badly damaged by shot; just be sure to dry the duck thoroughly afterward. A piece of celery or onion in the duck cavity while it is aging in the refrigerator is the accepted method of eliminating the last vestiges of strong flavor; always discard it before cooking.

In contrast to domestic ducks, wild ducks need larding or basting to prevent the flesh from drying out, especially under intense heat. Most people prefer wild duck at least slightly rare, which requires only a *total* of 18 to 25 minutes in a 450° F. to 475° F. oven. If you like duck well done, then use one of the recipes where moist heat is used. Do not attempt to roast or broil ducks to the well-done stage, for they are apt to be tough and dry.

Braised Duckling

Brace of ducks
Butter
Salt and pepper
1 cup orange juice
1 cup chicken broth
²/₃ cup golden raisins
¹/₂ cup tart jelly
Roux

Cut a brace of ducks into serving pieces. Brown in melted butter in Dutch oven; season with salt and pepper. Add orange juice, chicken broth and golden raisins. Cover and simmer gently until tender. Remove birds, blend in tart jelly and thicken, if necessary, with a bit of roux. Pour the sauce over the birds and serve with rice.

Since orange and grapefruit crystals are now available for campers, this dish can easily be prepared at camp. Just add water in the proportions directed, dissolve a bouillon cube in water for the broth, and there you are. Raisins should be no problem; if you don't already include them in your camp kit for quick energy, do so next time. Our hunting jacket pockets always have a few mini-boxes tucked into them.

 Broiled Duck Cantonese Style

Basting sauce:
¹/₄ cup honey
1 clove of garlic, crushed
3 tablespoons soy sauce
¹/₄ cup sherry
2 slices fresh ginger, minced
¹/₄ teaspoon dry mustard

Combine the above ingredients. Season the cavities of young ducks with salt and pepper, place a piece of celery and a slice of lemon in each cavity. Balance and truss on a spit. Broil over moderate coals, turning and basting frequently with sauce, for approximately 20 minutes.

Serve with rice and glazed gingered fruit (*see* Chapter 10).

Bohemian Duck with Turnip

3 cups yellow turnip, peeled and diced
¹/₄ cup butter
Salt and pepper
Paprika
¹/₂ cup white wine
¹/₂ cup sour cream

Brace of ducks (older birds would be fine)

In a flameproof casserole, cook turnip, covered, with 2 tablespoons butter, salt and pepper, paprika and wine for 15

Bohemian Duck with Turnip (cont.)

minutes. In a large skillet, season and brown ducks in 2 tablespoons butter. Place birds atop turnips, pour over the butter in which the ducks were browned. Cover the casserole and simmer until the ducks are tender.

Remove ducks to heated platter, drain off any excess liquid in the casserole, blend the sour cream with the turnip and then arrange around the birds. Sprinkle with paprika and serve.

Canard à l'Orange

Wild ducks
Apricot-Rice Stuffing (*see* page 205)
¹/₂ cup orange juice
2 tablespoons butter
Roux
Tart orange marmalade

Preheat oven to 450° F.

Stuff ducks with Apricot-Rice Stuffing and truss. Combine orange juice and butter for basting sauce. Roast ducks for ¹/₂ hour, basting frequently.

Prepare gravy by boiling up pan juices, stirring to loosen any browned particles, and adding a bit more orange juice if necessary. Thicken slightly with a bit of roux and stir in several tablespoons tart orange marmalade.

Garnish the platter with glazed orange slices (*see* Chapter 10) and watercress; serve with wild rice.

Filets of Duck (or Woodcock)

Duck breasts, boned
Butter
Cumberland Sauce (*see* page 172)

With a boning knife, carefully remove breast from breastbone. Sauté filets on both sides in butter and serve with Cumberland Sauce.

Clay Bird

This one is fun to do and the results are delicious. I have done it myself, so I offer it here with the necessary warnings: *IF* you have time while preparing breakfast, packing lunch, getting decoys and sneak box ready to go at 3:00 A.M., blessings on you! If one of your hunting buddies elects to stay in camp and loaf one day, this is a good one to remember.

Eviscerated, unplucked wild ducks
Naturally sticky clay

Apple and/or onion
Celery

Clay Bird (cont.)

Find yourself some good sticky clay. Nothing else will do, so if it's not available, forget it till next time. Dig a pit and build a good fire that will burn down to lasting coals. Stuff a cleaned but unplucked duck with apple and/or onion and piece of celery, fasten the openings closed and fold the feathers over to keep out the clay.

Then plaster the bird liberally with clay; the sticky overcoat should be at least an inch thick, if not more. Scrape aside some of the coals, set the bird in the coals and pile others on top. Seal the pit and forget about it till you're ready to eat. Dig the bird out carefully, knock off the hardened clay (the feathers will come, too) and start eating!

Roast Duck with Sauerkraut

Wild ducks
Apple
Onions
Juniper berries
Salt
Freshly ground black pepper
Bacon slices
2 tablespoons butter
3 cups sauerkraut
1½ teaspoons caraway seeds

Insert a piece of apple and half a small onion in the cavity of each duck, along with a juniper berry, if desired. Season ducks with salt and pepper and lard with bacon slices. Set ducks aside while you prepare the sauerkraut and preheat the oven to 425° F.

Combine and brown in saucepan butter and 2 diced bacon slices. Add sauerkraut and caraway seeds. Blend well and simmer 20 minutes. Place the sauerkraut in the roaster, arrange the ducks on top and roast 18 to 25 minutes, depending on the size of the ducks. Baste with melted butter at least once during roasting.

Roast Duck with Savory Wild Rice

Wild ducks, cleaned and plucked
Savory Wild Rice (see page 206)
Freshly ground black pepper
Salt if desired
Bacon slices
Port wine
Butter
Red currant jelly (optional)

Preheat oven to 450° F.

Stuff ducks with savory wild rice; season with salt and pepper and lard with bacon slices. Roast 25 minutes, basting frequently with port wine and butter. Several spoons of red currant jelly may be melted in the pan juices for gravy.

Salmi of Duck in Red Wine

Marinade:
2 cups red wine
¼ cup brandy
1 onion, sliced
2 carrots, sliced
2 stalks celery, sliced
4 sprigs parsley
1 teaspoon salt
½ teaspoon pepper
Pinch of thyme and marjoram

**Brace of older ducks, cut into serving
  pieces**
Butter
Roux
**½ pound mushrooms, sautéed in
  butter**

In a glass or ceramic bowl, combine all ingredients for marinade. Marinate the ducks 2 to 3 hours; drain. Brown the pieces in hot butter in flameproof casserole. Add the marinade, including the sliced vegetables, and simmer over low heat until tender, about 1 hour; remove the duck pieces to a hot platter. Strain the marinade into a saucepan, thickening with roux and stirring until smooth; gently blend in sautéed mushrooms.

Serve with wild rice.

WILD GEESE

It is hard to say whether goose or turkey shooting ranks higher among gunners. Both goose and turkey are a challenge to the hunter's skill and both are splendid for the table. The geese most often found in North America include the blue, brant, Canada, white-fronted and snow, both greater and lesser. The lesser snow goose is preferred for table use, as its diet makes the flesh more palatable than that of the greater snow goose.

Depending on the species, wild geese average between 5 and 9 pounds. Older birds, more suitably cooked by moist heat methods, are identified by coarse plumage and very large wingspurs. The young geese are most delicious roasted with a tart fruit stuffing to enhance the succulence of their dark meat.

Braised Goose

1 mature goose
Sage and Onion Stuffing (*see* page 203)
½ cup carrots, chopped
½ cup celery, chopped
½ cup onion, chopped
½ cup ham, chopped
2 cups game bird stock

2 juniper berries
Roux
½ glass white wine

Preheat over to 425° F.

Stuff an older goose with sage and onion bread dressing. Place in Dutch

Braised Goose (cont.)

oven or roaster with a tight-fitting lid, along with chopped carrot, celery, onion and ham. Add 1 cup stock and juniper berries. Braise in hot oven, covered, for 1½ hours or until tender.

Meanwhile, reduce over low heat 1 cup game bird stock until it reaches the jelly stage. Remove the goose to a heated platter, brush with the glaze and keep hot. Strain the juices from the Dutch oven into a saucepan, thicken with roux, bring to a boil, stirring constantly. Add ½ glass white wine and simmer for another minute. Pour into preheated sauce boat.

Serve with glazed apple rings or raw cranberry relish in orange cups (*see* Chapter 10).

Braised Goose with Apples

1 mature goose
Celery, sliced
Onion, sliced
Freshly ground black pepper
Salt if desired
3 large tart cooking apples, thickly
    sliced
Apple cider

Stuff an older goose with celery and onion slices. Season with salt and pepper and place in covered roaster. Peel and core cooking apples, cut into thick slices and place around the goose.

Roast, covered, at 425° F. for 20 to 25 minutes per pound, basting frequently with cider. Uncover the roaster the last few minutes to allow the goose to brown. Remove onion and celery before serving.

Jugged Goose

1 mature goose, cooked in stock
1 egg
1 tablespoon dry white wine
Seasoned bread crumbs
Butter
Madeira, Apricot *or* White Wine Sauce

Clean an older goose and cook as directed under game bird stock (*see* page 190). Simmer until tender, remove the goose from the broth and cool. Cut into serving portions.

Beat egg with dry white wine. Dip each piece of goose into egg, then into seasoned fine dry bread crumbs. Sauté gently in butter until golden brown.

Serve with any of the following sauces: Madeira Sauce, Apricot Game Sauce, or White Wine Sauce (*see* Chapter 10). If you prepare White Wine Sauce, boil up 2 cups of the stock in which the goose was cooked until it is reduced by half.

Roast Young Goose

1 young goose
Cranberry, Chestnut, Apricot or Prune
    and Apple Stuffing (*see* Chapter 11)
Freshly ground black pepper
Salt if desired
Pinch ginger or cloves

Basting Liquid:
Melted butter plus
Apple cider *or*
Apple juice *or*
Orange juice *or*
Red or white wine

1/2 cup clear tart jelly (optional)

Clean the goose and stuff with any preferred dressing.

Season the outside of the goose with salt and pepper and a light sprinkling of ginger or cloves (whichever complements the stuffing best).

Roast at 325° F. for 18 to 20 minutes per pound, basting frequently. The basting liquid should be made up of melted butter plus whatever flavor will blend best with the stuffing. When the goose is tender, the thigh joint will move easily.

Since roast goose is a festive dish, you may wish to add another special touch at this point—glazing the goose. Combine 2 tablespoons of basting liquid with tart jelly and brush over the bird. Return to the oven for 15 minutes.

Prepare gravy from the pan juices, plus stock or the liquid in which the giblets were cooked. Garnish appropriately, according to the stuffing used.

Wild Goose with Rum-Soaked Apples

6 large apples
White rum
Sage and Onion Stuffing (*see* page 203)
Goose liver
Nutmeg
Ground ginger
Freshly ground black pepper
3 slices bacon
Red wine
Roux
Glazed Apple Rings (*see* page 178)

Peel, core and coarsely chop 6 large apples and soak them in white rum for about 4 hours. Prepare Sage and Onion Stuffing, but omit the herbs; add the drained apples, the goose liver, chopped, and a fresh grating of nutmeg. Stuff and truss the bird.

Sprinkle the bird with ground ginger and freshly ground black pepper and place atop a few slices of bacon. Roast as indicated in above recipe, basting with red wine. Make pan gravy, thickening with roux, and serve garnished with glazed apples.

CHAPTER 7

LITTLE CRITTERS

Small game, often found right in your own backyard or pretty close to it, can be equally as delicious as the prime roasts from the deer or elk you traveled so far to bag.

Not 10 minutes' drive from our place are beaver and muskrat, and right in our backyard we have rabbits, chucks, opossum, raccoon and squirrel. Unfortunately, we are just within the village limits, so I can't take a poke at them from the doorstep. Not that I haven't been tempted to—especially by the rabbits which have gorged themselves on my young vegetable and flower plants, and by the squirrels which constantly rob my bird feeders.

Frogs (which I have tacked to the end of this chapter) are only a menace to my ears, and although they are not strictly small game animals, they are very edible little creatures (legs only).

Keep in mind when preparing these animals (frogs excepted) that the younger ones may be roasted or broiled successfully (with an occasional parboiling first to remove some of the fat), while the older critters should be plopped right in the stew pot or casserole dish for braising.

BEAVER

As Mrs. Dalziel says in her recipe for beaver tail (*see* page 219), "First you must get acquainted with a beaver hunter," to which I must add "or trapper," for in most areas these animals are trapped for their valuable pelts. There is a lot of good eating on a beaver; a mature animal will weigh up to 50 or 60 pounds. However, if you are offered a choice by your trapper friend, take a younger animal, for the meat will be more tender. Young beaver, with its dark rich meat, is delicious roasted. The older ones will make a good pot roast or stew.

Barbecued Beaver

1 young beaver
Salted water
1 onion
4 to 6 peppercorns
Barbecue Sauce (*see* Chapter 10)

Parboil a young beaver in salted water with an onion and a few peppercorns for about ¹/₂ hour or so. Cut the beaver into serving portions and, using any of the barbecue sauces in Chapter 10, allow the meat to sit in the sauce for 2 hours, turning after the first hour. Barbecue over medium-hot coals until crisp and tender.

 Beaver Stew

3 pounds boned beaver, cut into cubes
Drippings
Flour
Salt and pepper
Water to cover
Bay leaf
Dash of Worcestershire Sauce
Carrots, diced
Potatoes, diced
Onions, diced
Turnips and cabbage, if available, diced
Flour and water paste

Strip all possible fat from the beaver meat; flour the cubes and brown on all sides in small amount of fat in a Dutch oven. Season with salt and pepper, add water to cover, bay leaf and Worcestershire Sauce. Cover and simmer until tender; the time will vary, naturally.

When the meat is nearly tender, add the diced carrots, potatoes, onions and whatever else is available. Cover and simmer until the vegetables are tender but well recognizable. Thicken the gravy, if needed, with flour and water paste.

 Chicken-Fried Beaver

1 young beaver
Salted water
1 onion (optional)
Dry bread crumbs *or*
Flour seasoned with salt, pepper, sage
    or thyme
Butter *or* drippings
Dehydrated soup
Water

Cut the beaver into serving portions. Parboil in salted water with an onion, if desired, until the beaver is nearly tender. This parboiling helps to remove any excess fat. Drain the beaver pieces; roll in crumbs or seasoned flour, and then brown slowly in a heavy skillet in butter or drippings. Make gravy by blending into the pan drippings any of the dehydrated soup mixes with an appropriate amount of water.

Roast Young Beaver

1 young beaver
Freshly ground black pepper
Salt
1 onion, sliced (optional)

Strip all possible fat from the beaver. Preheat oven to 450° F., season with salt and pepper and place on a rack in the roaster. Cook at this high heat for 15 to 20 minutes to sear the outside, then lower the heat to 325° F. to 350° F. and roast for 30 minutes per pound. Slice an onion over the top of the roast if you wish. In contrast to the big game animals, this critter needs no basting; the rack is advisable so that the fat still within the beaver will not collect around the roast itself.

MUSKRAT

Muskrat is another dark-meated bonus from the trapper. I see no reason not to call a spade a spade or a muskrat by its own name, so forget about the "Marsh-rabbit," "Swamp-rabbit," or "Marsh-hare." If your lady-fair has accepted and done well by other game you've brought home, she'll accept this one, too—and on its own merits. Just be sure, before you present it for her fond attention in the kitchen, that you've removed all the small kernels or glands which could impair the otherwise delicious flavor.

 ## Braised Muskrat

1 mature muskrat
Seasoned flour
Butter or pan drippings
2 onions, sliced
1 cup sour cream *or*
1 10³/₄-ounce can cream of mushroom soup

Cut muskrat into serving pieces; roll in seasoned flour and brown with onions in Dutch oven, using butter or drippings. When all is evenly browned, reduce heat and add either sour cream or cream of mushroom soup. Cover tightly and simmer until tender.

Muskrat in Creole Sauce

1 muskrat
Oil or butter
Creole Sauce (*see* page 174)

Cut muskrat into serving pieces, brown well in oil or butter in skillet which has a tight-fitting lid. Add Creole Sauce to cover and simmer until very tender over low heat. Check occasionally to be sure the sauce is not sticking to the pan. Serve with fluffy rice.

Roast Muskrat

1 muskrat
Freshly ground black pepper
Salt if desired
Sage and Onion *or* Prune and Apple
    Stuffing (*see* Chapter 11)
Bacon slices
Butter, melted

Preheat oven to 350° F.

    Season inside and out with salt and pepper. Stuff with a bread Sage and Onion Dressing or a Prune and Apple Stuffing. Sew or skewer openings, lard with bacon slices or brush liberally with butter.

    Roast on a rack in a moderate oven, basting frequently with the pan drippings and a bit of hot water. When the muskrat is tender, remove the bacon slices and allow the meat to brown attractively the last 15 minutes.

OPOSSUM

Although I have seen 'possum in Illinois and near our former home in the East, I would not have cooked them in either case. 'Possum will eat anything, and those found near civilization are apt to be carrion and garbage eaters. Their meat can be unappetizing under such circumstances. However, friends from the South tell me that they are superb when they have been feeding on persimmons and berries.

    Because of the glands in the small of the back and inside the forelegs, some hunters prefer to skin these animals, removing the glands at that time. Other 'possum chasers treat the animal's outer layer like a pig's: they dunk the whole critter in a kettle of boiling water for a minute or so, then scrape off the fur with a dull blade. Age for a few days in the refrigerator as directed in Chapter 1 and be certain to strip off all excess fat.

Southern-Style Roast 'Possum

There are two ways to proceed with this favorite dish of the Old South. Both are designed to rid the 'possum of excess fat.

1 'possum
Salted water
Freshly ground black pepper
Salt if desired
Sage *or* poultry seasoning
Sweet potatoes
Brown sugar
Butter

1. Parboil in salted water to cover for about 1 hour. Pat dry, then place in a roaster into a 350° F. oven, draining off fat as it accumulates. After the roast has browned a bit, season with salt and pepper and a sprinkle of sage or poultry seasoning.

    After an hour of roasting, add sweet

Southern-Style Roast 'Possum (cont.)

potatoes which have been parboiled 20 minutes in their jackets and then skinned and cut into thick slices. Sprinkle the sweet potato slices with brown sugar and add a dot of butter to each slice, if you wish. Continue roasting until 'possum and potatoes are tender, about ½ hour.

2. Preheat oven to 450° F., place the 'possum on a rack in the roaster and roast for 15 to 20 minutes. Reduce the oven heat to 350° F., season with salt and pepper and roast uncovered for about an hour, draining off fat as it accumulates. Place scrubbed sweet potatoes in their jackets in the roaster and continue baking till both are tender.

Braised 'Possum with Sauerkraut

1 'possum, cut into serving pieces
Flour seasoned with black pepper and garlic powder
4 to 6 slices bacon, cubed
1 cup onion, chopped
½ bay leaf
8 to 10 juniper berries
2 cups dry white wine (plus a little water, if necessary)
Freshly ground black pepper
2 to 3 pounds sauerkraut, rinsed and drained
1 teaspoon caraway seeds

Preheat oven to 350° F.

Dredge the 'possum pieces in seasoned flour. In a large skillet, fry the bacon cubes and, when done, remove with a slotted spoon. In the bacon drippings, brown 'possum on all sides; arrange in a large casserole dish with lid. Sauté onion in remaining bacon drippings and cover the 'possum pieces. Pour in 1 cup wine; add the bay leaf, juniper berries and a sprinkling of fresh pepper. Cover and bake 1 to 1½ hours, making sure the liquid does not cook out.

Add sauerkraut to casserole with caraway seeds and arrange so all pieces of meat are surrounded by the kraut. Pour in the remaining cup of wine to moisten and bake about another hour, until meat is very tender.

Campfire 'Possum

1 young 'possum
Seasoning of your choosing
Sweet potatoes

Cut a young 'possum into serving pieces and season as desired. Broil over the coals of your campfire, turning frequently so the pieces are nicely browned. Serve with sweet potatoes which have been roasting in their jackets in the embers of the fire.

PORCUPINE

The porcupine is protected by law and/or tradition in most places to provide food for the lost and hungry. The slow-moving porky does not attack or "shoot" its quills, as so many people believe. The porcupine can be done in with a rock or a club, but even when he is dead, his quills can do damage. If you're that hungry, do as the Indians did—just throw the porky on the coals of a fire, heap with more coals and roast for about an hour. Then remove the burned hide and eat the flesh. However, if you're not in such a tearing hurry, it is better to skin the porky, in order to remove the excess fat. Approach the skinning job from the smooth underside of the beast and you should have little trouble.

Broiled Porcupine

Since porky fat has the same tallowy consistency as lamb or mutton, it is best to cook the meat over the coals of an open fire. If you have a small young one, spit the entire beast; a larger one can be cut into pieces and broiled in the same manner. Done in this way, the excess fat will drip out into the fire and the remainder can then be eaten cold as you go on your way.

Porcupine Stew

If you have an older porcupine, you may have up to 40 pounds of meat, and that should be enough to sustain you for some time. Parboil the meat in salted water to remove the excess fat and to help tenderize the meat. Finish the cooking over the open fire or make a stew if you happen to have any other supplies with you. As I have said before, hunger is the best seasoning and in an emergency, whatever you can devise is just dandy.

RABBIT AND HARE

Rabbits and hares are still the most abundant and popular game animals in North America. As a matter of fact, these furry vegetarians are favorites all over the world. The meat is mild in flavor, very similar to chicken, and can be prepared in the same way as chicken. The best indication of age, and therefore of your cooking method, is the ear. If the ear is soft and splits easily, the rabbit or hare is young and may be fried or roasted. A tough ear means a critter for the stew pot or Dutch oven. I mentioned it before, but it bears repeating—rabbit should always be well done to avoid any possible infection from tularemia.

Broiled Rabbit

2 young rabbits
Salt and pepper
Bacon slices
Butter (optional)

Split rabbits in half, season with salt and pepper, wrap in bacon slices or baste liberally with butter while broiling slowly over moderate coals. A judicious slit with your knife near the bone will indicate whether or not the meat is well done.

Civet de Lievre

1 hare or large rabbit, cut into serving
    pieces
Salt and freshly ground black pepper
Flour
¹/₂ pound bacon or salt pork, diced
2 onions, coarsely chopped
Dry red wine to cover or equal amounts
    of wine and stock
Bouquet garni of thyme, bay leaf,
    parsley, small garlic clove
¹/₂ pound fresh mushrooms
4 tablespoons butter
Rabbit liver, firm and dark with no
    spots
18 to 20 small white onions
Flour and water paste

Season rabbit pieces with salt and pepper and coat with flour. In a covered skillet or Dutch oven, brown bacon lightly, then remove with a slotted spoon. Brown rabbit on all sides in the same fat, adding the chopped onion during the last of the browning process so it does not scorch. Add wine and stock to cover the rabbit, bouquet garni and bacon pieces. Cover and simmer over low heat until tender, about 2 hours.

In another skillet, sauté mushrooms in butter for 5 minutes, add rabbit liver, chopped, and sauté another 2 to 3 minutes. Add liver and mushrooms to rabbit in Dutch oven, along with onions which have been parboiled in salted water for 15 minutes and then drained. Combine and heat thoroughly.

Remove the bouquet garni and place rabbit and vegetables on warm serving platter. Thicken gravy with flour and water paste, stir until boiling and let the gravy simmer for 2 to 3 minutes. Pour over rabbit and serve.

 Rabbit Fricassee

1 older rabbit or hare, cut in serving
    pieces
Flour seasoned with salt and pepper
Butter or drippings
Water or stock to cover

Celery, chopped
Carrot, chopped
Bay leaf
Sprigs of parsley
Pinch of thyme

Rabbit Fricassee (cont.)

Dredge rabbit pieces in seasoned flour; brown in hot butter in Dutch oven. Add stock or water to cover, vegetables and herbs. Cover Dutch oven and set over a slow fire or low heat to simmer until rabbit is tender. Thicken gravy if necessary.

If you want dumplings, add them to the bubbling liquid, cover tightly and steam for 20 minutes more—don't lift the lid! Place rabbit and dumplings on a hot platter and strain the gravy into a heated sauce boat (*see* Chapter 11 for dumplings).

Hasenpfeffer

**1 large rabbit or hare or 2 smaller ones,
    cut into serving pieces**
Seasoned flour
Drippings
1 tablespoon flour
1/4 cup sour cream

Marinade:
**Equal parts of wine vinegar and water
    to cover rabbit**
4 teaspoons sugar to each cup of liquid
1/2 teaspoon salt per cup of liquid
Few peppercorns
2 onions, sliced
2 stalks celery or celery knob, sliced
2 carrots, sliced
2 or 3 juniper berries
Bay leaf
2 or 3 whole cloves

Combine the ingredients for the marinade in a glass or ceramic bowl and add the rabbit pieces. Cover and marinate for 2 days in a cool place, turning the rabbit pieces twice daily. Drain and dry the rabbit, reserving the marinade.

Coat the rabbit pieces with seasoned flour and brown in drippings in Dutch oven. Reduce heat, add marinade and vegetables, cover and simmer until tender. Remove rabbit to heated platter and keep warm. Strain the sauce through a sieve, pressing the vegetables through also. Blend flour with sour cream and add slowly to the strained sauce, heating just to the boiling point. Serve with dumplings.

Pan-Fried Rabbit

Young rabbits
1 egg, beaten with 1 tablespoon water
**Flour or fine dry crumbs seasoned with
    salt, pepper and thyme**
Butter
Lemon juice (optional)

Cut young rabbits into serving pieces. Dip into beaten egg, then roll in

seasoned flour or fine crumbs. Heat butter in a heavy skillet and brown the rabbit over low heat until golden brown.

Cover and let the skillet sit at the edge of your fire until the rabbit is well done. A sprinkling of lemon juice, if available, is a welcome addition when serving. Or serve with pan gravy.

Rabbit Sicilian

To the uninitiated, Italian cooking means "tomatoes." Nothing could be further from the truth. In Northern Italy, French, Swiss and German influences filter through, and in the South as well as the island of Sicily, where this recipe originated, there is a strong Greek "presence" that goes back to Ancient times. My adaptation of this authentic Sicilian recipe—"Coniglio con Olive Verdi" (Rabbit with Green Olives)— features green olives and capers, very "un-Italian" with *no* tomatoes.

1 to 2 cottontails, cut into serving pieces
2 tablespoons bacon drippings
2 tablespoons olive oil
1 cup onion, chopped
2 cloves garlic, chopped
2 stalks celery, chopped
2 tablespoons flour
1¹/₂ to 2 cups water or chicken stock
¹/₄ teaspoon dried basil or a few fresh basil leaves
¹/₂ bay leaf
Pinch dried ground rosemary
Freshly ground black pepper
Handful (¹/₂ cup) green olives, pitted and drained
1 tablespoon capers, drained

In a large skillet or Dutch oven, heat the bacon drippings and olive oil. Brown the rabbit pieces on both sides and remove from pan. Add the onion, garlic, celery and sauté lightly. Stir in the flour so it is well blended, then add the water or stock, stirring until gravy is smooth and thickened. Add the herbs and return the meat to the skillet. Season with fresh black pepper and simmer, covered, for about 1 hour or until the rabbit is tender and thoroughly cooked.

Add the olives and capers and heat through, about 10 minutes. Serve with your favorite pasta and fresh bread. Delicioso! Serves 4.

Rabbit in White Wine Sauce

1 large rabbit or hare or 2 small ones
Larding pork or bacon slices
2 or 3 tablespoons butter
1 onion, thinly sliced
1 carrot, thinly sliced
2 stalks celery, finely diced
1 parsnip or parsley root, diced
Salt and pepper
2 or 3 allspice berries
Pinch of thyme or marjoram
2 tablespoons vinegar
1 glass dry white wine
Rabbit stock
Flour
1 tablespoon lemon juice

Grated lemon rind
1 teaspoon capers
2 tablespoons tomato paste
¹/₄ cup sour cream

Cut away the forelegs, breast and belly flesh of the rabbit, retaining only the saddle and hindlegs for the roast. Cover the forelegs, etc., with salted water and simmer to make stock for the casserole. In a covered flameproof casserole, melt butter, sauté vegetables lightly. Place rabbit and seasonings on top of vegetables; add vinegar, wine and enough stock to cover the bottom of the casserole ½-inch deep. Cover and simmer until rabbit is tender, adding more stock only if necessary to prevent sticking. Remove meat to warming oven.

Dust vegetables lightly with flour, stir until flour is blended. Add a ladle of rabbit stock, the lemon juice and rind, capers, tomato paste and sour cream. Stir until thoroughly blended and thickened. Put the sauce through a sieve, forcing the vegetables through also. Cut the rabbit into serving pieces, place on platter with dumplings and pour sauce over all.

Forelegs, breast and any leftovers can be used to make pâté or *see* "Leftovers and Luncheon Ideas."

Roast Rabbit

Young rabbits
Sage and Onion Stuffing (*see* page 203)
Salt and freshly ground black pepper
Flour
Bacon slices
Stock or chicken broth
Roux
Heavy cream (optional)

Preheat oven to 350° F.

Stuff young rabbits with a celery and onion bread dressing, skewer or sew up openings. Season outside with salt and pepper and dust lightly with flour. Cover the rabbits with bacon slices and place in roaster with enough stock or chicken broth to cover the bottom of the roaster. Cover the roaster and place in oven for 1 to 1½ hours, basting several times with the pan juices.

When the rabbits are tender, remove the bacon slices and return the roaster to the oven, uncovered, so that the rabbits can brown for a few minutes. Remove the rabbits to a heated platter and prepare gravy from the pan juices with a bit of roux and stock or cream.

Sweet 'n Sour Rabbit

See page 215. Once you taste this, you'll realize that just about any game goes well with this recipe.

RACCOON

There must be something to this 'coon hunting, where grown men go out at night and pursue Mr. Ringtail with hounds. Personally, I've never been able to get excited about chasing cross country, stumbling over stones, through brush and swamp—when it's so dark you can't see your hand in front of your face. But I do get a thrill out of listening to a pack of hounds as they pick up the scent, begin trailing and finally end in an orgy of barking "treed."

Old "rackety-coon" is perfectly adjusted to living a lonely existence in the wilds, but he also likes to live near people, sometimes waking them in the early dawn by knocking over the trash cans. If you hear a weird sound in the night—like a baby being tortured—friend 'coon is on the prowl. Not so amusing is the fact that Mr. Ringtail is a fierce fighter when backed into a corner by the hounds. More than one 'coon hound has lost his life when the 'coon enticed him into the water and then turned to the attack.

'Coon hunting is a matter of taste, but one fact you can't deny is that 'coon, properly prepared in the roaster, may be more to your taste than chasing him—I know I like it better!

Small Game Gumbo

1/2 **pound game sausage, smoked, if possible***
1 **tablespoon liquid smoke (optional)**
Olive or peanut oil
2 **to 3 young raccoon, rabbits, squirrels, etc., or a combination, cut into serving pieces**
1/4 **pound smoked ham, cubed**
1/4 **cup butter**
6 **tablespoons flour**
1 **cup onion, chopped**
3 **cloves garlic, chopped**
2 **quarts water or chicken stock**
1 **tablespoon paprika**
Salt
Freshly ground black pepper
1 **bay leaf**
1/2 **teaspoon dried thyme**
1/2 **pound shrimp, shelled and deveined**
1/2 **to 1 pound oysters (6 to 12, depending on size), shucked, with their liquor**
1 **tablespoon gumbo filé powder****
2 **tablespoons parsley, chopped**

In a Dutch oven, heat 2 tablespoons oil and brown sausage on all sides. If the sausage was not previously smoked, add the liquid smoke to the oil; brown; cool; cut into serving slices about 1/4-inch thick. Add the cut-up small game and the smoked ham cubes to the pan and brown, adding more oil if necessary; return sausage slices to the pan.

In a small skillet (iron, if possible), prepare a brown roux by combining the butter with the flour; stir constantly until smooth and golden brown, 10 to 15 minutes. Add the onion and garlic and lightly sauté. Add this mixture to the Dutch oven, scraping the skillet to get all the roux.

Pour in the water or stock and the oyster liquid (enough to cover the meat); season with paprika, salt, black pepper, bay leaf and thyme. Cover and simmer until game is tender; this will vary according to the game.

Add shrimp and oysters to the gumbo pot and simmer until shellfish is cooked, about 15 minutes. Stir in gumbo filé powder and chopped parsley and keep hot, but do not let this delectable Southern stew come to a boil again. Serves 4.

Serve over rice in large soup bowls, with toasty garlic bread.

* For game sausage, you may substitute hot Italian sausage or Creole hot sausage.

** If you don't live in the South, where gumbo filé powder is easily obtainable, you can purchase it at most food specialty stores. Do not eliminate it from the recipe, however, for it is *the* essential ingredient that makes this dish an authentic Creole one.

Broiled 'Coon

1 young raccoon
Seasonings

If you've found yourself a youngster, broil him over a good bed of coals. Cut the meat into cubes, season well and thread on green sticks or skewers. Broil slowly until well browned and crisp on the outside. Have some apples and onions baking in the coals in foil packages nearby.

 'Coon Stew

1 4-pound 'coon, cut into cubes
2 or 3 onions, sliced
2 to 3 cups canned tomatoes, coarsely chopped
Salt and pepper
Bay leaf
Dash of Worcestershire Sauce
Carrots
Onions
Potatoes
Turnips

Brown the meat cubes slowly in a Dutch oven. There should be enough fat within the tissues that no additional oil is required. Add the onions during the last of the browning process so they won't become scorched. Reduce the heat, add enough tomatoes and liquid to cover the meat, season and cover. Simmer over low heat until almost completely tender.

Add cubed vegetables of your choice and continue to simmer until vegetables are tender. Check seasoning—you may want more salt—and serve with hot biscuits.

Stuffed Roast 'Coon

Any tart fruit stuffing goes well with Mr. Ringtail, as the flavor of the meat is very similar to the dark meat of chicken.

1 raccoon
Salted water
Carrots, onion, celery, peppercorns (optional)
Apple-Raisin Stuffing (see page 202)
Apple juice

Parboil the 'coon in salted water to cover, adding carrots, onion, celery and a few peppercorns if you desire. Simmer for 30 to 60 minutes, depending on the size and age of the 'coon. As with 'possum, this helps remove some of the excess fat in the tissues. Drain and dry.

Stuff with Apple-Raisin Stuffing. Skewer and place on a rack in the roaster, adding a bit of apple juice to the bottom of the pan. Roast at 350° F. for 40 to 45 minutes per pound. If the 'coon is a wily oldster, you may wish to cover the roast for a part of the cooking time, but be sure to uncover it the last 1/2 hour or so to allow him to brown nicely.

SQUIRREL

Beloved target of small and not-so-small boys, the squirrel ranks second only to the rabbit in popularity. The squirrel was an important item in the diet of the early settlers and is still a welcome addition to the game bag. The delicately flavored meat needs fat—either bacon or butter—in cooking and can be broiled, baked or stewed in the same manner as rabbit.

The most famous dish for squirrel is Brunswick Stew—a most delectable concoction to which I was introduced in Williamsburg, Va., while my husband and I were on our honeymoon. Nothing would do but for me to duplicate the recipe at home as soon as we had obtained the necessary ingredients. I was still accustomed to helping cook for a large family, so I did not question the amounts in the recipe which had been given to me. The two of us ate Brunswick Stew for almost a full week!

P.S.—I still use the same recipe, sometimes doubling it if there's a large crowd to feed. It freezes successfully and is a handy item for the "emergency" corner of my freezer.

Brunswick Stew

The original recipe calls for squirrel only, but a combination of any or all of the following may be used with equally delicious results: squirrel, rabbit, woodchuck, pheasant—even chicken!

4 or 5 pounds small game, disjointed
Diced bacon, fried and fat reserved
3 onions, sliced
Salt and pepper to taste
Water or stock to cover
3 or 4 potatoes, peeled and diced
2 quarts of tomatoes, drained
1/4 to 1/2 teaspoon cayenne pepper
Liberal sprinkling of thyme
2 cups fresh lima beans or the equivalent in frozen ones
2 cups fresh corn or the equivalent in frozen niblets
2 cups okra, if available fresh—I find the frozen not too satisfactory in this dish

Brown the meat and onions in hot bacon fat in a Dutch oven. Season with salt and pepper, add water or stock to cover the meat and simmer until tender. Remove the meat from the bones, return to the liquid and add potatoes, tomatoes, cayenne and thyme. Cook slowly for 1/2 hour, then add the fresh limas, corn and okra and cook until all is tender. (If frozen vegetables are used, they will require less time than the fresh ones.) Adjust seasonings before serving.

Brunswick Stew is usually served in soup plates, since it has the consistency of a thick soup. However, if you prefer, you may thicken it further with the addition of a bit of roux or some fine dry bread crumbs. Corn 'Pone or any corn bread is the traditional accompaniment (*see* Chapter 15).

Baked Squirrel

For lovers of bacon, this great-tasting dish not only imparts the bacon flavor to the meat, but also seals in the delicate juices of the squirrel at the same time. Good also for rabbit, hare and game birds.

2 squirrels, cut into serving pieces (quartered)
Freshly ground black pepper
Garlic powder
Paprika
Flour
Rendered bacon drippings, strained
Fine dry bread crumbs, seasoned, if you wish, with dried basil and/or oregano

Preheat oven to 375° F.

Since squirrels tend to be small, I find that quartering them provides a more substantial serving. Dry the meat, season it and lightly flour the pieces. Then dip in and completely moisten with bacon drippings. Dredge in bread crumbs and arrange in a baking dish.

Bake for ½ hour to 45 minutes on one side, turn and bake on the other side for the same amount of time, until well browned and tender. Serves 4.

WOODCHUCK

Woodchuck, as well as their cousins the prairie dogs, have long been favored targets of the varmint shooters. Unfortunately, they have been neglected to a great extent in the culinary department. Young 'chucks, plump after a summer's gorging on grains and greens, are delicious roasted or broiled in the same fashion as 'coon, allowing of course for the difference in size.

Just don't forget to strip off the fat and remove the gland kernels. If your 'chuck is a senior citizen, parboil him for half an hour in salted water and proceed as in Rabbit Fricassee—or set him aside in the freezer to add to the next Brunswick Stew!

FROGS

Frogs aren't considered small game animals, and they aren't mammals—they're amphibians that seem to feel at home on land or in the water. But they are little leaping creatures that the hunter often encounters around woodland lakes and ponds. Most important, they are good eating.

We know of one hunter/fisherman who, after a few days of fruitless hunting, spent an afternoon with string, a safety pin and a strip of red cloth pulling frogs out of a pond. We laughed as we watched (the frogs kept jumping back into the water before he could remove the legs), but what a mighty fine meal he enjoyed the following day!

If you can get your hands on some fresh frogs' legs, here are two ways to prepare them deliciously.

Fried Frogs' Legs in Beer Batter

Fresh frogs' legs, soaked overnight in milk
Flour seasoned with black pepper and garlic powder
Beer batter (*see* page 161)
Vegetable oil for deep-frying

The purpose of soaking the legs in milk is to remove some of the marshy flavor. Dry and dredge in seasoned flour first, then dip in beer batter. Fry on both sides in vegetable oil until crisp, tender and golden.

Frogs' Legs Scampi

Frogs' legs, soaked overnight in milk
Salt and freshly ground black pepper
Paprika
2 tablespoons unsalted butter
2 tablespoons olive oil
4 to 6 cloves garlic, minced
Flat Italian parsley, chopped
Lemon slices

Dry the legs and season them highly with salt, pepper and paprika. In a skillet, melt the butter, stir in the oil and, when hot, brown the frogs' legs on both sides. Add the garlic and parsley, cover the pan and simmer, allowing the flavors to meld and the legs to cook through. Serve with the garlic "gravy" poured over and slices of lemon.

CHAPTER 8

VARIETY MEATS AND SAUSAGE

It surprises me to discover how many hunters discard—or completely ignore—the heart, kidney, liver and tongue of the big game animals. You will seldom find hunters of the old school—present-day Eskimos included—who do not celebrate the conclusion of a successful hunt with one of these delicacies. One great advantage to these meats is the fact that they can be prepared the same day the beast is shot and, in fact, they are at their very best when fresh. In addition, these organs, or variety meats, are a rich source of quality protein, vitamins A, B complex, C and minerals such as zinc. They also keep well in the freezer for three to four months and are so delicious that they should never be wasted.

Sausage can be mixed with a variety of meat products and by-products and has been prepared using liver, blood and, well, you name it and it's probably been tried. My recipe for sausage requires only the lesser cuts of game, added pork fat and essential flavorings. In short, it's simple and savory. If you've never dared to do your own, give it a try—you'll be pleasantly surprised.

HEART

Heart requires long, slow cooking with moist heat to be at its flavorful best. It cannot be hurried, but is well worth waiting for. Remove the veins, arteries, connective tissue and fat and rinse thoroughly in cold water.

 **Braised Heart**

1 game heart
3 slices bacon, diced
Celery
Carrots
Onion
Parsley root
Stock or water to cover
Freshly ground black pepper
Salt to taste
3 to 4 tablespoons sour cream

Cut heart into ½-inch slices. In heavy skillet, brown the diced bacon, along with celery, carrot, onion and parsley root, cut into small pieces. When vegetables are nearly browned, push to one side of skillet and brown heart lightly. Add just enough stock or water to cover and simmer, covered, until heart is fork tender.

Press vegetables through a sieve and return to gravy; season to taste with salt and pepper, blend in sour cream and heat just to boiling point. Serve with noodles, rice or dumplings.

 Hunter's-Style Heart

1 game heart
Flour seasoned with garlic powder,
    freshly ground black pepper and
    thyme
Butter or pan drippings
½ package dehydrated
    beef vegetable soup
1½ cups water

Freshly ground black pepper
Salt if desired

Slice heart ½-inch thick. Roll in seasoned flour and brown slowly in butter or drippings. Add dehydrated soup and water. Cover and simmer until heart is tender. Season to taste.

Stuffed Heart

1 game heart
Freshly ground black pepper
Salt if desired
Bread or rice stuffing
Flour seasoned with a pinch of
    marjoram and rosemary
1 cup stock or beef bouillon
Flour and water paste

Clean heart. Season inside and out with pepper and salt. Stuff with any favorite stuffing, using either bread or rice as a base. Since the heart will be cooked by moist heat, keep the stuffing on the dry side and don't pack the cavity too full—allow room for the stuffing to expand. Sew or tie the heart together firmly and dredge with seasoned flour.

Brown in hot fat in Dutch oven, add 1 cup stock or beef bouillon and simmer slowly until tender. Remove heart from Dutch oven, thicken gravy with a flour and water paste, adding more stock or bouillon, if necessary. Stir over low heat until smooth and thick.

KIDNEYS

Remove covering membrane and soak in cold salted water for 30 to 60 minutes, depending on the size. Kidneys from a young animal should be cooked very briefly—kidneys the size of a beef kidney (about 1 pound) may be browned and added to a stew.

Game Steak and Kidney Pie

This hearty traditional English dish is perfect for winter appetites.

1¹/₂ pounds round steak (deer, moose or elk)
³/₄ pound kidneys (beef kidneys may be substituted if game kidneys have already been used)
Flour seasoned with salt and pepper
3 tablespoons fat or drippings
3 or 4 carrots, cut in ¹/₂-inch slices
3 or 4 stalks celery, cut in ¹/₂-inch slices
1 large onion, sliced
2 tablespoons parsley, chopped
Generous sprinkling of thyme and rosemary
3 cups stock or beef bouillon
Unbaked pie crust

Remove white center and tubes from kidneys and any gristle or connective tissue from round steak. Cut both in 1-inch cubes and dredge with seasoned flour. Brown slowly in hot fat in heavy skillet or Dutch oven. Brown only enough cubes at one time to be uncrowded in the bottom of the pan. When the meat is all browned, place vegetables in pan and brown these also, adding parsley, thyme and rosemary at this time. Add bouillon or stock and stir vigorously, scraping the bottom of the pan to loosen all browned particles. Return meat to the pan, cover and simmer on very low heat until meat is nearly tender.

Pour into large casserole or individual ones, top with pie crust, seal edges and cut slits in the crust for steam to escape. Bake at 325° F. until crust is golden brown.

I have also used for the crust leftover mashed potatoes, whipped fluffy again with an egg and a bit of milk.

 Sautéed Kidneys

3 or 4 small kidneys
¹/₄ cup butter
1 tablespoon onion, minced
Pepper
Marjoram
Juice of ¹/₂ lemon

Cut the kidneys in thin slices. Sauté gently with onion in butter until they begin to brown. Add pepper, marjoram and lemon juice and simmer one or two minutes more. Serve over rice or with cornmeal dumplings.

LIVER

Although it is the organ most often saved, it is also the one most often misunderstood. Just because the liver comes from an old, and perhaps tough, animal, it does not mean that it will require the same long, slow cooking that the meat will. Liver is not muscular tissue and the only thing that makes it tough and hard is overcooking.

Baked Big Game Liver

1 big game liver, thinly sliced
Mushroom or sage bread stuffing
³/₄ cup game stock or beef bouillon

Preheat oven to 350° F.
    Allow two slices per serving. Spread each slice with mushroom or sage bread stuffing; roll and tie or skewer together. Place in buttered casserole, add ³/₄ cup game stock or beef bouillon and cover. Bake for 30 to 40 minutes, basting once or twice with the pan juices.

Canadian Logger Liver

Fresh game liver, sliced
Flour seasoned with freshly ground
    black pepper
Bacon drippings
1 or 2 onions, sliced
2 cloves garlic, sliced lengthwise
¹/₂ cup or so white wine
¹/₂ bay leaf
Scant ¹/₄ teaspoon thyme

Dredge liver slices in flour. In a large heavy skillet (my old iron skillet still works the best), heat the bacon drippings and lightly sauté the onions and garlic. Add the liver slices and quickly brown them on both sides. Add the white wine, bay leaf and thyme and season with a sprinkling of black pepper; cover and simmer 5 to 10 minutes. Serve with French bread and green vegetables.

Celebration Supper

Fresh venison liver
Butter or bacon fat

The liver has already been rinsed with water and drained during the field dressing. Remove it from the plastic bag, give it another quick rinse in cold water and cut the liver into slices. We prefer liver still pink on the inside, so we cut slices at least ¹/₂-inch thick. If someone in your party is of the "well done" school, then cut his slices thinner than that. Remove the membrane covering the edges of the slices by inserting the tip of your knife under the membrane and then pulling it away from the liver. Have everything else ready to eat and your diners assembled before the liver ever touches the frying pan.
    Use butter or bacon fat, whichever

Celebration Supper (cont.)

you prefer, flour the liver if you wish, but leave the salt and pepper on the table—it has no place here until the liver is cooked! Now into the pan—sear quickly on one side, turn and repeat on the other side—and that's it! The only exception I will make as far as rare liver is concerned is with bear, because of the possibility of trichinosis, and with rabbit, because of the danger of tularemia.

Deer Liver (Hirschleber)—European Style

1 deer liver
Butter or drippings
1 to 2 medium onions, sliced
Freshly ground black pepper
Salt
Garlic powder
¼ cup vinegar

This is the way the Central European hunters would do it. Remove outer membrane and slice liver. In butter or drippings, simmer sliced onions until golden brown; add liver slices and sauté only until no longer bloody. Remove liver to hot serving plate.

To the hot drippings in the pan add salt and pepper, a sprinkling of garlic powder and ¼ cup vinegar. Quickly bring to a boil, stirring to loosen all crusty particles in the pan. Pour over liver and serve piping hot.

Liver Loaf

This is first cousin to many of the fine pâtés, suitable for those who like their liver well done.

2 pounds liver
6 to 8 slices bacon
1 teaspoon anchovy paste
1 onion, diced
½ green pepper, diced
2 cups mashed potatoes
3 eggs
Salt and pepper to taste
1 cup mayonnaise
4 to 5 tablespoons tomato puree
1 tablespoon capers
Cayenne pepper

Cover liver with boiling water; let stand 10 minutes. Drain thoroughly, then put liver and bacon through the fine blade of a food chopper or process in your food processor. Beat eggs, add remaining ingredients and blend thoroughly. Season to taste. Butter a loaf pan liberally, pack in the mixture and bake at 300° F. for 1½ hours. Serve cold with a sauce made of the mayonnaise, tomato puree, capers and cayenne pepper.

Or bake the liver mixture in a greased ring mold and serve hot, with the center of the mold filled with creamed spinach.

Stuffed Deer Liver

This is a marvelous recipe for a fairly small liver, as the whole liver should be consumed at one sitting—one taste and you won't have any problems selling second helpings.

1 whole deer liver
Cheesecloth
Bacon slices
Mixture of the following, finely chopped: 1/4 cup onion, 1/4 cup bacon, 1/4 cup anchovies
Butter

Remove outer membrane covering and tubes running through the liver. Place on a piece of cheesecloth large enough to enclose the entire liver. Cut deep gashes crosswise on the liver, but don't cut all the way through. In the first gash, place a whole strip of bacon; in the next gash, the mixture of chopped onion, bacon and anchovies. Continue to stuff the gashes, alternating bacon slices and mixture; tie the liver securely in the cheesecloth.

Sear on both sides in butter in a heavy skillet. Cover and cook *only* until liver is no longer bloody. Do not overcook, as this toughens it. Remove cheesecloth and slice at right angles to the gashes, so each slice has portions of the two stuffings. Serve with parsley potato balls.

Pheasant Livers—Italian Style

1/2 pound pheasant livers
Butter
1 quart Italian Tomato Sauce (*see* page 71)

Sauté pheasant (or other bird livers) in butter. Pour over Italian Tomato Sauce and heat through. Serve over spaghetti or rice.

Pheasant Livers with Wild Rice

When we did a great deal of bird shooting in the East, I used to save the pheasant livers in the freezer until I had enough for this dish.

3 onions, sliced
1/2 pound butter
1 dozen pheasant livers, coarsely chopped
Salt and pepper to taste
2 cups wild rice, rinsed twice in boiling water
1 quart game bird stock or chicken bouillon

Sauté onions in butter in flameproof casserole until golden. Add pheasant livers, salt and pepper to taste and continue to stir over medium heat until browned. Add rice and stock and stir until water is bubbling again.

Cover and place in preheated 350°F. oven; bake until rice is tender, about 40 minutes. At the end of 30 minutes, add additional stock if rice is dry and not yet tender. Serve with fresh green peas and braised celery.

Rabbit Liver (Hasenleber)

Rabbit or hare livers
Sweet milk
2 tablespoons butter, per liver
1/2 onion, minced, per liver
Fresh parsley, chopped
2 tablespoons sour cream, per liver
Freshly ground black pepper
Salt, if desired

Be sure liver is firm and free from spots, which would indicate the presence of tularemia. Do not wash the livers, but soak in sweet milk for 24 hours. For each large rabbit or hare liver (or 2 small ones), melt 2 tablespoons butter and in it simmer 1/2 minced onion and 3 or 4 sprigs of chopped parsley.

Coarsely chop the livers and add to the onions and parsley; simmer briskly for 10 minutes. When livers are done, put in for each liver 2 tablespoons sour cream and salt and pepper to taste. Allow to simmer for 1 more minute, stirring constantly.

Serve with French-fried potatoes and green salad.

NOSE

Moose Nose

Mrs. G.C.F. Dalziel of Watson Lake, Yukon, gives a full account of the preparation of this Northern specialty.

"Moose nose is a great delicacy with the Telegraph Creek Indians. When I first cooked it . . ., I thought someone was joking but tried it anyway and it turned out to be just as good as they said it would be.

"The only distasteful part of it is that the nose must be cooked for the first hour or so—complete with hide and hair—and to peek into the pot and see all that fur bubbling like a drowned muskrat will make you put the lid back on fast!

"After at least an hour of cooking, cool the nose till you can skin the hide off easily and wash off thoroughly with cold water. Return to a kettle of cold water to cover, add salt, ground pepper and a few bay leaves and boil till tender. Remove and chill. Serve chilled on toasted squares or crackers."

TONGUE

The tongue, like the heart, has received considerable exercise during the animal's life and therefore needs long slow cooking to make it tender. If you are not planning on a head mount from your animal, remove the tongue, wash it and place it—skin and roots still on—in a kettle of cold water over a moderate fire while you go about skinning your animal. By the time you're ready for a break, the tongue will be ready for some further attention from you.

Incidentally, if you've never removed a tongue before, you'll find that especially with larger game animals—the moose, for example—this organ contains a lot of meat.

 **Boiled Fresh Tongue**

Salted water
3 to 4 whole cloves
1 or 2 bay leaves
4 to 6 peppercorns
1 onion

Assuming that the tongue has already been simmering for about an hour, drain off this water, rinse the kettle and the tongue and replace with fresh hot water to cover, adding 1 teaspoon salt per quart of water. Add whole cloves, bay leaves, peppercorns and an onion. Cover the kettle and simmer until the tongue is tender. For a small deer tongue, this may take only another hour or so; for a moose or elk tongue, the time required will probably be about 5 hours.

When the tongue is tender, allow it to cool in the stock until you can handle it. While it is still warm, remove from the broth, slice off the root and trim any excess fat. The skin will peel off easily. Serve the tongue sliced, hot or cold with any of the sauces listed in Chapter 10. It will also make marvelous sandwiches for the next day. And don't forget the lentil or pea soup that is an extra bonus on this deal. If you've been planning ahead, you probably have those legumes soaking already!

MAKING YOUR OWN SAUSAGE

Making your own sausage is one good way of preserving the meat you really don't know what else to do with—or perhaps you're just tired of all that burger and want to do something different. Preparing your own sausage is simple, especially if you own (or can borrow) a meat grinder. Beyond that, the other ingredients are readily available.

I would recommend, regardless of what ingredients you mix, that you freeze sausage "loose" as well as in casings. You can package it in 1-pound freezer bags and also shape it into patties. This way the end results can be utilized in a variety of ways. Hog casings (the kind I've seen and used most often) are relatively easy to come by at local butchers. Often sold by the yard, their cost is minimal. They are salted, so must be soaked before you fill them.

Here is the basic recipe I use, but of course, based on what I intend the sausage for or the mood I'm in, the seasonings vary. Incidentally, sausage is good made with game other than venison. I've had it with rabbit, and a mixture of small game, that was delicious. So be bold. Experiment with the type of game you like best. Remember, years ago (and with many Europeans even today), sausage was made with just about anything, including blood.

Basic Game Sausage

5 pounds meat—venison or other game (trimmed of all fat) plus pork butts and salt pork—usually in a ratio of 3 pounds game to 2 pounds pork
5 teaspoons salt (1 teaspoon salt per pound of meat)
5 teaspoons fennel seeds (1 teaspoon fennel per pound of meat)
1 teaspoon garlic powder
1 tablespoon paprika
2 to 3 teaspoons freshly ground black pepper
1 teaspoon allspice

Run the meat through the grinder once (medium disk), combine well with seasonings (you may have to use your hands for this, just dig in). Then run the seasoned meat through the grinder again. Most meat grinders, both manual and electric types, come equipped with a funnel-like attachment over which you slip the casings and out of which will come the sausage. That's how easy it is.

If you wish to vary the seasonings, you can substitute sage for the fennel or add finely chopped onion and green pepper to taste.

If you're going to freeze the sausage, be sure to wrap it well to prevent freezer burn, and use it within 4 to 6 months. Like burger, it does not keep well long.

Baked Sour Cream-Sausage Supreme

5 medium potatoes
4 eggs
3 links game sausage, 4 to 6 inches long
1 to 2 tablespoons vegetable oil
6 slices bacon
Freshly ground black pepper
1 pint sour cream
Paprika

Place potatoes and eggs in a large saucepan; cover with cold water; heat to boiling; reduce heat and simmer 30 to 40 minutes until potatoes are tender. Drain; rinse with cold water and cool.

Meanwhile, in a heavy skillet, brown the sausage in oil on all sides. Add a little water to the bottom; cover and simmer about 1 hour, or until tender. (Or you could use leftover sausage). Sauté the bacon separately; drain and reserve the drippings.

Peel the cooled potatoes and eggs. Cut the potatoes into 3/8-inch slices and slice the eggs with an egg slicer. Cut the sausage into about 3/8-inch slices, too. Preheat oven to 350° F.

Drizzle a little of the bacon drippings into a 2-quart casserole and swirl around to cover the bottom. Arrange some of the *potato* slices in a layer on the bottom, cover with a layer of *sausage*, then a layer of *eggs* and crumble 2 slices of *bacon* over. Season with black pepper and cover with a layer of *sour cream*. Repeat the same order of layers two more times. Over the top layer of sour cream, sprinkle paprika and drizzle the remaining bacon drippings, letting them ooze down the sides of the casserole.

With a conventional oven, bake about 1/2 hour, uncovered, until heated through. (If you have a microwave oven, heat on high 10 minutes, covered, turning a quarter turn after the first 5 minutes.) Serves 4.

Game Sausage Agliata

For garlic lovers only!

1 pound game sausage, thinly sliced
Olive oil (about 1 cup in all)
16 to 20 cloves garlic, peeled
1 pound pasta (small shells go well)
Freshly ground black pepper
Fresh parsley, chopped
Freshly grated Locatelli or Pecorino
(Romano) Cheese

Peel the garlic and in a small saucepan, pour about ³/₄ cup olive oil and let the garlic "sit" in it while you tend to the other ingredients. If we're really in the mood for garlic, I even crush a few of the cloves to add more flavor.

In a large skillet, sauté the sausage slices in a little oil and, while they are cooking, put the water on to boil the pasta. I add 1 teaspoon oil to the water instead of salt. Brown the sausage on both sides; drain on paper towels and reserve. Cook the pasta according to package directions and reserve about 1 cup of pasta liquid before you drain and rinse the noodles.

Heat the garlic/olive oil and slowly brown the cloves on all sides. As they cook, they will become soft and the taste will become mellow and "nutty." Add to the saucepan the cup of reserved pasta liquid and heat through.

Return the pasta to the pot in which you cooked it; add the garlic/olive oil mixture and the sausage slices and heat through. Serve 4 with a sprinkling of black pepper, parsley and a generous grating of cheese.

 ## Game Sausage Patties with Eggs

As you're making your game sausage, leave some loose to make patties with. You can fry these for breakfast, brunch or a light I-don't-know-what-to-serve-for-supper dish. Serve 'em up with scrambled eggs into which you've blended some cream cheese, top them with poached eggs or use as an accompaniment to your favorite omelet.

 ## Game Sausage with Brown Rice

1 cup brown rice, uncooked
1 pound loose game sausage
¹/₄ cup vegetable oil
¹/₂ teaspoon fennel seeds (if sausage is
not seasoned with it)
Scant ¹/₄ teaspoon coriander, crushed
1 medium onion, chopped
2 cloves garlic, chopped (optional)

2¹/₂ to 3 cups zucchini, washed well
and coarsely chopped (or in
combination with peeled, chopped
eggplant)
Freshly ground black pepper
1 to 2 tablespoons fresh parsley,
chopped

Game Sausage with Brown Rice (cont.)

Cook brown rice according to package directions and cool.

In a large heavy skillet, heat 2 tablespoons vegetable oil and sauté loose sausage, breaking up any big chunks with a wooden spoon. Add fennel and coriander, cover and cook over low heat until thoroughly cooked and tender. Remove with a slotted spoon and reserve.

Sauté onion and garlic in pan juices (adding more oil if necessary) for about 5 minutes, till onion turns pale and soft. Add zucchini pieces and sauté, stirring to turn the vegetable so it does not burn, but cooks through. Do not overcook, however; the squash should not be mushy.

Add the sausage and the cooked rice to the zucchini mixture and continue stirring to heat all the ingredients thoroughly. Season with black pepper and just before serving, stir in the fresh parsley. Serves 4.

 Game Sausage with Peppers and Pasta

¹/₂ ounce dried Italian porcini mushrooms*
¹/₄ cup olive oil
6 whole cloves garlic, peeled
2 pounds game sausage, cut into 4- to 6-inch pieces
1 cup onion, sliced
1 pound Italian frying peppers (banana variety), sliced lengthwise
1 heaping tablespoon flour
¹/₂ to 1 cup water or game stock *or* one-half dry vermouth to one-half water/stock
1 pound pasta (spaghetti, linguini)
Fresh parsley, chopped
Locatelli or Pecorino (Romano) cheese, freshly grated

Place the dried mushrooms in a small saucepan and cover with water. Bring to a boil, lower heat and simmer 20 minutes. Drain, reserving liquid.

While you're waiting for the mushrooms to soften and expand, heat the olive oil in a large skillet. Add the garlic and lightly brown on all sides (this gives the oil a nice nutty flavor that enhances the dish). Remove garlic and reserve. Add sausage to skillet and brown that on all sides; remove and slice into thinner serving pieces; reserve.

Now sauté the peppers and onions lightly, then return the sausage slices and the garlic to the pan. Sprinkle the flour over the mixture and stir to blend. Add the mushroom liquid (you should have about ¹/₂ cup) and ¹/₂ cup of water or stock or vermouth combination. Cover and simmer about 1 hour, until the sausage is thoroughly cooked and tender. Add the mushrooms and heat through.

Before the sausage and peppers are fully ready, cook the pasta according to package directions (I usually omit the salt, but substitute 1 teaspoon vegetable oil). Don't drain the pasta, however, until you have removed about 1 cup of its cooking liquid. Add that to the skillet

* You may substitute 1 cup fresh mushrooms, thickly sliced, for the dried Italian variety. In that case, also substitute game stock or water for the mushroom liquid. Incidentally, the porcini mushrooms can be found in most Italian specialty or gourmet food stores.

because by now, if you've prepared this dish outdoors on a grill, the sauce has cooked down considerably. The pasta liquid not only stretches the gravy, but its starch content also thickens it at the same time.

Now drain the pasta and arrange it on a platter. Top with the sausage/pepper mixture and its sauce; garnish with fresh parsley. Pass the cheese to each diner. This serves 3 to 4.

Hunter's Ziti with Sausage

1 pound game sausage, cut into large chunks
2 tablespoons olive oil
1¹/₂ quarts Italian tomato sauce
1 pound ziti
¹/₂ pound Mozzarella cheese, coarsely grated
Freshly ground black pepper
Freshly grated Locatelli or Pecorino (Romano) cheese

In a large heavy skillet, heat the olive oil and brown the sausage on all sides. Drain on paper towels.

Pour the tomato sauce into a heavy saucepan and add the game sausage, simmering for about 1 hour, until meat is thoroughly cooked and tender.

Remove meat, cut into smaller serving slices and return to sauce.

Meanwhile, cook the ziti according to package directions for a casserole; drain and rinse. Place a few tablespoons tomato sauce in the bottom of a 2¹/₂-quart casserole and swirl to coat. Add a thick layer of ziti, a layer of tomato sauce with sausage slices, grated Mozzarella cheese and a sprinkling of black pepper. Repeat layers two more times and top casserole with grated Romano cheese. Bake in 350° F. oven till heated through, or about 30 to 40 minutes. (In a microwave oven, heat 10 minutes on high, turn a quarter turn, then heat another 5 to 10 minutes.)

Sausage-Stuffed Eggplant

¹/₄ to ¹/₂ cup olive oil
¹/₂ pound loose game sausage, *or* encased sausage, chopped
2 to 3 medium-sized eggplants
3 cloves garlic, chopped
1 tablespoon fresh parsley, chopped

1 tablespoon capers
¹/₂ teaspoon dried basil
¹/₂ teaspoon dried oregano
1 cup (approx.) fresh bread crumbs
Freshly ground black pepper
2 fresh, ripe tomatoes, sliced

Sausage-Stuffed Eggplant (cont.)

Preheat oven to 350° F.

In a large heavy skillet, heat about 2 tablespoons olive oil and brown sausage on all sides; remove with a slotted spoon; drain on paper towels and reserve.

Slice the eggplants in half lengthwise and carefully scoop out the pulp (I use a grapefruit spoon). Chop and sauté the pulp in the skillet, adding more oil as necessary.

Off heat, add the garlic, parsley, capers, basil and oregano and stir to blend. Add the sausage to the mixture and the bread crumbs—enough so that the ingredients adhere and form somewhat of a paste. Season to taste with black pepper.

Place the eggplant halves on a baking sheet and fill with the sausage mixture. Top with tomato slices in an overlapping layer. Sprinkle with black pepper, a.f.g. oregano and a light drizzling of olive oil. Bake about 30 to 40 minutes until heated through. (If you're using a microwave oven, place in a low glass casserole, heat on high for 10 minutes, turn dish a quarter turn and microwave another 5 to 10 minutes.)

Savory Sausage Soufflé

Eggs and sausage always go so well together and, although this is not a true soufflé, the results would have you think so.

$\frac{1}{2}$ to 1 pound game sausage, sliced
$\frac{1}{4}$ cup or so olive oil
2 cloves garlic, chopped
1 medium onion, chopped
3 cups zucchini squash, washed well
　　and sliced into $1\frac{1}{2}$-inch pieces
1 teaspoon fresh basil, chopped, or
　　$\frac{1}{2}$ teaspoon dried basil
1 teaspoon fresh marjoram, chopped,
　　or $\frac{1}{2}$ teaspoon ground marjoram
2 tablespoons fresh parsley, chopped
Freshly ground black pepper
Salt if desired
5 large eggs
$\frac{1}{4}$ cup light cream or half/half
$\frac{3}{4}$ cup Swiss cheese, coarsely grated
$\frac{1}{4}$ cup Romano cheese, grated
1 tablespoon butter

Preheat oven to 350° F.

In a large heavy skillet, heat 1 to 2 tablespoons oil and brown the sausage on both sides; remove with a slotted spoon; drain on paper towels and reserve.

In the same skillet, adding more oil if necessary, lightly sauté the garlic and onion, then add the zucchini, stirring to brown the vegetable slices lightly and evenly. Blend in the herbs, and season to taste.

Pour the zucchini mixture into a $2\frac{1}{2}$-quart casserole and arrange sausage slices in a layer over it. In a mixing bowl, beat the eggs and cream together; stir in the cheeses. Pour over zucchini and sausage layers; dot with butter. Bake about a $\frac{1}{2}$ hour or so, until eggs have "set" and turned golden brown. Serves 4.

CHAPTER 9

FISH WITH A FLAIR

Although this is primarily a game cookbook, many lovers of the outdoors enjoy both hunting and fishing. There are many spots in North America where the hunter packs a fishing rod along with his guns and is able to enjoy the best of two worlds on one trip. With others, the fishing rods come out of the closet when the guns are retired for the summer.

In either case, everyone will agree that nothing can compare with fish freshly caught and cooked on the spot. Many's the lunch I've shared with my Dad on Strawberry Island—a thermos of tea, bread and butter and fish, fresh from Niagara River, sizzling over the campfire. Perhaps it's the fresh air and the thrill of having caught some of the fish yourself that adds extra zest to the meal, but the finest of sea food restaurants just can't compete as far as I'm concerned.

There are times when a larger catch could be brought home to share with family and friends. If you want to preserve that fresh-caught flavor, treat the fish in the same careful manner you do game. Clean them thoroughly and carefully as soon as feasible, remove any excess moisture after the cleaning process and then keep the fish cool. Ice, of course, is fine and dandy as long as the fish are not swimming in the water as the ice melts. Plastic bags are all right, too, as long as they're not punctured. The best combination we've found is Scotch Ice and a portable cooler, but I'm sure you have your own ideas on the subject. The main thing is to be prepared.

Fish may be broiled, fried, baked in a sauce, stuffed or poached—whatever suits your fancy and the ingredients at hand. There is only one rule to be followed without exception: DO NOT OVERCOOK! Even with a large fish to be baked whole, compute your cooking time carefully and have everything else ready, so the meal can be served the minute the fish is done.

Fish rich in fat—striped bass, halibut, mackerel, pompano, salmon, tuna and whitefish—respond well to wine, vinegar or lemon juice when they are baked or broiled. The lean fish are often baked in, or served with, a rich sauce. When broiled, they should be basted frequently to prevent dryness.

It is almost impossible to cover this subject extensively in one chapter. I can only set down a few guidelines and let you take it from there, adding your own personal touches, experimenting and substituting as you wish.

BAKED FISH

The recipes listed in this section are interchangeable for various fish, both fresh and saltwater. They are intended to serve only as guides for the fat and the lean fish—change and adapt them as you wish—use your own imagination.

Alsatian Fish Pâté

2¹/₂ pounds salmon, pike or trout
1 cup dry white wine
³/₄ pound cod
¹/₂ cup dry bread crumbs
¹/₂ cup mushrooms, finely chopped and sautéed
2 egg yolks, well beaten
1¹/₂ tablespoons melted butter
Salt and freshly ground black pepper
Several sprigs of parsley, chopped

Bone and skin the salmon; cut into 1-inch pieces. In a glass or ceramic bowl, marinate in white wine for 4 hours, turning once or twice. Chop the cod very fine and blend well with remaining ingredients, seasoning to taste with salt and pepper. Add the wine in which the salmon has been marinating, mixing well.

Preheat oven to 350° F. Butter a covered casserole, place in it a layer of salmon, spread over ¹/₂ the dressing, add the remainder of the salmon and then the balance of the dressing. Cover and bake for 45 minutes. Uncover and bake 15 minutes more to brown dressing.

Baked Cape Cod Turkey

4- to 5-pound cod, boned if you're skillful with the knife
Salt and freshly ground black pepper
Fresh lemon juice and slices
Butter
Sage and Onion Bread Stuffing *or* Crab Meat Stuffing (Chapter 11)
Water or white wine
Parsley

Stuff cod and skewer closed; place on buttered foil in baking pan and sprinkle with salt and pepper. Add a sprinkling of lemon juice and dot the cod with bits of butter. Pour in enough water or white wine to cover just the bottom of the pan. Bake at 350° F. for 15 minutes per pound, basting several times with the pan juices. Lift from the pan to the platter with the help of the foil and a broad spatula. Garnish with a necklace of parsley and a row of overlapping lemon slices down the length of the fish.

Baked Halibut

Suitable also for striped bass, mackerel and whitefish.

Fish
Fresh lemon juice and slices
Salt
Cayenne pepper
1 onion, minced
3 to 4 tablespoons butter
2 tablespoons white wine
Parsley or watercress for garnish

In a glass or ceramic bowl, marinate fish in lemon juice seasoned with salt and cayenne pepper for 1 to 1½ hours. Place fish in greased baking dish, top with minced onion and dot with butter cut into small pieces. Sprinkle over white wine.

Bake at 400° to 450° F. until fish flakes easily. Baste several times with pan juices, adding more white wine and butter if necessary. Transfer with a broad spatula to a heated platter, pour pan juices over the fish and garnish with lemon and parsley or watercress.

Baked Pollack with Eggplant

1 medium-large eggplant
Flour
Olive oil
2 pounds pollack, fileted
1 fresh lemon
Freshly ground black pepper
¼ cup bread crumbs

Tomato-Herb Sauce:
2 cups plain tomato sauce
2 tablespoons fresh lemon juice
1 teaspoon coriander seed, finely
**   crushed**
½ teaspoon garlic powder
Freshly ground black pepper
1 teaspoon dehydrated minced onion
2 teaspoons fresh dill (*or* 1 teaspoon
**   dried)**
2 tablespoons fresh parsley, chopped

Peel and cut eggplant into thick (about ⅜-inch) slices; you'll need about 12 slices. Place in a bowl, cover with warm water and weight down so eggplant stays submerged; let stand for about 1 hour. Drain, rinse and dry slices; dredge lightly in flour. In a heavy skillet, pour olive oil about ¼-inch deep; heat, but not to smoking point. Sauté eggplant on both sides; drain on paper towels; reserve.

While the eggplant is soaking, prepare the *Tomato-Herb Sauce:* Combine all ingredients in a small saucepan; bring to a boil, lower heat and simmer 10 minutes. Remove from heat.

Preheat oven to 400° F. I use a 9-inch square or rectangular glass casserole to prepare the final dish, but a stainless steel or other heavy pan would do; *do not* use aluminum, however. If you're at camp, you can prepare this as a skillet dish, just cover it as it cooks over low heat.

Pour a little olive oil in the bottom of the pan and swirl it around. You want just enough barely to cover the bottom. Sprinkle in a light covering of bread

Baked Pollack with Eggplant (cont.)

crumbs. Arrange filets in pan; season with pepper and squeeze some lemon juice on each slice. Arrange eggplant in overlapping layers atop the filets; sprinkle with some more bread crumbs.

Pour the sauce over all to cover completely and arrange a few lemon slices as a garnish. Bake 30 to 40 minutes. Serves 4.

Baked Squid

Squid is becoming more popular these days as a less expensive "fish" to come by and is very tasty when prepared properly. Don't throw away the tentacles that you cut off while cleaning, for they make a delicious hors d'oeuvre (*see* Squid Minceur).

2 pounds squid, cleaned and washed
Olive oil
Garlic powder
Freshly ground black pepper
Bread crumbs
Fresh parsley sprigs

Arrange the pieces of squid in a lightly oiled casserole. Sprinkle with garlic powder, black pepper, a few tablespoons of oil and the bread crumbs. Garnish with fresh parsley sprigs. Bake in preheated 350° F. oven for about 20 minutes, or until the flesh turns white. Do not overcook, for the squid will turn rubbery.

Baked Tuna Provençale

This is a tasty dish that I usually make in large quantity (if I'm lucky enough to have enough fresh tuna) and freeze it in serving portions. It does not have the customary "fishy" flavor, for it is marinated in olive oil and lemon juice first. (You could prepare swordfish steaks this way, also.)

Thick tuna steaks (trimmed of dark meat)

Marinade:
2 tablespoons lemon juice
Olive oil
Freshly ground black pepper
Sea salt

1 tablespoon flour
1 tablespoon butter, softened
1 tablespoon parsley, chopped

Provençale (Tomato) Sauce:
2 onions, chopped
3 cloves garlic, chopped
2 to 3 pounds fresh tomatoes, peeled and chopped
Freshly ground black pepper
1/2 teaspoon dried oregano
1/4 teaspoon dried thyme
1 teaspoon chili powder
2 to 3 fresh basil leaves, crushed
Salt if desired
1 cup dry white wine

Baked Tuna Provençale (cont.)

Combine lemon juice, 1/3 cup olive oil, black pepper and sea salt. Arrange tuna slices in a shallow glass or ceramic casserole; pour over marinade and cover. Let stand 1 hour; turn steaks over, cover well with marinade and let stand another hour. Remove fish from dish and dry on paper towels.

While the fish is marinating, prepare the **Provençale Sauce:** In a large saucepan, heat a little olive oil and lightly sauté the onion and garlic in it. Add the tomatoes and all the other ingredients, checking the seasoning to taste, and simmer about 30 minutes to 1 hour, until the sauce starts to thicken.

In a heavy skillet, heat some olive oil and brown the tuna steaks on both sides. Arrange in a large casserole and pour over the sauce. Place in a preheated 350° F. oven and bake, covered, for about 30 minutes, until the dish is piping hot, and the fish is tender. Remove the steaks from the sauce to a warm platter momentarily.

Into the sauce, stir the flour which you have mashed together with the butter and add the parsley, then spoon over the fish. Serve with rice.

Camp Baked Bass

Trout and perch are also delicious prepared this way.

Bass
Canned tomatoes
Sliced onions
Basil or oregano

Grease a shallow pan. Place in it seasoned fish and cover with canned tomatoes, sliced onions and a sprinkle of basil or oregano, if you have it along. Place in hot reflector oven and bake until fish flakes easily, basting once in a while with the liquid in the pan.

Filets in Cream

Pike, muskellunge, flounder or bass filets may be used.

Fish filets
Melted butter
Salt and freshly ground black pepper
3/4 cup cream of celery soup, undiluted
1/2 cup heavy cream
1/4 cup sherry wine
**Grated Parmesan or sharp cheddar
cheese**

Place filets in a shallow buttered baking dish. Brush liberally with melted butter, season with salt and pepper. Combine the soup, heavy cream and sherry and pour over the filets. Sprinkle with the cheese and bake for about 30 minutes in a 350° F. oven.

Filets in Wine

Most suited to the fat fish, although most any others could be substituted.

2 pounds filets
Salt and pepper
4 or 5 thinly sliced scallions, including a bit of the green tops
Several sprigs of snipped parsley
Soft fresh bread crumbs
Butter
White wine

Place the filets in a buttered baking dish that can go to the table. Sprinkle fish with salt and pepper, scatter scallions and parsley on the filets, and top with a sprinkle of bread crumbs. Dot each filet with several pieces of butter. Pour in enough white wine to cover the filets about halfway.

Bake at 450° F. until crumbs are browned and fish flakes easily, about 15 to 20 minutes.

4 to 5 servings.

Filets Piquant

1¹/₂ pounds cod or bluefish filets
¹/₄ cup butter
3 onions, sliced
Salt and pepper
¹/₂ cup sour cream
2 teaspoons lemon rind, grated
3 tablespoons fresh lemon juice
Several sprigs parsley, minced
3 to 4 tablespoons capers

Preheat oven to 325° F.

Place filets in buttered baking dish. Lightly sauté onion slices in butter, surround the fish with them and season with salt and pepper. Combine sour cream with remaining ingredients and pour over fish. Bake, covered, until fish is flaky. The lower oven temperature is used to prevent the sour cream from separating; therefore, the cooking time will be slightly longer.

Serve with fluffy white long-grain rice to 3 or 4.

Fish Baked in Clay

If you have good sticky clay in your camping area, you're in luck. Plaster a good thick layer of the stuff on a whole fish just as it comes from the water. Bury it in the embers of your fire, place more coals on top of the package and let it bake for about 20 minutes per pound. This is no time to fib about how much that fish weighed or it will be overdone! Crack open the hard block, scales and skin will be attached to the hardened clay and the entrails will have shriveled up.

Season the steaming fish and dig in!

Fish Florentine

1 ¹/₂ to 2 pounds lean fish filets
Double recipe of creamed spinach (*see* page 245)
Parmesan cheese
Salt and freshly ground black pepper
Paprika
Melted butter

Preheat oven to 375° F.

Butter a casserole which can go to the table. Spoon in the spinach, place the filets on top. Brush the filets liberally with melted butter, season with salt and pepper. Bake for 15 minutes, then sprinkle on Parmesan cheese and return to oven until fish flakes easily, probably another 5 to 10 minutes. Sprinkle with paprika before serving.

Little Barndoor Salmon

Fresh salmon
Butter
Sliced onions
Freshly ground black pepper
Salt
Milk

Little Barndoor Island on Lake Winnipesaukee, N.H., was the scene of many an outdoor feast. Among my fondest memories is "the day of the land-locked salmon" and Jim Warner's recipe for same. It is, of course, applicable to most any fish.

Melt butter in shallow pan, brown sliced onions slowly, place seasoned fish (either whole or in filets) on top of onions, brush top of fish with butter and pour milk around the fish. Place in reflector oven and bake until fish is easily flaked. Baste occasionally with the pan juices.

Rolled Stuffed Filets

6 thin filets of flounder, or any other delicate lean fish
Freshly ground black pepper
Salt
Shrimp or Crab Meat Stuffing (*see* Chapter 11)
¹/₂ cup white wine
1 tablespoon fresh lemon juice
Parmesan cheese
White Wine Sauce (*see* Chapter 10), substituting fish stock for game bird stock
Large pieces of crab claw meat or whole shrimp for garnish

Season filets with pepper and salt, spread with stuffing and roll up, securing with toothpicks. Place in buttered casserole, pour over wine and lemon juice and bake at 375° F. until fish is flaky but still moist, about ¹/₂ hour.

Transfer filets to ovenproof platter, and remove toothpicks. Pour over warm White Wine Sauce, sprinkle with Parmesan cheese and garnish with shrimp or crab that has been brushed with butter. Slide under broiler on medium heat for a minute or two until cheese is melted and the sauce is slightly browned.

Striper in Creole Sauce

4- to 5-pound striped bass
Butter
Salt and pepper
2 cups Creole Sauce (*see* Chapter 10)
1/2 cup white wine or tomato juice

Place seasoned fish in buttered baking dish. Thin Creole Sauce with half of the extra liquid and pour over the fish. Bake at 350°F. about 35 to 40 minutes, basting the fish several times and adding more of the liquid if the sauce seems too thick.

Serve with rice and green vegetables of your choosing.

One Dish Fish Dinner

2 pounds filets of your choice
2 to 3 cups cooked rice
4 tablespoons butter
1 pound or so asparagus *or* broccoli
     stalks, steamed
1 cup Lemon Tarragon Sauce or any of
     the other appropriate sauces found
     in Chapter 10
Freshly ground black pepper
Paprika

Preheat oven to 350° F. Butter a large casserole dish and place the cooked rice in it. Stuff each filet with a few asparagus or broccoli stalks and roll up, securing with toothpicks. Arrange atop rice. Season with black pepper and paprika and dot all with butter. Pour sauce over and bake about 30 minutes until fish is done.

BROILED FISH

Broiled Filets

Fish filets
Melted butter
Lemon juice
Dill, marjoram *or* chives

Preheat broiler, grease rack or aluminum foil before putting fish in to broil. With filets up to 1-inch thick, it is not necessary to turn the filets, so place skin side down on the rack and broil 6 to 10 minutes, basting with melted butter and lemon juice plus seasonings of your choice—dill, marjoram or chives are all good. When the fish is delicately browned and flakes easily with a fork, rush it to the table.

You might like to try the following variation of the basic recipe.

Filets with a Flair

Any fish would be appropriate, but I enjoy snapper, flounder or bass for this.

2 pounds fish filets
Salt and freshly ground black pepper
Melted butter
¹/₂ cup mayonnaise
1 tablespoon fresh lemon juice
1 teaspoon onion, finely minced
2 egg whites, stiffly beaten
Dash of cayenne
¹/₂ cup slivered almonds, toasted

Broil the filets as described above, seasoning with salt and freshly ground black pepper and basting with melted butter. While the filets are broiling, combine mayonnaise, lemon juice and onion. Fold in stiffly beaten egg whites, spread the topping on the filets as soon as they flake easily. Dust the topping with a light sprinkling of cayenne and top with the almonds. Return to the broiler, about 5 inches from the heat, and broil only until the topping is lightly browned and puffy. Watch carefully.

Broiled Filets with Lemon Tarragon Sauce

This is a very simple dish that will get raves every time. The key to its success is the light flouring of the fish.

Filets of your choosing
Flour
Freshly ground black pepper
Paprika
Garlic powder (optional)
Butter
Lemon Tarragon Sauce (see page 174)
Fresh parsley, chopped

Lightly flour (you can even sift the flour) the filets first; season them with the black pepper and paprika, garlic powder if you wish; then dot with butter. Broil briefly till done and serve with Lemon Tarragon Sauce, garnished with fresh parsley.

Broiled Fish Steaks

2-inch fish steaks
Butter
Lemon *or* lime juice
Marjoram *or* chervil
Salt
Freshly ground black pepper
Cucumber, Caper *or* Dill Sauce (see Chapter 10)

Steaks cut from the round of larger fish are usually cut to 2″ thick and should be turned midway in the broiling. Six to 16 minutes is the maximum, depending on the thickness of the steaks. Fresh salmon, cod or muskellunge are prime examples. Allow one steak per serving, combine equal amounts of butter and

Broiled Fish Steaks (cont.)

lemon or lime juice if fish is lean, less butter if fish is more fat. Broil on greased rack or foil, baste with combined juice and butter, adding marjoram or chervil plus salt and pepper. With thicker steaks, have the broiler 4 inches rather than the usual 3 inches from the flame.

Serve with Cucumber Sauce, Caper Sauce to which chopped hard-boiled eggs have been added or Dill Sauce with sour cream.

Broiled Fresh Tuna Filets

I have heard many fishermen along the Eastern shore say they found fresh tuna too oily for their taste. A veteran saltwater fisherman soon put us wise to the solution with these delectable saltwater fish. The oiliness in tuna is concentrated in the dark red meat midway along each side, so after skinning the fish, carefully trim this dark flesh away and discard it or feed it to the dogs. Remove the remaining white flesh the full length of the fish and wrap and freeze the long strips whole (they resemble a boneless pork loin on a good-size school tuna).

Tuna steaks
Melted butter
Lime juice
Paprika
Lime wedges

When ready to serve, cut crosswise slices about 1-inch thick from the thawed fish, broil on buttered foil, basting with equal amounts of melted butter and lime juice.

Sprinkle with paprika and serve with lime wedges.

If you've never tried lime in place of lemon with the more delicately flavored fish, you've been missing something! (The softer belly flesh on tuna should be poached in court bouillon—page 163—and used in salads and casseroles; *see* also "Baked Tuna Provençale," which removes the oily flavor by marinating.)

Flounder à la Jacqueline

This recipe was born while we were guests at Montauk for some shark fishing. Our host and my husband did some bay fishing for a change one morning and presented us with "a whole mess of flounder." While we were preparing them for the freezer, I wondered out loud what we could do for variety in preparation. Our hostess mentioned that she had once been served whole flounder stuffed with shrimp—that's all, no details. That casual remark came to mind later in the year and I started "fussing around" in the kitchen. My "experiment" was such a success with the family that I was persuaded to enter it in a cooking contest in our local paper, the *Bergen Evening Record,* of Hackensack, N.J. To my complete amazement, I was awarded third prize!

Flounder à la Jacqueline (cont.)

**6 small whole flounder, cleaned and
    heads removed**
Melted butter
Lawry's seasoned salt
Parsley
Lime wedges
Shrimp Stuffing (*see* **page 204**)

Preheat broiler to medium temperature.
Enlarge pocket for stuffing with slender
boning knife. Prepare shrimp stuffing,
reserving 6 whole cooked shrimp for
garnish. Stuff pockets (or if whole ones
not available, use small filets and place
stuffing between 2 filets and skewer).
Place on buttered broiler pan or foil,
brush with melted butter, sprinkle with
seasoned salt and broil 3 inches from
heat until browned and flaky. Turn fish,
baste with butter and broil other side,
placing reserved shrimp on each portion
1 minute before the fish is done. Remove
to heated platter, garnish with parsley
and lime wedges.

Broiled Whole Fish

Whole or split boned fish
Lemon butter *or* **Italian herb dressing**
Lemon slices *or* **pimiento strips**
    (garnish)

Larger fish may be boned and spread flat
for broiling or broiled "in the round," as
you prefer. In the latter case, a few
gashes on the skin will facilitate the
cooking. These gashes may be garnished
when serving with slivers of lemon or
strips of pimiento. Pike, bass, bluefish
or trout are most attractive cooked this
way. Brush with lemon butter or an
Italian herb dressing for a change of
pace. Turn as soon as the flesh has
become opaque and flaky on one side
and continue broiling the other, basting
as before. You may wish to broil
tomatoes and/or mushrooms along with
the fish.

Grilled Black Fish

Black fish is a flavorful, meaty fish that, although is dark at the start, cooks white.
Grill over medium-hot coals about 10 minutes, rarely longer.

2 pounds black fish, cleaned and fileted
Aluminum foil
**Celery tops with leaves (*not* the lower
    stalks)**
Garlic powder
Freshly ground black pepper
Paprika
Fresh basil leaves

1 Bermuda or Spanish onion, sliced
1 medium tomato, sliced
1 fresh lemon, sliced
Fresh parsley
Italian salad dressing

Tear off enough aluminum foil to hold at
least two filets each. Gently crumble the

Grilled Black Fish (cont.)

foil, then flatten it out again. The wrinkles that remain will help prevent the fish from burning. Place the celery tops on the aluminum foil, then arrange filets over them.

Season fish with garlic powder, black pepper and paprika. Arrange basil leaves atop, then place layers of onion and tomato and sprinkle on more black pepper. Garnish with lemon slices and parsley sprigs. Sprinkle each filet with about 1 to 2 tablespoons salad dressing to moisten. Place another piece of aluminum foil over the filets and fold the two pieces of foil together around all four sides. By "tenting" the fish, you in effect steam it over the coals and retain all the juices, which you'll find are delicious. Serves 4.

 Over-the-Coals Broiling

Lean, cleaned fish
Salt and pepper
Bacon strips

Fish may be broiled over the coals, of course. Wrap lean fish in bacon strips after they have been seasoned lightly with salt and pepper, skewering the bacon in place with toothpicks. Lay flat on a grill or impale on a peeled sweet wood stick, turning to cook evenly. Watch the bacon drippings so they don't catch fire—a drip pan of foil is helpful in this case.

 FRIED FISH

This seems to be the favorite method of cooking fish, indoors or over a campfire. You have a great deal of latitude within the basic recipe, as well as in the various sauces and garnishes, so that even fried fish need never become monotonous. Filets, steaks or whole fish are done this way—the cooking time is always brief, but does depend to some extent on the thickness of the fish. *Don't overcook and don't let it wait!* From the frying pan to the plates, with everything else ready and waiting, including the hungry guests.

Fry or sauté the fish without any adornment, lightly dredged in seasoned flour or prepared in this way.

Dip the fish first into: (pick one)

Milk
Evaporated milk
Egg beaten with 2 tablespoons
lemon juice *or*
white wine

Thin pancake batter
Savory bottled salad dressing

Season with salt and pepper. Dredge in crumbs such as:

Fried Fish (cont.)

Dry bread crumbs seasoned with herbs and cheese
Cracker meal
Corn meal
Any dry cereal, crushed to fine crumbs
Crumbled potato chips
Plain flour
Biscuit Mix (*see* page 250)

Or try "Beer Batter" (recipe follows).

Heat oil, shortening or butter in skillet until hot, but not smoking. If using butter, it should be bubbling but not browned. Sauté quickly over a medium flame until golden on underside (1 or 2 minutes), turn carefully and repeat. Place fish on heated platter, quickly add a dash of lemon to the butter in the pan, stir for a few seconds and pour over the fish. Garnish with olive slices, watercress, parsley, snipped chives or serve with your favorite tartar sauce in lemon cups. A number of sauces mentioned in Chapter 10 would also be appropriate.

If done properly with a minimum of fat in the pan, there should be no greasiness to the fish—just a lovely crisp crust. However, in deep-fat frying, fish must be drained thoroughly on paper towels or some such before serving. If you do deep fry, be sure the fat or oil has reached 365° F. to 370° F. before you begin. Fry only a small amount of fish at one time so the temperature of the fat remains constant. Otherwise, the crust will not be sealed quickly and the greasy results will have you searching for the bicarbonate of soda.

Beer Batter

³/₄ cup flat light beer
¹/₂ cup all-purpose flour
1 teaspoon salt
1¹/₂ teaspoons paprika
Flour seasoned with black pepper and garlic powder

Pour beer into a small mixing bowl. Sift in the flour, salt and paprika and lightly beat with a wire whisk. Dredge fish (soft-shelled crabs, shrimp or frogs' legs are fantastic in this) in seasoned flour *first*, then dip in beer batter.

Tempura-Style Fish with Vegetables

The Japanese people consume a great deal of fish and prepare it in many interesting ways. Their light tempura batter is a real treat, especially when fixed with sliced vegetables "fried" the same way.

1 to 2 pounds fresh fish filets, sliced
Any assortment of vegetables, such as carrots, zucchini, eggplant,
mushrooms, all sliced about the same size
Peanut or other vegetable oil

Tempura Batter:
1 egg beaten with 1 cup water
1 cup flour

Additional flour
Soy Sauce
Prepared Duck Sauce

Prepare the fish and vegetables and arrange them attractively on a serving platter. Incidentally, this is the type of dish that probably works best when cooked at the table, so each diner can enjoy it as it is piping hot and fresh.

For the batter, in a small mixing bowl, beat the egg with the water and sift in the flour; lightly beat (just to combine) with a wire whisk. If you are preparing this at the table, you can use a small wok (electric ones are available now that make this really easy), or a fondue pot in which you have heated the oil. Starting with the vegetables, dip each slice into flour first, then into the batter, then into the hot oil. It takes only minutes for them to "cook." Serve them immediately, with each diner dipping them in Soy Sauce or Duck Sauce. Cook the fish last, as it may impart a perhaps unwanted flavor to the oil. Serves 4.

POACHED FISH

Poaching fish is a most delectable way of preparing it—if done properly. Otherwise, it is disastrous.

Lean fish are usually recommended for poaching, since they do not disintegrate as easily as the fatter fleshed ones. There are always exceptions that prove the rule, the most notable in this case being the salmon, followed by the halibut, mackerel, shad and whitefish. Court bouillon, a seasoned broth for poaching fish, is prepared first in a kettle that will accommodate the fish (*see* recipe below).

Large whole cleaned fish are wrapped in parchment or cheesecloth to help them retain their shape, then placed on a rack with cold court bouillon to cover. The liquid is brought rapidly to the boiling point, skimmed and then simmered *very* slowly, with the liquid barely bubbling, until the fish is done. Six to 10 minutes per pound, depending on the thickness of the fish, is the recommended poaching time.

For small whole fish, slices or filets, the method is slightly different. First of all, the slices or filets must be fairly thick. They are placed on a Pyrex plate or in a wire basket with cheesecloth wrapped around the entire thing, then lowered into *boiling* court bouillon. This is done to seal the outside of the pieces as quickly as possible to prevent loss of flavor and to keep the slices from falling apart. The temperature is then lowered so the water is scarcely bubbling. Slices or filets are poached for 10 to 20 minutes, depending on their thickness.

Hot poached fish is traditionally served with melted butter, Hollandaise, a rich cream sauce with chopped hard-boiled egg, Caper Sauce or Cucumber Sauce. If the fish is to be served cold, allow it to cool in the court bouillon to prevent drying. A cold savory sauce with mayonnaise or sour cream may be used to dress the chilled fish.

Court Bouillon

2 quarts water and ½ cup vinegar *or*
1 quart water and 1 cup white wine
1 tablespoon salt
2 sliced carrots
1 large onion
6 to 8 peppercorns

Bouquet garni of parsley, bay leaf and celery

Combine all ingredients in a large saucepan or kettle, simmer 30 minutes and strain. Use to poach fish.

CHAPTER 10

SAUCES AND GARNISHES

An entire book could be written on sauces alone. The French consider sauce making the high point of their cuisine and the saucier rules supreme in the kitchen. However, it is not my intent to compete with Escoffier and I have included here only a few of the thousands of flavor combinations possible—those most suited to game cookery.

Discretion should be the watchword in making and serving sauces. Use seasonings subtly to achieve sauces that are neither too bland nor too blatant—herbs and spices add much to a sauce, but should never dominate. Serve sauces with the same restraint—vegetables with sauce combine well with simple broiled meats or fish, while meats served with sauce require vegetables dressed only with butter and seasoning.

Sauces fall into two main categories—white and brown—both of which use a roux, or blend of butter and flour, as the base. Brown sauce is the foundation of most highly seasoned and savory sauces and is made with the venison stock (or beef stock) described in Chapter 11. White sauces are made with milk, cream and/or stock from fowl, as described in Chapter 10, or fish stock. These are usually more delicate in flavor.

Roux may be made up in quantity and stored in a covered container in the refrigerator, to be used as needed to thicken gravies and sauces.

In addition to the white and brown sauces are the flavorful wine sauces, such as Cumberland, Italian Game Bird and Viennese Game Sauce. Other game sauces—classic English Bread Sauce, Creole Sauce and homemade Bar-B-Q sauces as well as seasoned butters—are excellent game enhancers.

For that extra touch for a special occasion, do try some of the glazed fruit garnishes or the herb and wild fruit jellies.

Roux for Gravies and Sauces

¹/₂ cup butter
¹/₂ cup flour

Melt butter over low heat, blend in flour gradually and stir constantly until the mixture is smooth and bubbly. If the roux is not allowed to darken at all, it may be used for the most delicate of white sauces, as well as for thickening all gravies. This amount makes ³/₄ cup of roux and is used as follows.

When a recipe calls for:

Butter and flour (in tablespoons)			*Roux* (in tablespoons)
1 each	→	use	1¹/₂
2 each	→	use	3

The roux may be reheated in a double boiler over hot water and the liquid added slowly, or the roux may be added directly to the warm liquid, as in a fricassee gravy. In either case, constant stirring over low heat is essential to producing a smooth sauce.

If a **brown roux** is desired, combine ¹/₂ cup butter, ³/₄ cup flour.

Proceed as above, but continue to cook, stirring constantly until a rich brown color is achieved. The larger amount of flour is necessary, since flour loses some of its thickening power as it is browned.

WHITE SAUCES

Basic White Sauce

To prepare a basic white sauce, blend **1 cup of milk** with:

1¹/₂ tablespoons roux for a *thin* sauce
3 tablespoons roux for a *medium* sauce
4¹/₂ tablespoons roux for a *thick* sauce

Add milk slowly to melted roux, stirring constantly over low heat, or in a double boiler, until smooth and thickened. Season to taste with freshly ground black pepper (white pepper if you want it a pure white) and salt if desired.

Allemande Sauce—*for vegetables*

1 cup white sauce, made with half
    stock, half cream
1 egg yolk
1 tablespoon cream
Pinch nutmeg
1¹/₂ teaspoons lemon juice

Reduce the white sauce by half over low heat, set over hot water and slowly add beaten egg yolk, stirring vigorously. Add cream, nutmeg and lemon juice, stirring until thick and creamy.

Béchamel Sauce—*for fowl and vegetables*

1 cup strong stock (game bird or
    chicken)
1 slice onion
Few peppercorns
4¹/₂ tablespoons roux
1 cup milk
Salt to taste
1 egg yolk, if desired

Simmer the stock with onion and peppercorns for 10 minutes, then strain. Melt the roux, slowly add broth, then milk, stirring constantly until thickened. Season to taste with salt. If desired, the egg yolk may be beaten with a few spoons of the hot sauce, then slowly added to the sauce, stirring vigorously. Do not allow the sauce to boil once the egg yolk has been added.

Caper Sauce—*for fish, sheep or cold meats*

4¹/₂ tablespoons roux
1¹/₂ cups stock in which meat or fish
    was cooked
Salt and pepper to taste
2 tablespoons butter
3 tablespoons capers
1 teaspoon lemon juice

Combine roux, stock and seasonings and simmer, stirring constantly until thick, or use 1¹/₂ cups Béchamel Sauce (above). Add butter, capers and lemon juice. Continue to stir over low heat until well blended.

Cheese Sauce—*for fish, vegetables, or leftover game birds*

1 cup white or Béchamel Sauce (made
    with the appropriate stock)
¹/₂ cup grated cheddar, Swiss, Gruyère,
    Romano or Parmesan cheese
Bit of grated onion if desired
Dash of cayenne pepper

Stir all ingredients over low heat until cheese is melted and well blended.

Cucumber Sauce—*for boiled fish*

1 cup white or Béchamel Sauce (made
    with fish stock)
1¹/₂ teaspoons lemon juice
Dash of paprika

¹/₂ to ³/₄ cup cucumber, peeled and
    finely diced

Combine all ingredients over low heat.

Dill Sauce I—*for vegetables or fish*

1 cup white sauce
1/2 cup sour cream
1 tablespoon freshly snipped dill leaves
1 teaspoon grated onion
1 tablespoon chopped parsley

Combine over low heat, but do not allow to boil once sour cream has been added.

Dill Sauce II—*for mountain goat or sheep*

3 tablespoons butter
3 tablespoons flour
1 1/2 cups chicken stock (or stock from same animal)
1/3 cup half-and-half *or* light cream
1 tablespoon lemon juice
2 tablespoons fresh dill, snipped
2 teaspoons sugar, or to taste
1 egg yolk, lightly beaten

Prepare a Béchamel Sauce made with the butter, flour, stock and cream. Simmer for about 10 minutes, then blend in the lemon juice, dill and sugar. Enrich the sauce with the egg yolk and correct the seasoning.

Horseradish Sauce—*for boiled fish, sheep or goat, tongue*

1 cup white sauce
4 to 5 tablespoons drained horseradish
1 tablespoon butter

Combine white sauce and horseradish, heat and blend thoroughly. Add butter bit by bit just before serving.

Madeira Sauce—*for game or poultry*

1 1/2 tablespoons roux
1/2 cup scalded cream *or*
1/2 cup game bird or vegetable stock
Salt and pepper
1/2 cup Madeira

Combine roux and stock or cream and stir over low heat until boiling point is reached. Season to taste and *slowly*, stirring constantly, add Madeira. Cook slowly another minute or so.

Mushroom Sauce—*for game birds or fish*

1 cup white or Béchamel Sauce
1/2 cup mushrooms, sliced
Butter
1 teaspoon parsley, chopped
1 teaspoon onion, minced

Sauté mushrooms in butter with the onion and parsley. Add sautéed mushroom mixture to white sauce in a saucepan and over low heat, stir till heated through.

Mustard Sauce—*for fish, vegetables*

1 cup white sauce
2 tablespoons heavy cream
1 egg yolk
2 tablespoons Dijon mustard
Freshly ground black pepper
Salt if desired

Lightly beat the egg yolk into the cream. Heat the white sauce in a small saucepan and beat in the egg/cream mixture with a wire whisk, until smooth and creamy. Blend in the mustard and correct the seasoning.

White Wine Sauce—*for broiled game birds*

1 1/2 tablespoons roux
1 cup strong game bird stock
1 cup cream
Grating of fresh nutmeg
Salt and pepper
2 tablespoons white wine
1 tablespoon butter

Combine and stir over low heat roux, stock and cream. Stir until thickened and smooth, season to taste, add white wine and butter, cook only a minute or so until blended.

BROWN SAUCES

Basic Brown Sauce

3 tablespoons brown roux
1 cup venison stock
   (or beef stock)
Freshly ground black pepper
Salt if desired

Combine roux and stock and cook over low heat until smooth and thickened, about 5 minutes. Season to taste with salt and pepper.

Bigarade Sauce—*for venison and duck*

Julienne strips of orange
    peel from 2 oranges
2 cups brown sauce
Juice of 1 orange
1 teaspoon lemon juice
Salt and pepper

Boil peel in water to cover for 5 minutes and then drain. Add to brown sauce and simmer until peel is tender. Add lemon and orange juices and season to taste. Heat until piping hot.

Black Pepper Sauce—*for all antlered game*

See page 33.

Bordelaise Sauce—*for venison steaks and chops*

Several slices bacon or salt pork
2 carrots, sliced
2 onions, sliced
Sprig of thyme
1 bay leaf
1 cup claret or Bordeaux
2 shallots, chopped
6 to 8 peppercorns
Dash of cayenne
1 clove garlic
1 tablespoon brown sauce
1 cup venison stock

Combine bacon, carrots, onions, thyme and bay leaf in pan and allow to simmer slowly in their own juices for 15 or 20 minutes. Add wine, shallots, peppercorns and garlic and continue to simmer gently until sauce is reduced, brown and sticky. Add brown sauce and stock, bring to the boiling point, skim any fat that rises to the surface and strain through a sieve. Reduce further by ⅓ by slow cooking.

Easy Curry Sauce—*for leftover meats or fowl*

(*See* page 212. With venison or antlered game, use game stock; with wildfowl, use game bird stock.)

Horseradish Sauce—*for all antlered game, pronghorn*

1 cup brown sauce
¼ cup onion, chopped
2 tablespoons butter
3 tablespoons prepared horseradish
White vinegar if necessary
Freshly ground black pepper

In a small skillet, sauté onion lightly in butter. Add to brown sauce with horseradish, extra vinegar (if you like it lively) and season with freshly ground black pepper. Heat through.

Mushroom Brown Sauce—*for broiled venison, smoked meats*

1 cup brown sauce
1/2 cup fresh mushrooms, sautéed in butter with minced parsley and onion
Black pepper to taste

Combine ingredients; season with freshly ground black pepper.

Mustard Brown Sauce—*for all game, tongue, boar, etc.*

1 cup brown sauce
1/4 cup onion, chopped
2 tablespoons butter
2 tablespoons Dijon mustard (or whatever kind you prefer)
1 tablespoon fresh parsley, chopped
Freshly ground black pepper
Salt if desired

In a small skillet, lightly sauté onion in butter. Add to brown sauce in a small saucepan along with other ingredients; heat through and check seasoning.

Raisin Sauce—*for tongue or boar*

1 teaspoon granulated sugar
1 teaspoon vinegar
1 cup brown sauce
1/3 cup raisins

Carmelize sugar over low heat; add vinegar and stir until sugar is dissolved and sirupy. Add brown sauce and raisins which have been blanched in hot water and then drained. Stir until well blended; correct seasoning.

Red, Red Game Sauce—*for all antlered game*

See page 30.

Sauce Geraldine—*for all antlered game*

This is my adaptation of the French Sauce Diane, which my husband humorously renamed, for obvious reasons.

3 cups game stock
1 cup dry red wine
3 tablespoons roux
1 cup heavy cream

2 tablespoons sweet butter
1 tablespoon Bourbon or Cognac
Freshly ground black pepper
Salt if desired

Sauce Geraldine—*for all antlered game* (cont.)

In a large saucepan, simmer the game stock and the red wine for about 1 hour to reduce by half. Add the roux and the cream, stirring constantly, until smooth and thickened; simmer another 10 minutes, and adjust roux or stock amount for the consistency you prefer. Before serving, stir in the butter and the Bourbon or Cognac and check the seasoning.

WINE SAUCES

Apricot Game Sauce—*for cold game birds*

Small glass apricot marmalade
Juice of ¹/₂ lemon and grated rind
¹/₂ glass white wine
1 to 2 teaspoons Dijon mustard or to taste

Blend together all ingredients.

Cumberland Sauce—*for all antlered game*

1 cup red currant jelly
1 wine glass port
Juice of 1 lemon
¹/₂ teaspoon ginger
Juice and shredded rind of 1 orange
1 teaspoon dry mustard
Cornstarch (2 teaspoons) if desired

Melt jelly with wine, reduce slightly, add juices and rind, seasonings and simmer 10 minutes, uncovered. Thicken with cornstarch, if desired. Also, try adding rind of 1 lemon for variation.

Italian Game Bird Sauce

3 tablespoons minced onion
¹/₄ cup chopped mushrooms
2 tablespoons butter
2 teaspoons flour
Grating of fresh nutmeg
1 tablespoon tomato puree
¹/₂ cup white wine
¹/₂ cup game bird stock
1 teaspoon herb blend for fowl

Sauté onion and mushrooms in butter; add flour and blend until smooth. Add nutmeg, tomato puree, wine and stock and simmer 10 minutes. Blend in herbs and serve.

Russian Game Sauce—*for all game*

2 tablespoons butter
1/4 cup grated onion
1 cup dry white wine
1 pint sour cream
Salt
Freshly ground black pepper

In small saucepan, melt butter and cook onion slowly until transparent, but not browned. Add wine and simmer until only 1/4 cup wine remains. Slowly stir in sour cream and continue stirring until sauce just reaches boiling point. Season to taste with salt and pepper, strain through a sieve and serve very hot.

Sour Cherry Sauce—*for quail and other wildfowl*

1/2 cup game bird or chicken stock
1/2 wine glass port
Shredded lemon peel
3 tablespoons red currant jelly
1/2 cup sour cherry compote
1 tablespoon lemon juice

Simmer stock, port and peel in pan in which birds were cooked for 8 to 10 minutes. Add jelly, sour cherries and lemon juice and simmer another 3 minutes.

Viennese Game Sauce—*for venison*

2 tablespoons pitted sour
    cherry compote
1/3 cup red wine
1/3 cup venison stock
1 tablespoon toasted bread crumbs
Shredded peel and juice of 1 lemon

Combine all ingredients and boil for 2 minutes.

OTHER GAME SAUCES

Blender Hollandaise—*for fowl, fish, vegetables*

2 egg yolks (from fresh eggs)
1 tablespoon fresh lemon juice
1/4 teaspoon freshly ground black
    pepper
1/4 teaspoon salt
1/4 pound butter, melted

Have egg yolks at room temperature. In a blender, combine the egg yolks, lemon juice, pepper and salt; beat together. *Slowly* drizzle in the melted butter, and continue blending until butter is used up and sauce is thick and smooth.

Bread Sauce—*classic English sauce for grouse or partridge*

1 cup milk
1 small onion studded with 1 whole
    clove
1 blade mace
2 ounces soft bread crumbs (2 slices)
Salt and freshly ground black pepper
1 tablespoon butter, in 2 portions
1 tablespoon cream

In a double boiler, slowly bring milk to scalding point with onion and mace; simmer 10 minutes, then remove onion and mace. Beat in crumbs with a whisk. Add salt and pepper to taste and half the butter. Cook for 10 minutes, stirring constantly. Add cream and remaining butter and blend well.

Creole Sauce—*for meat, fish, shellfish, poultry and game*

This sauce is so versatile that I usually make a good quantity of it and freeze it.

1/2 cup butter
2 onions, minced
2 green peppers, minced
1 cup mushrooms, chopped
2 cups stock
1 quart canned tomatoes, coarsely
    chopped
1/4 cup minced ham
Freshly ground black pepper to taste

Salt to taste
Cayenne
1 bay leaf
a.f.g. thyme

Sauté onions, peppers and mushrooms in butter for 5 to 8 minutes. Add remaining ingredients and simmer 30 minutes, or until thickened.

Lemon Tarragon Sauce—*for cold wildfowl, fish, vegetables*

This really falls into the mayonnaise category and is very easy to prepare, since it requires no cooking.

1/4 cup fresh lemon juice
2 egg yolks, at room temperature
1/2 cup light salad oil (safflower is good)
2 tablespoons prepared mayonnaise
1/4 teaspoon dried tarragon
1/4 teaspoon garlic powder
1/2 teaspoon sugar
Sprinkling of freshly ground black
    pepper

In a blender, blend together the lemon juice with the egg yolks. Add the salad oil slowly and continue to blend. Add all the other ingredients, and mix until well blended. Let stand for about 1 hour, until the flavors mellow.

Seasoned Butters

You can prepare these in two different ways. The traditional way is to soften the butter in a bowl, then with a spoon or fork, work the flavoring ingredients into the butter, mixing well. Chill and mold as you like.

The newest and easiest way is with a food processor. If you have one, start with the butter cold and hard. Cut it up into tablespoon-size chunks and place in the processor bowl; add the flavorings through the feed tube as you process lightly to blend the ingredients. Scoop out into a mold or any dish and chill.

Anchovy: 1 part anchovy to 3 parts butter

Garlic: pound 1 clove garlic in mortar, combine with ¼ cup butter

Garlic Herb: ½ cup butter combined with 3 pounded cloves garlic, 1 tablespoon fresh chopped parsley, 2 crushed basil leaves

Lemon: ½ cup butter, 1 tablespoon chopped parsley, salt, pepper and cayenne to taste, 1 tablespoon fresh lemon juice

Mint: ¼ cup each chopped mint and butter, 1 tablespoon fresh lemon juice

Paprika: 2 teaspoons paprika to 2 tablespoons butter

Savory: 2 tablespoons butter, ½ teaspoon each, freshly chopped parsley, chervil, tarragon, chives, shallots

Watercress: 1 tablespoon chopped watercress to 3 tablespoons butter

Tarragon: 1 teaspoon fresh tarragon (or ½ teaspoon dried) to 2 tablespoons butter

Sweet Mushroom Sauce—*all antlered game, pronghorn*

1 cup onion, sliced thin
¼ cup butter
1 cup mushrooms, sliced thick (wild mushrooms if possible)
1 tablespoon Bourbon
a.f.g. dried thyme
Freshly ground black pepper

In a skillet, sauté onion in melted butter until transparent; add mushrooms and barely heat through. Add Bourbon, thyme and black pepper and serve immediately.

Tangy Raisin Sauce—*for wild boar, javelina, tongue*

1 cup dark raisins
1¼ cups water
1½ tablespoons cornstarch
¾ cup light brown sugar
½ teaspoon dry mustard

¼ teaspoon ground cloves
Pinch of cinnamon and salt
¼ cup white vinegar
1 tablespoon sweet butter

Tangy Raisin Sauce (cont.)

In a small saucepan, blanch the raisins in boiling water 5 minutes. Mix together cornstarch, brown sugar, dry mustard and spices; add to raisins, stirring constantly, then blend in the vinegar. Simmer 10 minutes over low heat, stirring frequently. Just before serving, swirl in the butter.

BARBECUE SAUCES

Barney's Barbecue Sauce

1 teaspoon dry mustard
1 tablespoon flour
1 teaspoon celery salt
1/2 teaspoon cayenne
1/2 teaspoon cloves
1/4 cup vinegar
1/4 cup water
1/2 cup catsup

Blend all ingredients together in a saucepan; bring to boil; lower heat and simmer 10 minutes.

Barbecue Sauce I

1 cup Old-fashioned Chili Sauce (*see* recipe next page)
1/4 cup vinegar
2 tablespoons Worcestershire Sauce
1 teaspoon salt
1 teaspoon ground black pepper
1 teaspoon chili powder
Dash cayenne
1 1/2 cups water

Combine all ingredients and simmer together for 10 minutes.

Barbecue Sauce II

2 tablespoons butter
1 green pepper, chopped
1 onion, chopped
1/2 cup pickles, chopped
3/4 cup catsup
2 teaspoons prepared mustard
2 tablespoons sugar
1/2 cup vinegar
1 teaspoon lemon juice
Dash Worcestershire Sauce

In a skillet, brown the green pepper and onion in butter. Combine pickles with the remaining ingredients in a saucepan and simmer together for 10 minutes. Add the pepper/onion mixture and simmer for an additional 5 minutes.

B-B-Q Sauce with a Zip

1/2 cup ketchup
1/4 cup apple cider vinegar
1/4 cup light vegetable oil
2 tablespoons light brown sugar
1/2 envelope dry onion soup mix
1 tablespoon prepared country mustard
    (stone ground with horseradish)
1 clove garlic, minced, or 1/4 teaspoon
    garlic powder
1/2 cup water
1 tablespoon liquid smoke (optional)
Prepared hot pepper sauce (optional)

Combine all ingredients in a small saucepan; bring to boiling; lower heat and simmer about 10 minutes. Cool before using. This will yield about 2 cups and will marinate about 2 pounds of game kabobs.

If you like your B-B-Q Sauce more **Texas Style,** i.e., hot and smoky, add 1 tablespoon liquid smoke and a few dashes or more of hot pepper sauce.

Old-Fashioned Chili Sauce

This is my Grandmother's recipe, which has been handed down without change. It's as much a part of my childhood memories as the Christmas pudding and the English fruitcake. The whole family joined in the preparation of all of them.

1 peck red ripe tomatoes
6 large onions
1 large bunch celery
4 large green sweet peppers
2 large red sweet peppers
2 cups vinegar
4 level tablespoons salt
5 to 6 cups light brown sugar, packed
Spice bag (cheesecloth or muslin) filled with:

2 teaspoons ground ginger
4 teaspoons cinnamon
2 teaspoons cloves
2 teaspoons allspice
4 teaspoons grated nutmeg

Scald, peel, and cut up the tomatoes; put them on to boil while you chop the onions, celery and peppers. Add vegetables, vinegar, salt, sugar and spices. Do not make the spice bag too small or the flavor will not come out, but tie it tightly or the spices will make the chili sauce dark. (I usually tie one end of the string from the spice bag to the handle of my big kettle.) Simmer for at least 2 hours over very low heat and stir often, as it burns very easily. Pour into hot sterilized jars and seal. This should give you 6 or 7 quarts of chili sauce.

GARNISHES

Game is such a luxury in itself that it needs little in the way of embellishment. Some garnishes and accompaniments are traditional, however, and not only enhance and complement the flavor of the game, but please the eye as well.

Fruits and tart fruit jellies have a natural affinity for game. Often, they are used in the cooking of the meat itself or are added to the sauce. A few bright sprigs of parsley or watercress and a well-chosen fruit garnish, where appropriate, will add a festive touch to the platter without that "gussied-up" look most men detest.

Stuffed mushrooms are also a fitting garnish for game roasts. Since they double as an appetizer as well, please *see* pages 221–222.

Apple and Sage Jelly

The flavor of herbed jellies is subtle and different. They are particularly suited to game, but may be used with any meat or poultry.

1/2 cup fresh sage (or 1/4 cup dried sage leaves)
1 cup water
Apple juice
3 1/2 cups sugar
1/2 bottle liquid pectin
Sterilized jars, hot paraffin

Wash and crush fresh sage. In a small saucepan, add to water and bring to a boil; simmer, covered, 5 to 10 minutes. Strain through a jelly bag or very fine sieve and reserve the liquid. Measure the liquid and add enough apple juice to make 2 cups.

In a large kettle, combine juice with sugar and bring to a boil, stirring constantly. Add pectin, bring to a full rolling boil and boil hard for 1 minute, stirring constantly. Remove from heat, skim and pour at once into hot sterilized jars. Seal with hot paraffin.

Glazed Apple Rings

2 cups sugar
1 1/2 cups water or cranberry juice
1/4 cup fresh lemon juice
2 pieces stick cinnamon, if desired
2 or 3 whole cloves, if desired
6 large firm red apples

In a saucepan, combine all ingredients except apples, and boil for 5 minutes. Wash and core apples; slice, unpeeled, into fairly thick slices. Place in large flat baking pan, and cover with prepared syrup. Bake apple slices at 275° F. to 300° F. until transparent, basting occasionally with syrup.

These slices may be prepared in large quantities and frozen for later use. Pack into plastic containers, with a double fold of waxed paper between the layers. They may also be served as dessert with vanilla ice cream or a boiled custard.

Chokecherry Jelly

My introduction to chokecherries was a rude one—purple-footed dogs and people the summer we moved to the Midwest. Since then, I have discovered the delicious jelly they provide, in addition to food for the birds, so I now hold them in much higher esteem.

Chokecherry Jelly (cont.)

3½ pounds chokecherries
3 cups water
3 cups juice
6½ cups sugar
1 bottle liquid pectin

Simmer crushed berries in water, covered, for 15 minutes. Strain through a jelly bag and measure the juice.

Mix sugar and juice in a very large kettle over high heat. Bring to a boil, stirring constantly. Add pectin and bring to a full rolling boil and boil hard for 1 minute, stirring constantly. Remove from heat, skim and pour into hot sterilized jars at once. Seal with hot paraffin.

(If you're too busy to make jelly when the fruit is ready, extract the juice and store it in quart containers in the freezer until you have more time.)

Baked Cranberry Relish

4 cups cranberries
2 cups sugar
¾ cup toasted slivered almonds
1 cup citrus fruit marmalade
Juice of 1 lemon or lime

Combine washed and drained cranberries with sugar and place in a shallow pan, cover tightly and bake at 350° F. for 1 hour. Combine cranberries with remaining ingredients, mix well and chill.

Raw Cranberry or Blueberry Relish

Both cranberries and blueberries are delightful all year round, and are extremely versatile. When they are available in the market, purchase extra packages and freeze them as is. When ready to use them, pick them over while still frozen, then wash and use them immediately, just as you would fresh ones.

4 cups fresh or frozen cranberries or
    blueberries
2 oranges
1 lemon
1 lime, if available
1 cup granulated sugar (more if you
    prefer it quite sweet, less if you are
    using blueberries)

Quarter and seed the citrus fruits, keeping the peels on. Using your food processor or the medium blade of a food chopper, grind the berries with the citrus fruits. Mix well and add sugar to taste. We prefer it not too sweet, especially when served with fowl. Allow the relish to mellow in the refrigerator for at least several hours. This is also delicious served over vanilla ice cream as a change from too-rich desserts, especially at holiday time.

Spiced Cranberry Sauce

1½ cups water
1 orange, including juice and finely
　　chopped rind
2 cups sugar
1 piece stick cinnamon
4 cups fresh or frozen cranberries

In a large saucepan or kettle, cook together the water, orange (all of it), sugar and cinnamon for 5 minutes. Add the cranberries and cook until berries stop popping. Cool without stirring.

Wild Currant Jelly

I have been delighted to find currants growing wild right here on our land. They are seldom seen in the markets in urban areas anymore, since they are so easily crushed and bruised by handling. When picking currants for jelly, include some that are not completely ripe, as the pectin and acid content will be higher. If you use all ripe berries, then add liquid pectin.

4 pounds red currants
1 cup water
¾ cup sugar per cup of juice

To extract the juice, combine the red currants with the water in a large saucepan. Crush the fruit thoroughly and simmer, covered, for 10 minutes. Strain through a jelly bag or several folds of cheesecloth, wrung out of hot water. Measure the juice.

　　If some unripe fruit has been included, proceed as follows: Add ¾ cup granulated sugar for each cup of juice in a large saucepan. Stir until the sugar is dissolved and then boil rapidly until the jelly stage is reached. With currants, it will be only a few minutes until two

drops of the jelly will hang from the side of the spoon. Skim and pour at once into hot sterilized glasses. Seal with paraffin.

　　If you are using all ripe fruit, proceed as follows.

5 cups juice
7 cups sugar
½ bottle liquid pectin

Combine juice and sugar in a very large kettle, heat over high heat, stirring constantly until boiling. Add pectin, bring to a full rolling boil and boil hard for 1 minute, stirring constantly. Remove from heat, skim quickly and pour into hot sterilized glasses. Seal with paraffin.

Elderberry Jelly

Wild elderberries are becoming more and more difficult to come by these days, but they still can be found in many of our deciduous forests in late summer. I find only two problems with them: first, you must get to them before the birds; and second, you must pick literally hundreds of these tantalizing morsels to make it worth your while because they're so tiny. But worth your while it will be, especially when you serve up some elderberry jelly with a special game dinner.

Elderberry Jelly (cont.)

3 to 4 pounds ripe elderberries
1/2 cup fresh lemon or lime juice, strained
7 1/2 cups sugar
2 pouches liquid fruit pectin

Wash the berries, which you have removed from the stems. Place in a large kettle, crushing some of them, and simmer, covered, about 15 minutes or more to extract the juice. Strain through a jelly bag or very fine sieve. Measure the juice; you should have about 3 1/2 cups. If not, add some apple juice to make up the difference.

In a large kettle, place the berry juice, lemon or lime juice and sugar. Bring to a boil, stirring constantly. Add the pectin and bring to a full rolling boil and boil hard for 1 minute, stirring constantly. Remove from heat, skim and pour immediately into sterilized jars; seal with paraffin.

Sautéed Fruit

Peach halves, apricot halves or pineapple rings
Butter
Brown sugar, to taste
Curry powder (optional)

Canned peach halves, pineapple rings or apricot halves may be drained well, then sautéed in butter until they are delicately browned. Sprinkle with a bit of brown sugar and a light dash of curry powder, if desired, before serving.

Spiced Fruit

1 pound canned whole apricots, crab apples or pears
1/3 cup lemon juice or cider vinegar if you prefer
6 tablespoons sugar
12 whole cloves
2 sticks cinnamon

Drain the juice from the canned fruit, combine with sugar, lemon and spices and simmer 15 minutes. Pour over fruit and let it stand in the refrigerator for several days. If I have fresh lemons on hand, I often add a few thin slices of lemon to the syrup.

Gooseberry Sauce

Delicious with venison as well as boar.

1 quart gooseberries
Juice and grated rind of 1 lemon or orange, plus enough water to make a total of 2 cups liquid

1 piece stick cinnamon
2 or 3 whole cloves

Gooseberry Sauce (cont.)

Combine liquid, cinnamon and cloves and boil together for 15 minutes. Add washed gooseberries and simmer gently until tender. Remove gooseberries with a slotted spoon, take out spices, reduce syrup by half and pour over berries.

Grapefruit and Savory Jelly

¹/₂ cup savory leaves
1 cup water
Grapefruit juice
3¹/₂ cups sugar
¹/₂ bottle liquid pectin
Sterilized jars, hot paraffin

Infuse savory leaves as directed for sage leaves in Apple and Sage Jelly. Measure the strained juice and add enough canned grapefruit juice to make a total of 2 cups.

Combine juice with sugar in large saucepan and bring to a boil, stirring constantly. Add pectin, then bring to a full rolling boil and boil hard for 1 minute, stirring constantly. Remove from heat, skim, and pour at once into hot sterilized glasses. Seal with hot paraffin.

Glazed Oranges

2 cups sugar
1 cup water
2 tablespoons fresh lemon juice
3 or 4 large seedless oranges

Combine sugar, water and lemon juice in a large skillet. Bring to a boil on low heat and then simmer for 5 minutes. Meanwhile, wash oranges and cut fairly thick slices, leaving the skins on. Poach the orange slices gently in the syrup, turning at least once, until the skin of the oranges is transparent. Cool in the syrup and drain just before serving.

A flavor variation may be achieved by adding a few whole cloves or a small piece of dried ginger root to the syrup. Place a whole clove or a candied cranberry in the center of each slice, if desired. Also, try glazing other citrus fruit, such as lemons and limes.

Orange Herb Jelly

¹/₂ cup fresh marjoram leaves
  (or ¹/₄ cup dried)
1 cup water
3¹/₄ cups sugar
1 6-ounce can frozen orange juice
  concentrate, thawed
¹/₄ cup fresh lemon juice, strained

¹/₂ bottle liquid pectin
Sterilized jars, hot paraffin

Wash and crush fresh marjoram leaves. Combine with water, bring to a boil and simmer, covered, for 5 to 10 minutes. Strain through a jelly bag or very fine

Orange Herb Jelly (cont.)

sieve and measure the juice.

Combine juice with enough water to make 1 cup and place in large saucepan with sugar. Stirring constantly, bring to a boil and boil hard for 1 minute.

Remove from heat, add thawed orange juice concentrate and lemon juice. Add pectin and mix well. Skim and pour at once into hot sterilized glasses. Seal with paraffin.

Mint Apple Jelly

1½ cups fresh mint leaves, crushed
4 cups apple juice
4 cups sugar
Green food coloring
1 tablespoon fresh lemon juice,
    strained
1 pouch liquid fruit pectin

In a large kettle, combine the mint leaves with the apple juice. Bring to a boil, then remove from heat and let stand about 15 minutes. Remove mint leaves with a slotted spoon and add food coloring to the juice.

Heat the juice again, stirring in the sugar and the lemon juice and bring to a boil. Stir in the pectin, bring to a full rolling boil and boil hard for 1 minute, stirring constantly. Remove from heat, pour into sterilized jars and seal with paraffin.

Parsley Jelly

Several large bunches fresh parsley
Water
Sugar
Lemon extract

Remove the stalks from the parsley and wash thoroughly. Place in enamel saucepan and cover with water. Bring to a boil and then simmer for ½ to ¾ hour. Strain through jelly bag and measure juice. Combine sugar and juice, cup for cup, and boil, stirring constantly until jelly "sheets." Add ½ teaspoon lemon extract for each cup of jelly. Pour into hot sterilized glasses and seal with paraffin.

Pears Poached with Cranberries

1 cup cranberries, fresh or frozen
1 large can pear halves, drained and
    syrup reserved

In a saucepan, add cranberries to the syrup from the pears. Simmer until the skins pop, but do not cook so long that the berries become mushy. Remove the berries with a slotted spoon and set aside. Gently poach the pears until they have acquired a rosy hue, turning at least once in the syrup. To serve, place the cranberries in the centers of the pear halves.

CHAPTER 11

SOUPS AND STUFFINGS

Sadly, the old soup kettle has all but disappeared from the kitchen. In its place is a row of cans or a pile of foil envelopes on the pantry shelf. These modern convenience foods are not to be scorned; they are the product of much research, skill and technical know-how, and serve countless purposes in camp or kitchen. However, we are being needlessly wasteful if we never bring the soup kettle out of that far corner of the cupboard. Those bones rescued from the butchering and freezer preparation are an excellent source of nutrition: just ¼ pound of bones yields, with long slow cooking, the same amount of gelatine as two pounds of meat. Furthermore, the stock thus obtained can be used in so many ways—in soups, sauces and casseroles— that it would be a pity to resort to substitutes when the vastly superior ingredient is so easily prepared.

Making soup need not consume a great deal of time, either. I consider five or ten minutes extra in the kitchen morning and evening as time well spent for a reservoir of good soup to draw upon on those hectic days we all seem to have. While you're tending to breakfast dishes, haul a plastic sack of bones from the freezer and start the stock. By the time the kitchen is squared away, the stock can be skimmed and left to simmer with the vegetables without further attention until dinnertime. An electric crockpot is a marvelous convenience when preparing long-cooking soups, because you can leave it unattended rather safely for hours. In addition, many of the soups I have included here—potato, chestnut, for example—take no time at all.

Bones from veal and beef roasts and chops are well worth saving, in addition to those from the larger game animals. Chicken and turkey bones, as well as the carcasses of broiled or roasted game birds, should be collected for white stock. One other "saving" suggestion: when you are planning to serve tongue, ham or corned beef, be sure you have lentils, beans or split peas on hand. I find it a waste of space to freeze the large amount of liquid in which these meats have been cooked, so I plan to make soup—usually a double batch—by the next day, and then freeze the more concentrated finished product.

I have found it handy to save the waxed paper cartons from cottage cheese for storing stock and completed soups. The one-pound cartons are perfect for enough stock for a sauce or gravy recipe, while the two-pound size holds almost a full quart of soup. Using these cartons eliminates thawing time, for you just slit the carton and start cooking right away. This is particularly helpful when every minute counts.

If your soup kettle is large enough, by all means double or treble the recipe for any favorite soup. It's definitely a time saver when you have all the ingredients out anyway.

GAME STOCK AND DERIVATIVE SOUPS

Game (Venison) Stock

3 pounds cracked bones and meat trimmings (any antlered game)
2 quarts water or vegetable liquid
Pinch of thyme
Pinch of mace or marjoram
1 teaspoon whole peppercorns
2 bay leaves
3 sprigs parsley
4 cups chopped or sliced vegetables, including the following:
Onions, carrots
Celery and the leaves
Tomatoes, fresh or canned
Mushroom trimmings or a few dried ones
Any leftover vegetables on hand

Part of the bones and meat may be browned first in the oven for a richer color. Using a large kettle with a lid, cover bones and meat with cold water or vegetable liquid and slowly bring to a boil. Skim any foam that rises, add vegetables and seasonings and simmer gently over lowest heat all day (at least 5 hours).

Strain through a colander or sieve, cool and remove the fat that forms on top. Package and freeze. Makes about 2 quarts of stock. Bones from roasts and chops may be added to the stated quantity of uncooked bones.

Borscht

This national dish of the Russians and Poles has more variations than the spelling of its name. It may be served hot or cold, strained or as a thick soup, garnished with sour cream or not—but usually served with dark rye bread. This basic recipe may be varied according to the ingredients you have on hand. It freezes well, so double the quantities if you wish.

Borscht (cont.)

1 quart venison stock
1 cup beets, peeled and shredded
3 cups shredded or finely chopped
    vegetables, any combination of the
    following: onions, parsnip,
    cabbage, celery, carrot, green
    pepper, tomato, potato
Salt and pepper to taste
Pinch of marjoram
Sprinkle of dill or fennel

Combine all ingredients and simmer, covered, for several hours. Adjust seasonings, if necessary, at the end of the cooking period. We enjoy Polish sausage added to Borscht for a hearty supper on winter evenings; try your own homemade game sausage, too. This quantity makes 6 generous servings.

Camp Onion Soup

5 or 6 onions, thinly sliced
4 tablespoons butter
6 cups venison stock (or 6 to 8 bouillon
    cubes and 1 1/2 quarts water)
Salt and freshly ground black pepper to
    taste
Dash of Worcestershire Sauce

Brown the onions slowly in butter and cook over low heat for 15 to 20 minutes. Add venison stock or bouillon, season to taste and simmer an additional 20 minutes. Serve with toasted bread slices sprinkled with Parmesan cheese floating on each bowl.

Meat Glaze

Meat glaze is game bird or venison stock boiled down to the jelly stage and is used to add authority to gravy, sauces and stews. Store covered in the refrigerator.

Navy Bean Soup*

2 cups navy beans, soaked at least 3
    hours, drained
3 quarts venison stock
2 stalks celery, chopped
2 carrots, sliced
1 large potato, diced
1 onion, sliced, or 1 teaspoon dried
    onion
Salt and pepper to taste
Pinch of thyme and marjoram
2 cups tomatoes (if available)

Cook beans in stock for 2 hours, add remainder of vegetables and cook another hour. Strain and serve with a slice of lemon in each bowl.

    Camp suggestion for bean, split pea, or lentil soup:

    If fresh vegetables are not available, use dehydrated vegetable soup, legumes, bouillon cubes and water. Set the kettle over a slow part of your dinner fire and the soup will be ready when it's time to retire. A quick reheating the next day and you have the beginning of a fine dinner.

Game Consommé

This is simply clarified stock, which can be served with many attractive garnishes.

1 quart stock
1 egg white, slightly beaten, plus the crushed egg shell

In a saucepan combine stock with egg white and shell and heat slowly, stirring constantly. Boil 3 minutes, then simmer slowly for 20 minutes. Skim and strain through wet cheesecloth (or in a pinch I've even used a large coffee filter from my glass drip pot, which worked well).

Serving suggestions. (*See* Garnishes for Soups and Stews, page 196).

1. Reheat and garnish with sliced lemon.

2. Add 4 tablespoons Madeira or dry sherry wine.

3. Garnish with custard cubes.

4. Garnish with Viennese peas (Wiener Erbsen).

5. Add julienne strips of tongue or vegetables.

6. Float several liver dumplings (Leberknödel) on each serving.

7. Add several game quenelles to each serving.

8. Jellied consommé. If original stock has been cooked long enough, consommé will jell when chilled. If not, for 1 quart of stock, add 1 tablespoon unflavored gelatine softened in 1/2 cup cold consommé and dissolved in hot consommé. Chill; break lightly with fork when serving.

9. If consommé lacks zip, add a dash of Worcestershire Sauce or lemon juice.

10. Try consommé prepared Oriental style. Dilute first with water, then add soy sauce to taste and chopped scallions; garnish with game wontons.

Lentil Soup

Lentils are an excellent trail food—easy to carry, high in energy and nutritional content, and an outstanding source of protein and vitamin B. Soak the lentils overnight, though, then cook them in fresh liquid to prevent digestive upset.

1 1/2 to 2 cups lentils, soaked overnight in cold water, drained
2 quarts of tongue or ham broth or 2 quarts of water plus diced bacon
1 onion, sliced
Pinch of thyme or dried parsley
2 to 3 carrots, sliced
2 to 3 stalks celery, chopped, leaves, too
Salt and pepper to taste
Bay leaf

Combine all ingredients in a covered kettle; cook slowly for 2 hours, or until lentils are tender. Press through a coarse sieve or food mill and check seasoning.

Our favorite when reheating the next day: brown sliced onions and sliced franks in butter, add soup and heat 10 minutes or until very hot. Good on a rainy day in camp: serve for lunch with dark bread and canned fruit for dessert. Or simply add cooked, sliced game sausage.

Split Pea Soup

3 cups split green or yellow peas
2 quarts broth from tongue (or water)
Meaty ham bone or 2 pounds venison
    brisket
4 carrots
5 or 6 stalks of celery with leaves
2 onions, sliced
1½ cups tomatoes
Generous pinch thyme
2 bay leaves
Salt and pepper to taste

Combine ingredients and simmer in a covered kettle about 2 hours. Remove bones and meat, cut meat in small pieces and reserve. Put vegetables through a sieve or food mill, reheat with meat pieces. Garnish with croutons.

If the soup is too thick for your taste, it may be thinned with milk or cream, but one of our friends maintains that 'tain't good pea soup unless you can stand the spoon up in it! If you have cooked your moose or deer tongue in camp, this is a good one to remember.

Venison Barley Soup

8 cups game (venison) stock
1 pound venison, cooked and cubed
1 cup *each*: onions, potatoes, carrots,
    celery, peas or green beans
½ cup parsnips
1 large tomato
3 cloves garlic
1 bay leaf
2 tablespoons fresh parsley, chopped
Pinch thyme
Freshly ground black pepper
½ cup barley
1 cup dry red wine
2 tablespoons butter
3 tablespoons flour

In an 8-quart kettle with lid, pour in the game stock and add the cubed venison. Dice all the vegetables so they are all the same size and add them to the pot. Add the bay leaf, parsley, thyme and black pepper to taste. Stir in the barley and red wine and simmer, partially covered, until the vegetables are tender, about 1 hour or so.

Prepare a brown roux by melting the butter in a small pan and adding the flour, stirring constantly over low heat, about 7 minutes. Pour this into the soup and continue stirring until thickened. Serve immediately.

Wild Mushroom Consommé

Perfect for a festive game dinner.

3 cups fresh wild mushrooms, coarsely
    chopped, or 2 ounces dried wild
    mushrooms
3 stalks celery, chopped
1 medium onion, chopped
4 tablespoons butter

2 quarts stock (venison or pheasant)
A few peppercorns
Salt to taste
2 sprigs parsley
¾ cup Sauterne

Wild Mushroom Consommé (cont.)

Brown mushrooms, onion and celery in butter. Add stock, seasonings and parsley. Simmer 1 hour. Strain through a fine sieve or cheesecloth, pressing to extract the liquid from the vegetables.

Add Sauterne, reheat until piping hot, but do not boil.

(You can of course use cultivated mushrooms, but the wild variety seems so much more apropos.)

GAME BIRD STOCK AND DERIVATIVE SOUPS

Game Bird Stock

Bones from broiled or roasted game
    birds
Veal knuckle bone, cracked
Any older game bird (i.e., pheasant,
    wild turkey)
Water to cover (measure it as you add
    it)
1 cup of the following, chopped and
    blended, *per quart of water*:
Carrot
Celery with leaves
Onion

½ teaspoon peppercorns *per quart*
Several sprigs parsley *per quart*

Cover the bones and bird with cold water in a large covered kettle. Bring slowly to a boil, skim and add vegetables and seasonings. Simmer, covered, until the bird is tender. Remove the bird from the stock, strip the meat from the bones and set aside. Return the bones to the kettle and simmer another few hours. Strain, cool, skim any fat and freeze. The meat may be used for game pies, pâtés, creamed dishes or to garnish consommé.

Austrian Potato Soup (Kartoffelsuppe)

5 potatoes
2 or 3 carrots
1 celery knob or 3 stalks celery
1 medium onion, sliced
6 cups game bird stock
Salt and pepper
2 teaspoons caraway seeds
2 tablespoons butter
3 tablespoons flour
Parsley, finely chopped

Peel and cube the vegetables, cover with boiling game stock, add salt and pepper, caraway seeds. Simmer, covered, until vegetables are tender, about 1 hour.

Make a roux as follows: melt butter, stir in flour and cook over low heat until bubbly. Add 1 cup of liquid from the soup, stirring constantly until thickened and smooth. Blend into soup carefully so as not to mash vegetables and continue to cook for 5 to 10 minutes. Serve garnished with finely chopped parsley.

Avocado Cream Soup

2 cups stock from pheasant, grouse or
    partridge
1 chicken bouillon cube
1 tablespoon cornstarch
1 cup milk
1½ teaspoons onion, grated
1 avocado, peeled and mashed with a
    sprinkle of lemon juice
Salt to taste
Crisp bacon bits *or* shredded toasted
    almonds as garnish

Bring stock to a boil, dissolve bouillon cube in it; slowly add cornstarch dissolved in milk. Cook over medium heat, stirring until mixture thickens; do not boil. Add onion and mashed avocado. Continue to heat for another minute or two over low heat. Serve piping hot to 4 people. A garnish of crisp bacon bits or shredded toasted almonds is attractive.

Chestnut Soup

Chestnuts have a natural affinity for game. Do try this one!

2 cups blanched chestnuts
    (*see* page 239 for shelling
    instructions)
½ cup celery, chopped
¼ cup butter
2 tablespoons onion, finely minced
3 tablespoons flour
1 teaspoon salt
¼ teaspoon pepper
Blade of mace
2 whole cloves
2 cups game bird stock
1 cup cream

Cook chestnuts and celery in lightly salted water 15 to 20 minutes; drain and force through food mill; set puree aside. In large saucepan, melt butter and cook onion over low heat without browning for 5 minutes. Blend in flour until smooth and bubbly; add salt, pepper, mace and cloves. Slowly pour in stock, stirring constantly until it thickens. Remove mace and cloves. Combine cream and chestnut puree and blend into stock. Reheat until piping hot, but do not boil.

Game Bird Consommé

Clarify as directed earlier in this chapter and serve as suggested for Game (Venison) Consommé *or*:

1. Garnish with diced or julienne strips of fowl plus button mushrooms sautéed in butter.

2. Add ½ cup finely broken noodles or ½ cup rice per quart of consommé and simmer until rice or noodles are tender. Garnish with finely chopped parsley just before serving.

Green Pepper Consommé

I have included this recipe because it is unusual and never fails to intrigue with its delicate and delicious flavor. I like to serve it as a first course with grouse or quail.

4 large sweet peppers—may be green or tinged with red
3 medium fresh tomatoes, cut up
1 onion, sliced
6 cups water
1 teaspoon salt
Pinch ground cloves

Remove seeds and white membrane from peppers, cut into pieces. Combine all ingredients, heat to boiling, and simmer in covered saucepan for 2 hours. Strain and adjust seasonings. This may be served hot or cold.

Green Soup

3 to 4 tablespoons butter
1 cup onion, chopped
2 cups game bird stock
2 cups potatoes, cut up
2 cups spinach and watercress, coarsely chopped
2 cups lettuce, shredded
Parsley, dill, thyme (cook's choice)
Freshly ground black pepper

In a good-sized saucepan, melt the butter and sauté the onion until golden and soft. Pour in the game bird stock and add the potatoes; cook until soft, 30 to 40 minutes. Then add the green vegetables and seasoning of your choosing and cook for another 10 minutes or so.

Puree in a blender and serve hot with homemade herb croutons (*see* page 197).

Lemon Soup

Speedy to prepare, this soup is light and unusually delicious for a luncheon with a game bird soufflé or hot pâté.

2 eggs
Sprinkle of salt
4 teaspoons cold water
3 tablespoons lemon juice
Pinch of dried chervil, if desired
4 cups game bird consommé, heated

Combine all ingredients except consommé and beat well. Gradually stir in hot consommé, place over low heat and heat only to boiling point, stirring constantly. Strain through fine sieve into preheated bouillon cups and serve immediately to 4.

11/92

Mulligatawny

This dish has its origin in the East Indies and means "pepper wate[r]
traditionally made of chicken and rice, highly seasoned with curry
excellent way to use an older pheasant or a sage hen suspected to [be]

1 large pheasant or sage hen *—used 2-3 odd birds*
4 tablespoons butter, melted
1½ cups total of the following,
    chopped: onion, celery, green
    pepper, carrot
2 green apples, peeled and chopped *used 1 big apple*
1 tablespoon flour
1 tablespoon curry powder (start with
    less, if you prefer) *used >*
Pinch mace
2 quarts game bird stock *used 1½ qt chix broth*
1 8-ounce can tomato puree
Salt and black pepper to taste
Cooked rice

Disjoint bird. In a heavy kettle, brown the pieces in the melted butter. Add the chopped vegetables and apples as the bird is browning, st[irring]
evenly. Push the vege[tables to] one side; add flour, curry and mace, stirring until they are well blended and bubbly. Slowly pour in the stock and tomato puree, blending until smooth. Season to taste with salt and pepper. Bring to a boil, cover and reduce heat; simmer over low heat until the bird is tender.

Remove the bird, dice the meat into fairly large pieces, put the vegetables through a sieve or food mill, return diced fowl and vegetable puree to broth and heat well. Serve in a tureen, with a side dish of rice. Place some rice in each bowl and ladle the soup over it.

Vegetable Cream Soup

There are countless varieties of creamed soups; the choice is limited only by your own imagination. This is a basic recipe I have worked out, with a few suggestions for vegetable combinations. The rest is up to you.

2 cups vegetables (see below)
2 cups total of the following:
    Game bird stock (or chicken broth)
    plus liquid in which the vegetables
    were cooked
4 tablespoons roux (see page 166)
Salt and pepper to taste
2 cups light cream

Cook vegetables in lightly salted water to cover (don't drown the vegetables); drain and reserve the liquid. Combine
vegetable liquid with enough game bird stock to make 2 cups. Puree vegetables.

Melt roux in saucepan and stir over low heat until bubbly; add seasonings. Slowly stir in vegetable liquid and game bird stock, blending until smooth and thickened. Add cream and vegetable puree; continue to cook over low heat until very hot. Do not allow to boil once cream has been added. A bit of grated onion or a sprinkle of freshly grated nutmeg may add needed zest.

Suggested vegetable combinations:
Mushroom and celery
**Spinach and watercress (cook over low
      heat with only the water which
      clings to the leaves)**
**Asparagus and celery (reserve the
      asparagus tips for garnish)**
Carrot and onion
**Cabbage and onion (garnish with grated
      sharp cheddar cheese)**

**Cooked cucumber and celery, with 1
      tablespoon each chopped green
      pepper and onion**

Any leftover soup will be a welcome addition to a casserole. When I freeze these soups, I combine only the vegetable puree with the stock, preferring to add the cream in proper proportion after the stock has been reheated.

Vichyssoise

Every nation has its potato and onion soup. This is considered a French classic, although I understand it was originally created in an American hotel.

8 leeks, finely chopped
4 tablespoons butter
2 stalks celery, finely chopped
3 cups potatoes, finely diced
1 quart game bird consommé
2 cups heavy cream
Salt and pepper

Clean leeks very thoroughly, as they are apt to be gritty. Melt the butter in a large saucepan, and cook the leeks and celery over low heat, without browning, for 5 to 10 minutes. Add potatoes, stock and seasonings, cover and simmer until potatoes are very tender, about 25 minutes. Put through a sieve or food mill, blend in the cream and chill.

Serve in chilled bowls, garnished with chives, parsley or a dash of paprika. I usually make a double recipe of this soup and freeze only the onion and potato mixture, adding equal portions of cream to the thawed mixture when I am ready to serve it.

Zucchini Soup

4 tablespoons butter
1 cup onion, chopped
**1½ pounds zucchini squash, sliced
      and slices quartered (*not* peeled)**
2 quarts game bird stock
2 eggs, lightly beaten
2 tablespoons fresh parsley, chopped
¼ cup Romano cheese, freshly grated
Freshly ground black pepper

In a 4-quart kettle, melt the butter and sauté the onion until soft and golden. Add the zucchini pieces and cook them, stirring occasionally, so they sauté evenly. Pour in the game bird stock and cover; simmer 30 minutes or so, until vegetables are tender.

In a small bowl, combine the beaten eggs, parsley and cheese. Meanwhile,

Zucchini Soup (cont.)

puree the zucchini soup in a blender and return to the pot in which you cooked it. Ladle a tablespoon or two into the egg mixture, then whisk that into the pureed soup until well blended. Heat through, but do not boil. Serve immediately sprinkled with extra cheese and freshly ground black pepper.

FISH AND OTHER GAME SOUPS

Since most hunters enjoy fishing as well, here are two fish soup recipes that are particularly suited to camp cooking, and a recipe for rabbit soup.

 Fish Chowder

3 or 4 strips bacon, diced
1 large onion, sliced
2 pounds fish, cut into pieces
6 potatoes, sliced
Water to cover
1 tablespoon butter
1 tablespoon flour
2 cups milk (canned milk or equivalent dried milk and water)
1 teaspoon salt
Freshly ground black pepper to taste
Parsley, fresh or dried
1 can corn niblets, drained (optional)

Brown bacon in kettle; remove browned bits and set aside. In the bacon fat, cook sliced onion until golden brown. Add fish and potatoes, barely cover with water. Set beside the fire to simmer gently until the potatoes are tender. Blend butter and flour, thin with a small amount of the pot liquid, add to fish and potatoes and stir until thickened. Add milk and seasonings to taste; simmer 5 more minutes. A can of corn niblets is a nice addition to this chowder.

 Fish Mulligan

I have often wondered if the name "mulligan" has any relation to the East Indian mulligatawny—at any rate, it's a good camp dish—add, subtract or substitute whatever is handy.

2 pounds fish, cut into chunks
4 potatoes, diced
2 onions, sliced
1½ quarts water
⅓ cup raw rice

1 green pepper, diced
2 or 3 strips bacon, diced
Celery or celery salt
Carrots or any leftover vegetables

Fish Mulligan (cont.)

In a large kettle, combine fish, potatoes, onions and water. Bring to a vigorous boil, then add rice, green pepper and bacon, plus any other vegetables you may have on hand. Cover and remove to a spot on the cooking fire where it will just simmer until the potatoes are done, about 1/2 hour.

Rabbit Soup

If the rabbit population is overabundant, you might try this soup as a change from stewed, roasted, or fried rabbit. It's particularly suited to older critters.

1 old rabbit or hare, cut up
2 cups chopped soup vegetables,
**   including the following:**
**   carrot, onion, celery knob, turnip**
**   (or parsnip)**
2 or 3 sprigs parsley
1 bay leaf
Pinch rosemary
1/4 cup butter (or more, if necessary),
**   melted**
2 quarts stock
1 teaspoon grated lemon peel
Salt and pepper to taste
1 tablespoon roux (*see* page 166)

1 wine glass port or Sauterne

Brown disjointed rabbit with vegetables and herbs in melted butter. Add stock and lemon peel and simmer over low heat for several hours until rabbit is very tender. Season to taste with salt and pepper. Strain soup through colander, remove rabbit meat from bones and cut into cubes. Puree vegetables, and return puree to broth along with diced meat. Thicken with roux, stir until smooth; add wine and serve.

GARNISHES FOR SOUPS AND STEWS

While it is easy to serve soups and stews with rice or noodles, you can enliven an otherwise ordinary meal with dumplings or game quenelles, for example, that never fail to satisfy your eye—or your appetite.

 ## Dumplings for Stew

These are easy to prepare and tasty in that camp stew.

2 cups Biscuit Mix
**   (*see* page 250)**
1 teaspoon dried parsley flakes

1/2 teaspoon dehydrated minced onion
3/4 cup water

Dumplings for Stew (cont.)

In a small bowl, pour in the biscuit mix and blend in the dried parsley and onion; add the water and stir until "sticky" and of dumpling consistency.

Thicken stew, if necessary, before adding dumplings. Dip spoon into hot gravy, then spoon a gob of the dough onto the bubbling liquid (dipping the spoon in the gravy first helps the dough slide off the spoon), repeat this process quickly until the dough is used up. Be sure to leave space between the dumplings when you put them in the kettle—they need room to expand. Clap the lid on the kettle and cook 15 to 20 minutes. No peeking or you'll be eating cannonballs instead of fluffy dumplings!

Croutons

Bread
Butter
Herbs of your choosing

Trim crusts from bread with a very sharp knife; cut into cubes, diamonds or shapes. They may be fried in butter or just toasted in the oven. However, I prefer to brush the croutons liberally with melted butter and toast them on a flat baking sheet in a 300° F. oven, turning until delicately brown and very crisp on both sides.

Herb croutons may be made by adding a pinch of finely crushed dry herbs or finely chopped fresh ones to the melted butter. Two pleasing combinations for rather bland dishes would be chervil and thyme or tarragon and parsley.

Game Quenelles

$1/2$ pound cooked and finely ground game
$1/4$ cup butter
1 egg plus 1 egg yolk
Salt and pepper
2 tablespoons heavy cream
$1/4$ cup water
1 tablespoon butter
2 tablespoons flour

Combine all ingredients and work into a smooth paste. Season to taste and chill for an hour. Shape into small balls and poach gently in boiling stock. *Or:*

$1/2$ pound uncooked game
$1/2$ cup heavy cream
Salt and pepper
2 egg whites, stiffly beaten

Put the meat through a food chopper twice, using the fine blade. Season to taste and work in heavy cream. Chill for an hour or so, and then add egg whites. Form into small balls and poach gently in boiling stock for 10 to 15 minutes.

Custard Cubes for Consommé

⅓ cup milk or game stock, scalded
1 egg, slightly beaten with a pinch of salt and paprika

Slowly pour scalded liquid into egg, stirring rapidly as you pour. Strain through cheesecloth or a fine sieve into a shallow pan. Set in a larger pan on oven rack, fill outer pan with boiling water. Bake about 30 minutes at 325° F. or until custard is set. Cool, cut into cubes or fancy shapes and add to soup when ready to serve.

Game Wontons

Wontons can be prepared with any type of leftover game—no one will ever suspect. And they are easy to fix, and freeze well.

1 pound cooked game, ground or minced
2 slices fresh ginger, minced
2 scallions, minced
¼ teaspoon garlic powder
Pinch nutmeg
Freshly ground black pepper
Pinch salt
½ teaspoon sugar
2 tablespoons dry sherry
2 tablespoons soy sauce
Prepared wonton skins

In a mixing bowl, combine all ingredients, except wonton skins. Add a little bread crumbs, if necessary, to make the mixture adhere.

Wonton skins may be purchased in any supermarket and can be frozen until ready to use. They are approximately 4 inches square and usually come in 1-pound packages. To fill them, place a ½ teaspoon filling roughly in the center of each; fold in half so the corners meet (now you have a rectangle, not a square). Fold again in half in the same direction so the dough looks 1-inch high by 4 inches long. Now take the two ends, curl them around and overlap them slightly, using a little water to press them together. The end result looks like a nurse's cap. You should be able to prepare about 32 wontons with above amount of filling.

To cook them, place in a large pot of boiling water; bring water to boil again and wontons will rise to the top. Add some cold water to the pot, let the water boil again; this second boil will thoroughly cook these Oriental delights.

Remove from water with a slotted spoon. Gently lower into game consommé to which you have added soy sauce to taste and chopped scallion.

If you are not ready to use them, you may drain the wontons and rinse with cold water; arrange them in shallow freezer containers with lids and freeze. Do *not* thaw before boiling them again in water when you do wish to serve them.

For the record, most Oriental wonton recipes call for uncooked pork, but when I use game, I prefer to work with it cooked. This way when you heat the wontons in the soup, you'll know the meat is already edible and you won't have to worry about it.

Liver Dumplings (Leberknödel)

¹/₂ pound venison liver
1 cup boiling water
1 egg
¹/₃ cup cream
1 cup fine dry bread crumbs
¹/₄ cup onion, minced
1 small clove garlic, minced
1 tablespoon butter
Several sprigs parsley, chopped
Pinch marjoram
Salt and pepper to taste

Simmer liver in boiling water for 5 minutes; drain and remove membrane and tubes. Put through medium blade of food chopper. Beat egg with cream, blend in bread crumbs. Add onion and garlic which have been sautéed briefly in butter. Add liver and seasonings and blend well.

Shape into 1-inch balls and cook in boiling water or stock. Cook only a half dozen at a time and remove as they rise to the surface. Serve several dumplings in each bowl of soup. Any remaining may be frozen for a few weeks.

Potato Dumplings (Kartoffelknödel)

Kartoffelknödel are as essential to Sauerbraten as cheese is to apple pie. But keep in mind that they are favorites with stews and other gravy dishes, too!

5 medium potatoes
4 tablespoons farina
2 tablespoons butter
1 or 2 slices of bread, trimmed of crusts
    and cut into cubes
1 egg
1 teaspoon salt
Generous grating of nutmeg
³/₄ cup flour
2 quarts boiling water
2 teaspoons salt

In a large covered saucepan, boil peeled, cut-up potatoes in salted water until tender, 25 to 30 minutes. Drain and put through ricer; add farina, mix well and let rest for 1 hour. In a skillet, melt the butter and brown bread cubes lightly over low heat. Add egg, salt and nutmeg to potatoes and beat until fluffy. Add toasted bread cubes and half the flour; mix well. Continue sifting in flour and mixing until you have a soft dough.

Shape one 2-inch dumpling; roll in flour and cook in boiling, salted water. If it does not retain its shape, add more flour to the dough. When dough is of proper consistency, shape dumplings into 2-inch balls, roll lightly in flour and cook in rapidly boiling, salted water for 15 minutes, or until dumplings rise to the surface of the water.

Do not attempt to cook too many at once, as this will lower the temperature of the water. Drain with a slotted spoon and keep warm in the oven while cooking the remainder of the dumplings. Serve hot with melted butter. Leftover dumplings may be cut in half, sautéed in butter, sprinkled with parsley and served in place of potatoes the next day.

 **Soup Egg Garnish**

To the creative cook (or the camp "chef" who's looking for easy fixings), eggs are terrific because you can whip up so many varied dishes with them. This recipe results in a batter-type omelet, to be cut up into chunks or thin slices—either way a high-protein addition to a clear game broth.

1 onion
2 tablespoons parsley
2 eggs
Unsifted, unbleached all-purpose flour
Salt and freshly ground black pepper
Butter/oil or bacon drippings

Chop the onion and parsley. In a small bowl, beat the eggs lightly with a fork; add the onion and parsley and enough flour to make a thick batter. Season with salt and pepper.

In a 5- or 6-inch skillet, heat the shortening and pour in all of the batter; sauté on both sides until golden brown. Cut up as desired. Place in the pot of soup for a few minutes to heat through before serving in individual bowls.

 Viennese Peas (Wiener Erbsen)

I suppose you could call these deep-fried dumplings. At any rate, they are quick and easy to do, especially at camp.

Vegetable oil
1 egg
2 tablespoons milk
Pinch salt
¾ cup flour

Heat fat for deep frying to 375° F. Make the batter as follows: Beat the egg with the milk and a pinch of salt. Add all at once to flour and beat smooth. Dip tip of small spoon into hot fat and drop tiny balls of batter into hot fat. Cook until golden (only a minute or so), remove from fat and drain on paper towels.

BREAD STUFFINGS

Stuffing adds its flavor to meat and poultry, at the same time absorbing some of the flavor of the meat. Stuffings should therefore be chosen with care to provide the maximum in flavor.

Fruit stuffings, especially when they are tart or slightly acidic, are excellent with rich and rather fat meats or birds—goose, boar, muskrat. Stuffings for lean and somewhat drier meats and birds may be more rich and savory.

Stuffings expand considerably during the cooking process, so always stuff lightly to avoid a soggy mass of stuffing or a burst bird. Extra stuffing, especially when small birds are used, may be baked in a buttered casserole to provide extra servings.

When using bread as a base for stuffing, use bread that is at least a day old and slightly dry. Always toss ingredients lightly together with a fork to blend or you will have a soggy stuffing to start with. Birds or meats to be braised are often stuffed and here it is most important to start with a stuffing drier than usual. The steam generated in the braising kettle will moisten the stuffing to a great extent.

Regardless of what you may have read elsewhere, *never* stuff meats or fowl until you are ready to cook them. If you wish to make advance preparations, get your stuffing ingredients ready the day before—dice or crumb the bread, cook the rice, shell and peel chestnuts, steam prunes, etc. But do wait until you're ready to turn on the oven before you assemble the stuffing and fill the birds. (The only exception to this rule is the apple, onion or celery placed inside duck cavities to draw out any possible fishy taste.) After all, you are preparing a feast and you don't want it to turn into a disaster because of the development of dangerous toxins due to bacterial growth.

As a general rule, one cup of stuffing is figured on for each pound of bird, so adjust these recipes to the birds on hand and allow a bit extra to serve with them for second helpings.

Bacon-Swiss Chard Stuffing

**4 cups stale white bread cubes
    (French or Italian bread is fine)
3 slices bacon
2 tablespoons shallots, chopped
1/4 cup celery, chopped
1/4 pound Swiss chard, chopped
    (about 1 cup loosely packed)
2 eggs, beaten
1 1/2 to 2 cups Game Bird Stock (or
    chicken broth or water) to moisten
Freshly ground black pepper
Salt if desired
Fresh grating of nutmeg**

Place bread cubes in a large mixing bowl.

In a skillet, sauté the bacon, remove and break into small pieces. In the bacon drippings, sauté the shallots and celery; add the Swiss chard and sauté it to remove some of the moisture content; cool.

Combine bacon pieces and shallot/Swiss chard mixture with bread cubes. Add beaten eggs and enough liquid to moisten thoroughly. Season with pepper, salt if desired and the nutmeg. Makes about 4 to 6 cups.

This is a flavorful stuffing that does very well with the oft-times strong taste of game birds.

Apple and Raisin Stuffing

1/4 cup butter
1 cup celery, diced
1 quart bread crumbs
2/3 cup raisins
3 apples, diced
1/2 cup nut meats, coarsely broken
Pinch each of thyme and marjoram
Salt and pepper to taste
Apple juice or cider to moisten

In a skillet, cook celery in melted butter for 5 minutes without browning. In a mixing bowl, combine the remaining ingredients, add the celery and toss lightly to blend. Season to taste and add cider or apple juice to moisten if necessary. Makes about 6 cups stuffing.

Bread Stuffing for Fish

1/4 cup butter
1/2 onion, chopped
1 stalk celery, chopped
2 slices bread, pulled into soft crumbs
Pinch thyme
1/2 teaspoon sage, crumbled
3 or 4 sprigs parsley, chopped
3 to 4 tablespoons milk, water, or
    lemon juice
Salt and pepper

In a small skillet, cook onion and celery in butter for 5 minutes without browning; cool. Add to other ingredients, toss lightly and season to taste. Pour in only enough liquid to moisten—don't let the dressing become soggy. For variation, you might add 1/2 cup chopped mushrooms or 1/4 cup chopped pickle.

Chestnut Stuffing

1/4 cup raisins
1/2 cup butter
1/4 cup celery, chopped
1/4 cup onion, chopped
2 cups chestnuts, cooked and coarsely
    chopped
Parsley
Sage
Rosemary
Salt and pepper
Wine or broth to moisten

Briefly blanch raisins in boiling water; drain. In a skillet, melt butter and cook celery and onion for 5 minutes without browning. Combine all ingredients in a mixing bowl, toss lightly and season to taste. Moisten if desired with wine or broth.

Cornbread-Pecan Stuffing

See page 64.

Crabmeat Stuffing—*for fish*

2 tablespoons butter
1 1/2 teaspoons onion, finely chopped
1/4 cup celery, finely chopped
1 7 1/2-ounce can crabmeat, flaked
2 or 3 tablespoons green pepper,
    chopped
2/3 cup fine dry bread crumbs

2 tablespoons lemon juice
Pinch each thyme and nutmeg

In a skillet, sauté onion and celery lightly in butter, but do not brown; cool. Add to other ingredients and toss lightly to blend.

Cranberry Stuffing

2 cups cranberries, coarsely chopped
1/2 cup sugar
1/2 cup butter
1/2 cup celery, chopped
2 tablespoons onion, minced
1/4 cup snipped parsley
1 teaspoon marjoram or 1/2 teaspoon
    each thyme and marjoram
Salt and pepper to taste

2 quarts coarse bread crumbs
Water or white wine to moisten

Combine chopped cranberries and sugar; let stand for 1/2 hour. In a skillet, sauté celery, onion and parsley gently in butter for 5 minutes. Combine all ingredients and season to taste. Add wine or water to moisten slightly.

Prune and Apple Stuffing

2 cups prunes
2 cups tart apples, peeled and chopped
1 quart day-old bread crumbs
Salt
Generous grating fresh nutmeg
Apple juice to moisten
1/2 pound sausage (optional)

If prunes are not plump and tender,

steam them briefly or soak them for a short time; it is not necessary to cook them. Pit and chop the prunes, then combine all ingredients and toss lightly with apple juice to moisten. If appropriate for the meat or bird you are planning to stuff, 1/2 pound mild sausage meat, cooked and drained, may be added to this recipe.

Sage and Onion Stuffing

1/2 to 3/4 cup butter
6 large stalks celery, diced
3 large onions, chopped
3 quarts day-old bread crumbs
Salt and pepper to taste

2 teaspoons crumbled sage
3/4 teaspoon thyme
1/2 teaspoon rosemary *or*
1 1/2 tablespoons poultry seasoning in
    place of the 3 herbs

Sage and Onion Stuffing (cont.)

In a large skillet, melt butter over low heat, and cook onion and celery for 10 minutes without browning. Remove from heat and add to bread crumbs and seasonings in a large mixing bowl. Toss lightly with a fork to blend and check seasonings, adding more if you wish. If you prefer a moister dressing, add a bit of broth. Sufficient for a 10 to 12 pound turkey.

Chopped giblets, $1/2$ pound mushrooms, sautéed in butter, or $1/2$ pint drained and chopped oysters may be added for flavor variations.

Shrimp Stuffing—*for fish*

16 large raw shrimp, shelled and deveined
2 tablespoons butter
$1/4$ teaspoon salt
Dash of pepper
$1 1/2$ teaspoons onion, finely chopped
$1/4$ cup celery, finely chopped
2 sprigs fresh dill, chopped or $1/2$ teaspoon dill seed
2 tablespoons lime juice
$2/3$ cup fine dry bread crumbs

In a skillet, melt butter; add shrimp, season with salt and pepper and sauté just until pink and opaque; do not overcook. Remove from pan and chop. In same pan, cook onion and celery for 5 minutes, but do not brown. Add dill, lime juice, chopped shrimp and bread crumbs. Stir with fork to blend.

Wine Stuffing

1 quart day-old bread crumbs
$1/2$ cup butter, melted
$1/2$ cup dry white wine
8 to 10 sprigs parsley, snipped
$1/2$ cup mushrooms, sautéed in the butter or $1/2$ cup crisp bacon bits, well drained
Thyme and marjoram to taste

Combine all ingredients and toss lightly, seasoning to taste.

RICE STUFFINGS

Rice for stuffings should be cooked only until barely tender, as it will continue to cook during the roasting process. If you do not have a favorite method of producing fluffy rice that's not sticky or mushy, see the instructions suggested in Chapter 14.

Apricot-Rice Stuffing

4 tablespoons butter
4 tablespoons onion, diced
4 tablespoons celery, diced
1¹/₂ to 2 cups cooked rice
1 cup dried apricots, chopped
Salt and pepper
Grating of fresh nutmeg
1 orange, put through the food
    processor or medium blade of the
    food chopper, rind and all
¹/₄ cup brandy or white wine

In a skillet, cook onion and celery in melted butter for about 5 minutes without browning. Combine with other ingredients in a mixing bowl and toss lightly but thoroughly to blend.

Rice Stuffing—*for small birds*

The amounts will vary with the size of the birds, of course.

Bird liver
Butter or bacon fat
Minced onion
Cooked rice
Tart apple, diced
Brandy *or* white wine
Salt and pepper
Freshly grated nutmeg

Gently sauté the bird liver in butter or bacon drippings with a small amount of minced onion. Chop liver coarsely, add rice, a bit of diced tart apple, and moisten with brandy or white wine. Season to taste with salt and pepper and a grating of nutmeg.

Rice and Raisin Stuffing—*for birds*

1 cup cooked rice
2 tablespoons butter
1 teaspoon onion, grated
1 teaspoon parsley, minced
1 teaspoon orange rind, grated
2 tablespoons raisins blanched in
    boiling water
2 tablespoons slivered almonds
Salt and pepper to taste

Lightly toss all ingredients together in a mixing bowl; season to taste.

Savory Wild Rice Stuffing

1 cup raw wild rice
3 cups stock
¹/₂ pound mushrooms, sliced
1 cup smoked ham, chopped
¹/₂ cup celery, diced
¹/₄ cup onion, chopped
¹/₂ cup butter
Salt

Marjoram
Thyme

Cook wild rice in broth about 40 minutes, or until nearly tender. In a skillet, sauté mushrooms, ham, celery and onion in butter for 5 to 8 minutes. Combine with rice and season to taste.

OTHER STUFFINGS

Veal Forcemeat—*for stuffing small birds*

¹/₄ pound veal
¹/₄ pound smoked ham
1 roll, moistened with white wine
1 tablespoon mushroom, chopped
1 tablespoon onion, minced
4 tablespoons butter
Fresh parsley, chopped
Salt and pepper to taste
1 egg, beaten

Put veal and ham through the food chopper, using the fine blade. Sauté the mushrooms and onion briefly in butter. Pound all ingredients together until smooth and bind with the egg. *Or*:

Place all ingredients—veal, ham, roll, sautéed onions and mushrooms, seasonings—in food processor and with metal blade process until smooth, creamy and well blended. Add beaten egg and process until mixed well.

CHAPTER 12
LEFTOVERS AND LUNCHEON IDEAS

Game leftovers need present no problem to the creative cook, especially now that freezers are in such common use. With a bit of foresight and imagination, the leftovers can be equally as delicious as the original dish—for luncheons, Sunday night suppers or whatever.

I discovered long ago that cooking for two can be a bit difficult (as well as expensive) unless you develop a repertoire of what I call "planned leftovers." In my opinion, you can't cook a roast properly unless it's of fair size and there is a limit, especially in this household, to the number of times one can serve cold sliced roast. The same thing is true in most families, regardless of size.

I try to have at least some ideas in mind, and in many cases I do the advance preparation before I tuck the leftovers away in the freezer. Then after the original dish has been forgotten, I can present the leftovers in a completely new dish. Leftovers have been the featured attraction at "company luncheons" and at the cocktail hour preceding a dinner party. No one has been aware of their humble origins.

Food frozen raw can be safely refrozen after it has been cooked. However, the maximum time for freezer storage of leftovers is three months, so keep a record of leftovers that you have "squirreled away." Boiled potatoes and hard-boiled eggs should not be included in dishes you plan to freeze; the potatoes become watery and the eggs, tough and rubbery.

With a supply of stock from bones on hand and prepared soups in the cupboard to serve as the base for sauces, the flavor variations are limited only by your imagination. An extra flourish, such as fresh mushrooms or a bit of wine in a sauce, will help lift a casserole out of the doldrums. You'll still be ahead on your budget, for you've utilized the leftovers for another meal instead of feeding them to the dog.

To save freezer space and to prevent freezer burn from air trapped inside oddly shaped packages, I usually cut meat from the bones immediately, dice it or grind it, and then pack it in plastic containers. The gravy is frozen separately in small containers and then the two packages fastened together with freezer tape. Slices of breast meat from birds are wrapped in self-adhering plastic film with a double fold of wax paper or film between slices, then sealed carefully in freezer paper or plastic freezer bags.

GROUND MEAT OR FOWL

Croquettes

2 cups ground leftover meat or fowl
1/2 cup chopped mushrooms, sautéed in butter
2 eggs, beaten separately
1/2 cup bread crumbs
Lemon juice or Worcestershire Sauce
Minced onion
Chopped parsley or minced celery
Sufficient white sauce, canned soup or gravy to moisten
Dry bread crumbs
Sauce or gravy of your choice

Blend the first 8 ingredients together using only 1 beaten egg; season to taste, then chill for an hour or so before shaping into flat patties or the traditional cone-shaped croquettes.

Dip croquettes into the other beaten egg and then into bread crumbs; allow to "dry" on a rack for about 20 minutes. Deep fry in oil at 375° F. or pan fry in hot melted butter. Serve with any savory sauce that will blend with the meat flavor.

Pinwheels

Biscuit dough, using 1 cup mix (page 250)
Croquette mixture, above
Gravy

Prepare biscuits, using 1 cup mix.

Roll or pat dough into oblong shape on floured board a scant 1/2-inch thick.

Spread with croquette mixture described above and roll up from the long side of the oblong. Cut thick slices and place on greased cookie sheet. Bake at 350° F. for 20 to 25 minutes, until biscuits are browned. Serve with gravy which has been extended with tomato, mushroom or cream of celery soup.

Pheasant or Grouse Mousse

This is an elegant dish for a bridge luncheon and serves 4.

1 envelope (1 tablespoon) unflavored
    gelatine
1/4 cup dry white wine
1/2 cup hot game bird stock
2 egg yolks
1/2 cup milk
1 1/2 cups ground fowl
2 tablespoons mayonnaise
Several sprigs parsley, chopped
6 to 8 green olives, sliced
1 stalk celery, finely diced, *or* 3
    tablespoons slivered toasted
    almonds
Few drops lemon juice
Salt and pepper
Dash of onion salt
1/2 cup heavy cream
Paprika (optional)

Soften gelatine in wine. Beat egg yolks in top of double boiler, add milk and set over hot (not boiling) water and stir constantly. Add hot stock slowly and continue to stir until the mixture coats the spoon. Remove from the hot water and stir in the gelatine and wine until dissolved. Cool until mixture begins to thicken.

Lightly oil 4 individual molds with salad oil and turn upside down to drain. Blend together ground fowl, mayonnaise, parsley, celery, lemon juice and seasonings. Fold into thickening gelatine mixture. Whip cream and fold in with a dash of paprika, if desired. Spoon into molds and chill until set.

Unmold onto chilled plates and garnish with parsley, radish roses. Serve with hot rolls or cheese straws.

Moose Mousse

I couldn't resist doing a recipe for this, although any antlered game may be substituted.

2 cups strong game stock
1 bay leaf
6 juniper berries
2 tablespoons unflavored gelatine
1/4 cup white wine
1 1/2 cups leftover moose, finely ground
1/2 cup game liver pâté (*see* Chapter 13)
2 tablespoons onion, chopped
1 teaspoon Worcestershire Sauce
Freshly ground black pepper
Fresh grating nutmeg
2 tablespoons Cognac
1 cup heavy cream

Pour the game stock into a saucepan with the bay leaf and juniper berries; simmer about 20 to 30 minutes until reduced slightly (to 1 1/2 cups); remove bay leaf and berries and cool.

Sprinkle gelatine over white wine and let soften about 5 minutes; dissolve over hot water (or in a microwave oven in a nonmetal container).

Pour game stock, dissolved gelatine, ground moose, liver pâté and chopped onion in a blender and season with Worcestershire Sauce, black pepper, nutmeg and Cognac; puree until smooth. Pour into a metal bowl (if you have one) and chill until slightly set.

Whip the cream, then fold it into the partially set moose mixture. Pour into a lightly oiled 6-cup mold and chill until firmly set, at least 4 hours, and preferably overnight.

Unmold onto a chilled plate and surround with your choice of greens and cherry tomatoes.

Sandwich Spread

Coarsely ground meat or fowl
Minced onion
Mayonnaise
Chopped pickles or capers
Prepared mustard or anchovy paste

Mix meat with minced onion; moisten with mayonnaise and add pickles and capers plus a little mustard or anchovy paste for zest.

Turnovers or Pasties

2 cups ground leftover pot roast
Minced onion
Chopped parsley
1 egg, beaten
Dash of Worcestershire Sauce
Gravy to moisten
Pastry for double-crust pie

Mix meat with seasonings, egg and gravy. Roll out pastry and cut into 5- or 6-inch rounds. Place a heaping tablespoon of meat mixture on one half of each round, fold the other half over and seal edges with the tines of a fork. Cut several slits for steam to escape and brush with beaten egg yolk or milk.

Bake on ungreased cookie sheet at 450° F. for 10 minutes, reduce heat to 350° F. and bake until golden brown, about 20 minutes.

Serve hot with leftover gravy or mushroom sauce. These are also delicious made in miniature and served as hot canapés.

DICED MEAT OR FOWL

Cold Stuffed Avocados or Tomatoes

Diced game or fowl
Curry, Garlic or Mustard Mayonnaise
    (*see* page 61)

Diced celery
Minced onion
Avocado *or* fresh tomato halves

Cold Stuffed Avocados or Tomatoes (cont.)

Prepare curry, garlic or mustard mayonnaise to moisten diced fowl or game; add diced celery, minced onion to enhance the flavor and stuff avocado halves or fresh tomatoes, of which you've scooped out the pulp and seeds.

Serve on shredded lettuce.

Another type of mayonnaise you could try would resemble a **Thousand Island** dressing: combine with 1 cup mayonnaise, 2 to 3 tablespoons ketchup, a little lemon juice and horseradish or sweet relish or capers.

Cold Pasta Salad

Filling for Cold Stuffed Avocados
Raw broccoli flowerets
Carrots, shredded
Small pasta shells

Prepare above recipe with any of the suggested mayonnaises. In addition to celery and onion, you could add raw broccoli flowerets and shredded carrots and toss with small cooked pasta shells, ditalini or elbow macaroni.

Creamed Wild Turkey

This is a basic recipe that lends itself to great variation, with other fowl, as well as in serving.

4 tablespoons butter
1 medium onion, chopped
1 large stalk celery, chopped
4 tablespoons flour
1 cup game bird stock
1 cup milk
Freshly ground black pepper
Pinch salt, if desired
2 teaspoons Worcestershire Sauce
1 tablespoon ketchup
1¹/₂ cups leftover wild turkey, cubed
¹/₂ cup green peas
Mushrooms (optional)

In a large saucepan, melt the butter and in it lightly sauté the onion and celery. Blend in the flour, then add the game bird stock and the milk, stirring constantly until the sauce is thickened and smooth. Season it with black pepper, salt, if desired, Worcestershire Sauce and ketchup. Add the turkey and the peas and cook until the peas are tender. Watch for scorching on the bottom, however. Add the mushrooms last and just heat through.

To serve:
Pour over **1.** buttered toast points; **2.** baked puff pastry shells; **3.** rice; **4.** elbow macaroni; *or* **5.** Use as filling for "Palatschinken" (Austrian Crêpes); *or* **6.** Cook spinach egg noodles according to package directions; toss with creamed mixture and pour into buttered casserole; sprinkle with Romano cheese, dot with butter and bake at 350° F. for 30 to 40 minutes.

End-of-the-Line Quiche

My husband laughs at me because he says he never knows what to expect when we sit down to dinner. Sometimes I throw in everything but the kitchen sink and, really, it's due to the fact that I learned a good cook throws nothing, or at least very little, away. Here's a dish that proves my point.

Combine to make 4 cups total, diced:
> **Leftover fowl**
> **Leftover stuffing**
> **Carrots, steamed**
> **Green beans, steamed**
> **Onion, steamed**

4 eggs, beaten
Leftover gravy
Milk *or* half and half *or* light cream
1/2 cup Swiss cheese, grated, if desired
Freshly ground black pepper
Salt, if desired
3 tomato slices
1 partially baked 9-inch pie shell

Preheat oven to 350° F.

Steam the carrots, beans and onion for about 5 minutes and combine with leftover fowl and stuffing in a large mixing bowl.

In a small mixing bowl, beat the eggs lightly. Combine leftover gravy with enough milk/half and half/light cream to make 1 1/2 cups and blend into eggs. Add liquid to dry mixture to moisten and cover completely. Blend in cheese, if desired; season.

Pour into prebaked pie shell; garnish with tomato slices and bake about 1 hour, or until knife inserted in center comes out clean.

Easy Curry

Particularly good with fowl, sheep or goat.

2 tablespoons butter
1 onion, minced
Coarsely grated lime rind, if available
Pinch of cardamon
1 tablespoon curry powder
1 teaspoon ground ginger
2 tablespoons flour
2 cups stock
2 cups leftover meat, diced

Brown onion and lime in butter; add seasonings and simmer for 10 minutes over low heat. Blend in flour and add stock, stirring until thick and smooth. Add diced meat, check seasonings and heat thoroughly. Serve over fluffy rice.

Fried Brown Rice with Game

See page 245.

15-Minute Chinese Supper

1 pound leftover meat or fowl, diced
2 tablespoons peanut oil
2 tablespoons soy sauce
1 cup stock or 1/2 cup stock and 1/2 cup
    gravy
1/2 cup minced onion
1-pound can Chinese vegetables,
    drained
1 tablespoon cornstarch
1/4 teaspoon ground ginger
1 tablespoon honey or light molasses
1/4 cup dry sherry or water

Brown meat lightly in oil; add soy sauce, stock, onion and vegetables. Simmer 5 to 8 minutes, only until thoroughly heated. Meanwhile, combine cornstarch, ginger, honey and sherry and add to skillet, stirring only until thickened and clear.

Serve over rice or crisp Chinese noodles.

Game Bird Soufflé

4 tablespoons butter
4 tablespoons flour
1 cup milk
4 egg yolks
1 cup finely diced fowl
Salt and pepper
Celery salt
Cayenne or curry
Grated onion to taste
4 egg whites, stiffly beaten

Preheat oven to 350° F. Make a heavy white sauce with the butter, flour and milk; cool.

Add egg yolks to white sauce, one at a time, beating vigorously after each addition. Add fowl and seasonings to taste, then gently fold in egg whites. Spoon into buttered soufflé dish, set in a pan of hot water and bake for 45 minutes. Serve immediately with green salad and hot rolls. 4 servings.

Game Pies

2 cups diced meat or fowl
1 1/2 cups gravy *or* 1 cup stock, 1/2 cup
    cream and 3 tablespoons roux
    blended together
1/2 cup tiny whole onions, precooked 5
    minutes
1 package frozen peas, thawed but not
    cooked
1/2 cup carrots, sliced and precooked 5
    minutes
1/2 cup mushrooms, sautéed in butter
Fresh grating nutmeg
Freshly ground black pepper

Combine all ingredients, seasoning to taste, and pour into buttered casserole. Proceed as you wish:

1. Top with pastry, cut gashes for steam to escape, seal pastry to edge of casserole, bake at 400° F. until pastry is browned.

2. Cover casserole with a mashed potato crust; if desired, 1/2 cup grated sharp cheddar or Gruyère cheese may be blended into the potatoes.

3. Top with biscuits, bake at 375° F. for 45 minutes or until biscuits brown.

Game Pies (cont.)

4. Line individual pie plates (4 to 5 inches in diameter) with pastry. Use only enough gravy to moisten ingredients. Divide the filling among the pastry-lined pie plates and cover with a top crust, crimping the edges and cutting gashes as you would for any pie. Bake at 400° F. until the crust is brown. Carefully loosen the edges of the pies and slide each one onto a dinner plate. Pass remainder of the gravy hot in a separate sauce boat.

 Hash

2 cups leftover meat, diced or coarsely ground
1 cup boiled potatoes, diced
1 onion, chopped
Salt and pepper to taste
Chili sauce, catsup, or gravy to moisten

Lightly toss ingredients with a fork to blend. Place in heated, well-greased skillet, set over a slow fire or in reflector oven to brown and heat through. If desired, form wells in top of hash with back of spoon, and when hash has begun to brown, crack an egg into each hollow, season with salt and pepper and cover skillet until the eggs are done to your liking.

Palatschinken—Austrian Crêpes

This is lovely luncheon fare that goes well with many fillings, not only leftover game. The amount given in this recipe makes 18 pancakes, or 3 or 4 for a main course.

1 cup flour
1/2 teaspoon salt
3 eggs
1 cup milk
2 tablespoons butter, melted

Sift flour and salt together. In a large mixing bowl, beat eggs until very thick; add milk and melted butter, continuing to beat until all is well blended. Combine with sifted dry ingredients and beat smooth.

Lightly butter a 5- or 6-inch skillet and melt over moderate heat. Ladle into the skillet just enough batter to cover the bottom of the skillet, tilting the pan back and forth to spread the batter thin. Cook until the bottom of the pancake is light brown and the top is firm to the touch. Turn with spatula and brown the other side. Transfer to a hot platter and keep warm in the oven as you continue to cook crêpes one at a time. Because of the butter in the mix, it should be unnecessary to grease the skillet after each crêpe is made. To serve, fill and roll up with:

1. Cottage cheese and raisins; sprinkle rolls with cinnamon sugar.

2. Sardines, sprinkled with a bit of lemon juice.

3. Any game liver pâté and serve with mushroom sauce.

4. Creamed wild turkey.

Pilaf

1 cup long-grain rice
2 onions, sliced
¼ cup butter
Curry powder and cardamon for fowl
Bay leaf or oregano for game
Game stock *or* game bird stock *or*
      tomato juice
2 to 3 cups leftover game or fowl, diced
Mushrooms, sautéed in butter
      (optional)

Preheat oven to 350° F.

Wash rice 6 times in hot water, 6 times in cold water and set aside to drain on paper towels. Brown sliced onions in large flameproof casserole in butter. Remove onions while you brown the rice in the same casserole. Stir the rice constantly, adding more butter as needed, until the rice is a golden color. Add seasonings and enough stock to cover the rice completely. Stir over the heat until the stock is bubbling, add the diced meat and onions and blend in.

Cover the casserole and bake in oven until the rice is tender and the liquid is absorbed. If desired, add sautéed mushrooms just before serving, tossing lightly with a fork to blend.

 ## Quick Pilaf

2 to 3 cups leftover meat or fowl, diced
3 cups cooked rice
Minced onion
2 cups canned tomatoes, cut up
1 cup gravy or stock

Combine all ingredients, season to taste and put in a greased casserole. Top with buttered crumbs and bake at moderate heat in reflector oven about ½ hour.

 ## Quick Tomato Goulash

1 pound leftover meat, cubed
2 tablespoons fat or drippings
1 cup water
1 8-ounce can tomato sauce
1 package dehydrated vegetable soup
      mix
Dried onion flakes

Lightly brown leftover meat in fat. Stir in remaining ingredients and simmer over slow fire until vegetables have become tender. An extra pinch of dried onion flakes may be added also.

Sweet 'N Sour Wild Boar

Although any game in the pork family is delicious in this recipe, wildfowl—all varieties—are suitable, as well as antlered game. Try venison meatballs in miniature in this, too, as an hors d'oeuvre (in which case I'd dice all the vegetables and the fruit).

2 tablespoons peanut oil
1 cup green pepper, sliced lengthwise
½ cup onion, chopped (or sliced)
3 cloves garlic, chopped
1 cup chicken bouillon
1 tablespoon soy sauce
3 tablespoons white vinegar
¼ cup light brown sugar
1 teaspoon fresh ginger, chopped
½ teaspoon dry mustard
2 to 3 teaspoons cornstarch
1 3-pound pineapple, "dressed"
1½ cups game, large dice
1 cup straw or black mushrooms
1 8-ounce can bamboo shoots or water
    chestnuts (optional)

Prepare all ingredients beforehand. Clean the pineapple by chopping off the top and slicing down straight to remove the outer layer; then cut the inner core laterally into slices and cube the fruit. A 3-pound pineapple will yield about 1½ pounds of edible fruit. If you can't find fresh pineapple, use a 20-ounce can of pineapple chunks.

In a wok or large skillet, heat the peanut oil and lightly sauté the green pepper, onion and garlic; remove from pan. Make the sweet 'n sour sauce by pouring in the chicken bouillon, white vinegar, brown sugar, ginger and dry mustard; stir and heat through; thicken with cornstarch dissolved in a small amount of water, stirring constantly. Add the cubed pineapple and diced game and heat through. Return the green peppers and onions to the pan along with the mushrooms and bamboo shoots or water chestnuts, if desired.

Serve over rice; 3 to 4 servings.

SLICED MEATS

Oriental Medley

2 tablespoons peanut oil
1 medium onion, sliced
2 cloves garlic, chopped
Broccoli flowerets
Zucchini in julienne strips
1 cup game stock
2 tablespoons soy sauce
1 tablespoon hoisin sauce
Freshly ground black pepper
2 to 3 teaspoons cornstarch
Leftover venison, sliced
Dried black mushrooms, reconstituted

In a wok or large skillet, heat the peanut oil. Lightly sauté the onion and garlic, then add the broccoli and zucchini, stirring to cook through; cover pan for a few minutes to steam vegetables. Pour in game stock, soy sauce, hoisin sauce and season with black pepper; thicken with cornstarch dissolved in a small amount of water, stirring constantly. Add sliced venison and mushrooms and heat through.

Serve over rice.

Pheasant or Turkey Divan

Pheasant or wild turkey slices
Boiled ham
Broccoli or asparagus
2 cups thick white sauce
¼ cup Romano or Parmesan cheese
Minced onion

Preheat oven to 350° F.

Butter a shallow ovenproof casserole. Place in it slices of pheasant or wild turkey breast meat. Top each slice with a thin slice of boiled ham. Cook broccoli or asparagus until tender, but still crisp, and place several stalks of asparagus or one larger piece of broccoli on each portion. Cover with rich cream sauce to which has been added ¼ cup Romano or Parmesan cheese and a whisper of minced onion; sprinkle with another spoon or two of cheese.

Place in oven for 15 minutes and then slide briefly under the broiler until the sauce is bubbly and brown.

Pita Bread Repast

Pita bread
Sliced game or fowl
Cucumber slices
Zucchini slices
Avocado slices
Carrot, shredded
Cheese of your choice
Alfalfa or mung bean sprouts
Salad dressing of your choice

Fill Pita bread pockets with sliced game or fowl; add slices of cucumbers, zucchini or avocado plus shredded carrots and cheese, alfalfa or mung bean sprouts and pour over a little of your favorite salad dressing.

Serve with hot soup.

Reuben Grill

Leftover game
Pumpernickel *or* rye bread
Sauerkraut
Swiss cheese
Mustard

Slice cold, leftover antlered game, corned or smoked bear or boar and place on pumpernickel or rye bread; top with a layer of rinsed, drained sauerkraut and shredded or sliced Swiss cheese. Top with another slice of bread and grill on both sides. Serve with mustard.

Sliced game birds
Apricot Sauce (*see* Chapter 10)
Cold roast venison
Cumberland *or* Viennese Game Sauce

With cold sliced game birds, serve Apricot Sauce.

With cold sliced roast venison, serve Cumberland or Viennese Game Sauce.

Accompany with rice and mixed vegetables.

CHAPTER 13

GAME AND NON-GAME APPETIZERS

When I wrote the first edition of this book over 20 years ago, it was considered "poor form" to repeat as an appetizer the same food you'd be serving for the main course, even if it appeared in a different guise. I still tend to agree with that—not so much because it's poor form, but rather because today there's such a wide selection of foods you can choose from—why reintroduce the same thing. Nowadays with renewed interest in game, a passion for variety and the affluence to purchase or otherwise procure virtually anything money can buy, don't be surprised to see a combination of game served at one meal: a Rouennaise for the appetizer, chukars for the entrée and rack of venison for the main course. And do compliment the hostess when you dip into some "Hirsch" or "Hasen" pâté at the next fancy cocktail party you attend. Game has come of age, again.

Here are some of my favorite game appetizers—as well as non-game ones, some of which I often serve together.

GAME APPETIZERS

Beaver Tail

Herewith Mrs. Dalziel's recipe verbatim—the comments are as delightful as the beaver tail is delicious.

"It is a special 'Northern Recipe' enjoyed by most all trappers' families and I have both delighted and astonished some city slicker types with it. It is simple once you know how.

"First you must get acquainted with a beaver hunter (and don't start thinking of beaver coats), ask him to save the tail from one of his animals. First you thrust the tail into hot coals, or propane flame will do, till the black scaly outer skin puffs and blisters. Use heavy gloves for this or you may blister, too. Do this all over. Then, as soon as cool to handle, peel off the outer layer, simple as peeling a banana.

"Wash and put it in a large kettle of cold water, add salt, peppercorns, and a tablespoon of pickling spice, clove of garlic if desired. When tender—only an hour or so—place on platter and serve chilled, sliced—on cocktail crackers—a real conversation piece."

Broiled Bird Livers in Bacon

Pheasant livers, uncooked
Water chestnuts, sliced
Bacon, halved

If you have enough livers to try this, it's worth it. Take a half slice of bacon and in the center of it place a chunk of liver and a slice of water chestnut. Wrap the bacon around them and skewer with a toothpick. Broil, turning the liver, so all sides of the bacon are cooked. Since the bacon usually requires longer cooking time than the liver, when the bacon is done, so should the liver. Incidentally, frozen livers work well.

Game Jerky

The old and time-honored trail food is equally as delicious as a snack or nibble food with drinks. The pioneer method, still used in the bush today, was to cut the meat into thin strips and dry it in the sun and wind on racks over a low smoky fire to keep away insects, removing the water content without actually cooking the meat. The hard blackened strips kept indefinitely and provided a compact and highly nutritious food which could be "chawed" dry, or reconstituted in a stew. Most city folk would find it rather difficult to prepare jerky in this fashion, but with a few "substitutions" you can achieve the same results in your kitchen.

Lean game
Smoky seasoned salt *or* herb blend
Freshly ground black pepper

Trim the meat of all fat and gristle and slice as thin as possible with a sharp knife. You are not limited to fresh meat—any of the less tender cuts of venison in your freezer will do very nicely. As I have mentioned before, it is

Game Jerky (cont.)

easier to slice the meat while it is still partially frozen. Substitute any of the smoky seasoned salt or herb blends on the market for the smoke of the campfire, adding ground pepper if you wish. Substitute your oven racks for the rack of green willows the pioneers used, and dry in the oven instead of the sun, using the heat from the pilot flame if you have a gas range. If you have an electric oven with a very low temperature setting for keeping foods warm (140° to 170° F.), use that setting, but prop open the oven door, so the meat will be dried without being cooked. If the meat has been sliced thin enough, it will be dry overnight. With most men, I have found, there is no storage problem with jerky—it's gone in a twinkling. If you do have some left over, it will keep well in a tightly closed container—preferably hidden away in a far corner of the cupboard.

Moose Nose

Moose nose, prepared as described in Chapter 8, may be served chilled as is, or the meat may be cut into fine dice and jellied. Press the diced meat into a loaf pan or mold, pour over it enough of the cooking liquid to cover—about ½ cup— place a piece of foil on the meat and then weight it. Let it chill in the refrigerator for a day or so, then unmold and slice as described. This is very similar to head-cheese.

Pâté-Stuffed Mushrooms

Large mushrooms suitable for stuffing
Butter
Liver pâté (any found in this chapter)

Sauté mushrooms lightly in butter. Stuff with liver pâté and bake (in a hot 400° F. oven about 10 minutes) *or* broil a few minutes *or* microwave (30 to 60 seconds on high) to heat through. Serve warm, garnished with a sprig of parsley.

Sausage-Stuffed Mushrooms

This is a good recipe for leftover sausage, because you don't need much to fill the mushrooms. Even the suggestion of the flavor will enhance these appetizers.

Large mushrooms, suitable for stuffing
Butter or olive oil
Game sausage, cooked and crumbled
Bread crumbs

Romano cheese
Garlic powder
Freshly ground black pepper
Fresh parsley, chopped

Sausage-Stuffed Mushrooms (cont.)

Remove the stems from the mushrooms and coarsely chop them. Wipe the mushroom caps with a damp paper towel to clean them. Sauté stems in butter or olive oil and add the crumbled sausage; add some bread crumbs and cheese, sprinkle with garlic powder and black pepper and blend in the chopped parsley. You should have a thick mixture which should adhere like a stuffing. Stuff the mushrooms and bake them in a preheated 375° F. oven about 20 minutes.

Broiled Stuffed Mushrooms

An excellent garnish for venison filet mignon.

Large whole mushrooms
Butter
Minced onion
Bread crumbs
Minced parsley
Celery, finely diced
Garlic powder
Freshly ground black pepper
Salt if desired

Remove the stems from large whole mushrooms. Sauté the chopped stems in butter and combine with minced onion, dry bread crumbs, minced parsley, finely diced celery, garlic powder, salt and pepper. Dip caps in melted butter to coat thoroughly, stuff and broil 5 to 8 minutes.

Rouennaise

Bird livers
Butter
Pinch thyme
Dried onion flakes (optional)
Salt and pepper
Sherry or brandy
Croutons

Brown bird livers in butter for 2 or 3 minutes, season with thyme and salt and pepper, add a dash of sherry or brandy and cook an additional 1 to 2 minutes. Mash to a smooth paste and spread on croutons.

There is no reason not to enjoy this delicacy in camp. Sauté the bird livers gently in butter or margarine with a pinch of seasoning and perhaps a whiff of dried onion flakes. Do it over a slow part of the fire while the birds are broiling and the toast is browning. Put one whole liver on each piece of crisp toast, divide up the butter and drippings from the bird on the toast slices. It takes only a few minutes for the livers to be lightly browned, yet tender enough to be mashed to a paste on the toast.

Game-Filled Turnovers or Pasties

See page 210. Make in miniature and serve hot.

Tongue Rolls

Game tongue
Cream cheese
Chives *or* horseradish *or* mustard

Slice deer, moose or elk tongue very thin. Spread with cream cheese which has been beaten with one of the following: chives, horseradish or mustard to taste. Roll up and chill. Cut each roll into 2 or 3 pieces, depending on the size of the tongue slices. Serve on cocktail picks.

GAME PÂTÉS

These are all more or less interchangeable and will vary in flavor according to the game used. I have listed several to show how practically identical results may be obtained by different methods.

Game Bird Pâté

Game birds, cooked
Bird livers, giblets
Butter, softened
Freshly ground black pepper
Salt if desired
Mace *or* ginger
Clarified butter

Remove the skin of cooked game birds and bone. Grind the meat twice, using fine blade of food chopper. Leftover bird livers and giblets may be included. In the proportion of ½ pound fowl to ¼ pound butter, work the two to a smooth paste. Season to taste with salt and pepper, mace or ginger. Pack firmly in a small casserole and place in a slow oven to heat through. Press down again after it is heated, cover with clarified butter and chill.

Liver Paste

½ pound leftover sautéed liver
1 tablespoon butter
1 tablespoon onion juice
1 teaspoon celery salt
Dash cayenne
2 tablespoons lemon juice
Bit of prepared mustard, if desired

Grind the liver twice, using the fine blade of a food chopper. Work in butter and seasonings until it is a smooth paste. Pack in small jars and use as a spread for canapés. See also Pâté In Aspic.

Pâté in Aspic

1 tablespoon unflavored gelatine
¹/₄ cup cold water
1 10¹/₂-ounce can beef consommé,
    undiluted
1 tablespoon Worcestershire Sauce
Liver Paste (*see* preceding recipe)

Aspic. Soften the gelatine in cold water for 5 minutes, dissolve in hot consommé and add Worcestershire Sauce. Rinse one fancy 3 to 4 cup mold (or several individual ones) with cold water and drain. Pour in a thin layer of aspic and let it get sticky and almost set. Set the remaining aspic aside where it will not gel.

Pâté. Prepare Liver Paste as described previously. Shape into a ball slightly smaller than the mold you are using and firm up by setting in the freezer for ¹/₂ hour. Place the pâté on the sticky layer of gelatine and pour the remainder of the aspic around it. Chill for several hours or overnight. Unmold on a chilled plate, garnish with parsley or watercress, and serve with crackers or melba toast.

Partridge Pâté

This recipe from a very old Viennese cookbook uses, of course, the European grey partridge. An equivalent amount of quail or grouse may be substituted.

2 or 3 partridge
¹/₂ pound bacon
10 whole peppercorns
1 glass dry white wine
1 large hard roll
4 whole eggs
1 egg yolk
Salt and pepper to taste
1 goose liver, finely minced*
¹/₂ pound fresh mushrooms, finely
    minced

Clean and wipe birds, wrap in bacon and place in covered casserole with whole peppercorns. Simmer over very low heat or in a slow 275° F. oven until birds are tender. Add 1 glass white wine, simmer 10 additional minutes and allow birds to cool.

Remove meat from the bones, break hard roll into several pieces and place in casserole to soak up the juices. Put partridge, bacon and roll through fine blade of the food chopper twice. Beat eggs and extra yolk thoroughly, add meat and bacon mixture and season to taste with salt and freshly ground black pepper. Combine the chopped mushrooms and the liver. (Do not prepare mushrooms until you are ready

*Since goose liver is not readily available here, you may substitute 6 to 8 chicken livers plus 2 to 3 tablespoons melted butter.

Partridge Pâté (cont.)

to use them, as they will darken.)

Butter a mold liberally, pack in a layer of partridge, then some of the mushroom/liver mixture, and so on, ending with a layer of the partridge mixture. Cover mold with a layer of waxed paper and then one of heavy foil, tie securely and set on a rack in a kettle of boiling water. Cover kettle and steam 1 to 1½ hours.

Serve cold with thinly sliced hot buttered toast or watercress sandwiches.

Rabbit in Aspic—Viennese Style

This recipe was translated from a very old Viennese cookbook. It's strictly party fare, but well worth the effort. It would be most attractive served as an appetizer or for a cold buffet.

1 whole saddle of young hare or plump rabbit
Larding pork, cut into long thin strips
Clear aspic

Remove the entire saddle from a cleaned rabbit or hare and set aside while you prepare the aspic. Disjoint the remainder of the rabbit and place in a covered kettle. Cover rabbit with water and add *per quart*:

1 tablespoon salt
1 carrot
1 stalk celery, including the leaves
1 medium onion
Pinch of thyme
2 to 3 whole peppercorns

Cover and simmer over low heat. When the rabbit is tender, remove from the bones and reserve for future use. If stock is not strong enough at this point, return the bones to the kettle and reduce by boiling—or you may add 1 or 2 chicken bouillon cubes. Strain and clarify as directed in Chapter 11. There should be at least 3½ cups clarified stock.

For the aspic:
2 tablespoons unflavored gelatine
½ cup cold stock
1 cup hot stock
Saffron
1 tablespoon lemon juice

Soften the gelatine in the cold stock, then dissolve completely in the hot stock. Add a liberal pinch of saffron and the lemon juice, then stir until the saffron has released all of its color to the liquid. Strain through a fine sieve to remove saffron particles and combine with the remaining stock. Select a flat platter long enough to hold the saddle, rinse the platter in cold water and spoon a layer of aspic onto the platter and chill. Set the remaining aspic aside where it will not set.

Lard the saddle liberally with strips of pork fat in an attractive pattern, drawing the strips through the length of the saddle with a larding needle. Place in baking pan, tent with greaseproof paper or aluminum foil and roast at 350° F. to 375° F., basting frequently until tender but still juicy. This will take about an hour, but be sure that the larding pork is still visible and has not all cooked out. Remove from the oven and cool. When saddle is cold, remove the filets from the ribs carefully with a thin sharp knife. Place the two filets on the layer of aspic in such a way that the saddle appears to be whole. Spoon over it the remainder of the aspic which should by now have the consistency of unbeaten egg white. Set in the refrigerator to jell completely. It must appear as if the meat is covered with thick yellow glass. Garnish with watercress, freshly grated horseradish and red radishes.

Rabbit Paste (Hasenpastete)

½ pound leftover rabbit meat
1 tablespoon butter
2 teaspoons onion, minced
2 whole eggs plus 1 egg white, beaten well
⅓ cup dry bread crumbs
Salt and pepper to taste
Rabbit stock

Put rabbit meat through food chopper twice, using fine blade. Combine with other ingredients, adding only enough stock to moisten it—it should not be too liquid. Butter a small mold liberally, sprinkle with fine dry crumbs and fill with rabbit mixture. Cover mold with waxed paper and foil, tie securely and steam for 1 hour. Turn out of mold and chill. Serve with thinly sliced buttered toast.

Terrine de Foie de Venaison

2 pounds uncooked venison liver
½ pound pork fat
¾ pound lean leftover venison roast
1 tablespoon brandy
Juice of a lemon
Generous grating of nutmeg
Generous pinch of thyme
Thin slices of fat pork back

Using the fine blade, put the liver, pork fat and venison through a food chopper twice. Add brandy, lemon juice and seasonings and work to a smooth paste. Line a terrine or earthenware dish with thin slices of fat pork back, then pack in the pâté mixture and cover with additional slices of pork back. Cover the terrine and set in a boiling water bath almost to the top of the mold. Bake 2 hours at 375° F. Drain off liquid fat, weight down and chill. Serve cold—or reheat, slice and serve with a zesty tomato sauce.

Venison Paste (Hirschpastete)

¹/₂ pound leftover venison
1 slice bread
¹/₄ pound butter
2 eggs, beaten
2 teaspoons onion, finely minced
Pinch thyme
1 tablespoon Madeira wine
Salt and pepper to taste

Grind the venison and bread together twice, using the fine blade of a food chopper. Work into a smooth paste with the butter, eggs and seasonings. Steam for 1 hour in a greased covered mold—then chill.

Or roll out puff paste, fill with pâté, fold over and seal. Bake at 400° F. for 15 minutes, lower heat to 300° F. and bake until puff paste is golden and crisp.

NON-GAME APPETIZERS

Braunschweiger Spread

Some of my guests have come to believe (erroneously) that all my meat dishes—including the appetizers—are prepared with game. They are surprised when I tell them this pâté, although a compulsive one (once you taste it, you have to have more), is not.

2 8-ounce packages prepared braunschweiger
1 double package dry green onion dip mix (.56 ounce)
1 teaspoon sugar plus a little water
6 ounces cream cheese
Garlic powder
Dash or two hot pepper sauce
Milk

In a small mixing bowl, combine the green onion dip with the sugar and enough water to moisten. Add the braunschweiger and mush it all together. If you have a food processor, it's just as easy to place it all in there and blend it lightly. Chill the mixture until it can hold its shape and pat it into a ball on a small serving plate.

Soften the cream cheese, season with a little garlic powder and hot pepper sauce (don't use too much) and make a paste, blending in a teaspoon or two of milk. When it is creamy, smear it over the braunschweiger ball and garnish with a sprig of parsley or dill. I like to make this the day before I am to serve it; the flavors have a chance to meld and, incidentally, this gets better as it reaches room temperature again.

Cheese-Stuffed Pecans

About ¹/₂ pound large salted pecan halves
¹/₄ cup blue cheese
¹/₄ cup cream cheese

Combine the two cheeses thoroughly at room temperature. Place a small amount between pecan halves and press together. Chill before serving.

Cheese Mousse

1 tablespoon unflavored gelatine
1/4 cup cold water
1/2 cup Roquefort cheese
1/3 cup Camembert cheese
1 egg, separated
1 tablespoon sherry
Dash Worcestershire Sauce
3 tablespoons parsley, chopped
1/2 cup whipping cream

Soften gelatine in cold water for 5 minutes; set in pan of hot water and dissolve completely or use your microwave—30 to 60 seconds on high, using a glass or plastic bowl. In a small mixing bowl, cream the two cheeses together, beating until well blended. Beat in egg yolk, sherry and Worcestershire Sauce; add dissolved gelatine and blend well. If you have a food processor, "cream" the cheeses first, then add other ingredients through feed tube, one at a time. Beat egg white until stiff and fold into cheese mixture, along with chopped parsley. Whip cream in chilled bowl, fold into mixture and spoon into a wet 2-cup mold.

Chill until firm, several hours. Unmold onto chilled plate, garnish with pimiento and parsley.

Cheese-Olive Puffs

1 cup flour
1/2 teaspoon salt
1/2 teaspoon dry mustard
Dash of cayenne
1/4 pound butter, softened
2 cups grated sharp cheddar cheese
Small stuffed green olives, well drained
Paprika

Sift dry ingredients together. Work softened butter and cheese together and combine with dry ingredients. Mix thoroughly and wrap a spoon of the cheese mixture around each olive, covering the olive completely. Chill until firm. Just before serving, sprinkle each puff with paprika, and bake on ungreased baking sheet for 15 minutes at 400° F. Depending on the size of the olives, this will make 40 to 50 puffs.

Chick Pea Spread

2 cups chick peas, cooked and drained
3 to 4 cloves garlic, chopped
3 to 4 tablespoons prepared sesame
**   paste**
Juice of 1 or 2 fresh lemons,
**   depending on size**
1/4 cup olive oil or more
Freshly ground black pepper

I've made this several times now and I find that sometimes I like it more lemony and sometimes more garlicky, so I leave the exact proportions up to you.

In a food processor or blender, combine all the ingredients and adjust to taste. You should have a nice, thick paste when finished. Chill and serve with crackers or vegetable sticks.

Churag

This recipe was given to me by a neighbor many years ago. I believe it is Armenian in origin, but can't be positive. At any rate, the flavor is unique and delicious.

3 cups flour, sifted
3 teaspoons baking powder
3 tablespoons sugar
1/2 teaspoon salt
1 teaspoon anise seed, crushed
1 teaspoon sesame seed
1/2 cup milk
1/4 pound butter
1 egg plus 1 egg yolk

Sift the dry ingredients together, add the anise and sesame seeds. Scald the milk, then add butter and stir until butter is melted. Beat the egg and yolk with a fork and combine with the milk. Add liquid to the dry ingredients and work the resulting dough until thoroughly blended. Roll a small amount of the dough at a time into a long roll, without using any extra flour. Cut into 2-inch pieces, shape into crescents and place on buttered baking sheet. Brush with beaten egg and bake at 400° F. for 15 to 20 minutes, or until delicately browned.

Creamy Salmon Mousse

1 1/2 cups salmon, cooked (poached in white wine is best)
1 1/2 tablespoons unflavored gelatine
1/2 cup cold water
1/4 cup prepared mayonnaise
1/4 cup heavy cream
Dried tarragon
Fresh lemon juice
Freshly ground black pepper
a.f.g. cayenne pepper

In a glass measuring cup or small bowl, sprinkle the gelatine into the cold water and let it soak for five minutes. Dissolve over hot water, or put it in your microwave for 30 to 60 seconds on high.

Place the salmon in a blender or food processor and process until pasty. Add to it the dissolved gelatine, the mayonnaise, the heavy cream which you have whipped, and the remaining seasonings to taste. Process briefly until well-blended, smooth and creamy. Pour into a 3-cup oiled mold and chill for at least 4 hours. Unmold and serve with your favorite crackers.

Liptauer

This Viennese cheese spread has as many variations as the cooks who make it. With the exception of the butter and cheese, the other ingredients were added "to taste" and that's the way I've always made it. The taste-testing has been one of my husband's favorite chores; as a matter of fact, quite a bit of it disappears before he's finished with the "testing." However, we have standardized the recipe in order to share it with you.

1 8-ounce package cream cheese
¹/₂ pound butter
¹/₂ teaspoon salt
2 teaspoons dried minced onion
1¹/₂ teaspoons paprika
2 teaspoons caraway seeds
1 teaspoon prepared mustard
1 tablespoon capers, chopped
1 teaspoon anchovy paste
¹/₄ teaspoon freshly ground black
    pepper

Let butter and cream cheese soften and cream them together. Add other ingredients and beat until fluffy and well blended. If you have a food processor, no need to soften the butter and cheese; simply process them together and add the remaining ingredients through the feed tube. Serve at room temperature on thin rye bread or crackers. It is best to make this at least an hour ahead of time, so the flavors will have a chance to mellow and blend.

Although I am seldom able to rescue enough to freeze for future use, this spread may be frozen in small containers. It should be beaten again after thawing to restore the proper texture.

Miniature Cheese Puffs

¹/₂ cup flour
¹/₂ teaspoon salt
Pinch dry mustard
Pinch cayenne
¹/₄ cup butter
¹/₂ cup boiling water
²/₃ cup grated cheddar cheese
2 eggs

Sift flour, salt, mustard and cayenne together. Bring butter and water to a vigorous boil in a saucepan. Dump in flour all at once and beat with wooden spoon until mixture becomes a smooth ball and leaves the side of the pan. Remove from heat, add cheese and beat again until smooth. Add eggs, one at a time, beating vigorously after each addition until the mixture is smooth again. Drop small amounts from the tip of a spoon onto a lightly greased baking sheet. Bake at 400° F. 10 to 15 minutes until golden. Serve hot. (Dough may be wrapped in waxed paper and stored overnight in refrigerator.)

Pineapple-Cheese-Nut Ball

1 8-ounce package cream cheese
¹/₄ cup green pepper, finely chopped
¹/₂ cup crushed pineapple, drained
1 cup walnuts, finely chopped
Dash or two hot pepper sauce

In a small mixing bowl or food processor, combine all the ingredients, reserving ¹/₂ cup chopped walnuts for garnish. Chill the cream cheese mixture until it will hold its shape and mold into a ball. Pat remaining nuts all over.

Roquefort Mousse

2 tablespoons unflavored gelatine
1/2 cup cold dry white wine
1 cup (8 ounces) Roquefort or blue
    cheese
1/2 cup prepared mayonnaise
1/2 cup sour cream
1/2 cup onions, coarsely chopped
2 tablespoons fresh lemon juice
1/2 teaspoon Worcestershire Sauce
Hot pepper sauce (a dash or two)
1 cup heavy cream, whipped

In a glass measuring cup or small bowl, sprinkle the gelatine into the cold wine and let it soak for 5 minutes. Dissolve over hot water, or in your microwave for 30 to 60 seconds on high.

In a blender or food processor, combine the remaining ingredients, except the heavy cream, and add the dissolved gelatine; process until well-blended and smooth. Pour into a metal bowl and chill until it begins to "set." Whip the cream and with a wire whisk fold it into the gelatine mixture. Wet with cold water and shake a 6-cup mold and immediately pour the mousse into it. Chill at least 4 hours, or preferably overnight.

Unmold and serve with apple slices or your favorite crackers.

Sardine Spread

1 3³/4-ounce can sardines, drained and
    chopped
1/4 cup butter
1 teaspoon prepared mustard
1 teaspoon fresh lemon juice
Minced onion, to taste

Cream butter; beat in other ingredients and season to taste with onion. May be used as a spread for crackers or toast rounds, or to fill miniature cream puffs.

Shrimp Butter

1 can baby shrimp
1/4 cup butter
1 teaspoon fresh lemon juice
1 teaspoon celery, diced
1 teaspoon green pepper, diced
Minced onion

Shrimp butter may be made the same way as the Sardine Spread (above); just omit the mustard and add 1 teaspoon each finely diced celery and finely diced green pepper.

Sesame Seed Cheese Pastry

Originally an improvisation in answer to my own question, "What to do with the rest of this pastry?" this has become part of the repertoire. It has always been well received, for all its simplicity.

Toasted sesame seeds
1 cup grated sharp cheddar cheese
¹/₂ recipe for plain pastry (using 1 cup flour)

Roll pastry quite thin, spread half the grated cheese on half the pastry. Fold the pastry over the cheese, roll out not quite as thin as the first time, spread the remaining cheese on half the dough, and fold over again. Roll out to about ¹/₄ inch in thickness, sprinkle liberally with sesame seeds and roll just enough to press the sesame seeds into the pastry. Cut into straws or small fancy shapes with cocktail cutters and bake on ungreased cookie sheets at 425° F. for 10 minutes.

They will puff up almost like a puff paste, and should be served hot from the oven. These can be made weeks ahead of time and stored in the freezer to be baked as needed. For variety, sprinkle the tops with Lawry's seasoned salt instead of the sesame seeds.

Smoked Oyster Dip

6 ounces cream cheese
1 7¹/₂-ounce can smoked oysters, drained
1 tablespoon parsley, chopped
2 shallots, minced
¹/₄ teaspoon garlic powder
¹/₄ teaspoon Lawry's seasoned salt
1 tablespoon fresh lemon juice
2 tablespoons sour cream

Combine all ingredients in a blender or food processor and process until well blended. Chill and serve with your favorite crackers.

Squid Minceur

This is a thoroughly delicious and unexpected treat, especially when served over homemade melba toast or dry toast points.

Squid tentacles, cleaned and washed (from 3 to 4 squid)
2 tablespoons butter
2 to 3 teaspoons garlic, minced
Freshly ground black pepper
1 teaspoon fresh parsley, chopped
A little fresh lemon juice
Bread crumbs

In a small skillet, lightly sauté the garlic in butter. Let stand while you mince the tentacles very finely. Add squid to skillet and sauté till it changes color and flesh is cooked. Sprinkle with black pepper and blend in parsley and lemon juice. Add enough bread crumbs so the mixture adheres and forms a paste. Serve warm.

Wild Mushroom Delights

If you can get your hands on some fresh wild mushrooms, this recipe is an experience. If not, you could use dried ones, but unfortunately the flavor is not quite as exotic.

Wild mushrooms
Yellow onions
Mayonnaise
Freshly ground black pepper
Thin slices dry white toast
Yellow American *or* **Swiss cheese**

In a skillet, sauté in butter equal parts of finely chopped mushrooms and yellow onions. Blend in a little prepared mayonnaise and season with freshly ground black pepper. Take thin slices of dry white toast and cut them into squares; arrange on a baking sheet. Place a little mushroom/onion mixture on each square and top with a small square of yellow American or Swiss cheese. Run under the broiler a few seconds until the cheese starts to puff and brown; serve immediately.

CHAPTER 14
VEGETABLES AND HERBS

Many cooks of yesteryear cooked vegetables to death and then poured all the goodness down the drain. Today, with frozen vegetables so easily prepared, vegetables get even less attention from the average cook. Just throw them in a pot of water or the microwave and cook as directed on the package. I will admit, though, that we do have a better selection of packaged vegetables to choose from nowadays, including mixed vegetables with various international sauces.

My preference, however, is still for fresh vegetables, prepared lovingly and cooked lightly. Especially when you are creating a gala game dinner, fresh, properly cooked, attractively served vegetables can add an extra note of festivity. And, let's face it, even if your hunter husband is a meat 'n potatoes man, we all know that vegetables are part of a well-balanced diet and vital to good health.

To my mind, several basic rules of thumb should be followed when preparing vegetables:

—For maximum flavor, cook gently for a minimum amount of time in a minimum quantity of liquid; steam, if possible. Vegetables should be crisp tender, not soggy. This is where I think the microwave excels—vegetables can be cooked with almost *no* liquid and in a jiffy they are done.

—Serve at once for maximum color and vitamin content.

—Season subtly, but try a variety of "enhancers" besides salt and pepper, such as fresh herbs. *See* the section at the end of this chapter.

—Serve attractively. Sometimes a combination of vegetables cooked or served together will lift the vegetables out of the ordinary. Select your combinations with eye as well as flavor appeal. Colorful combinations and simple garnishes add so much.

VEGETABLES

Asparagus

The first sign of Spring and always most welcome in our house, asparagus deserves to stand alone.

Stand the cleaned stalks in a tall deep kettle, with only enough boiling salted water to cover the lower third of the stalks. Eight to 10 minutes should be sufficient to steam the tops and have the tougher bases tender. Lemon butter, buttered crumbs, or a sprinkling of Romano or Parmesan cheese over the butter is all that's necessary.

Beans—Green or Wax

Fresh or frozen, cook in a saucepan that has a tight-fitting lid. Pour in only enough water to cover the bottom of the skillet, add a good chunk of butter, salt. Add vegetable, rapidly bring to a boil, then cook over low heat until vegetables are barely tender; they will steam this way rather than boil. Or use a steamer, and steam for about 5 to 10 minutes.

1. For flavor variety try a pinch of tarragon, a bit of minced onion and fresh snipped dill, a fresh grating of nutmeg or a few crumbled rosemary leaves.

2. Or dress with lemon butter to which you have added a few crushed fennel seeds.

3. With green beans, particularly, I like to cut equal amounts of celery and beans in diagonal strips and cook in a small amount of bouillon with butter and a pinch of thyme.

Beets

Boil in the usual manner, peel and slice or dice.

1. Serve hot with butter to which you have added 1/2 teaspoon chopped chives and 2 teaspoons chopped watercress.

2. For Harvard beets, substitute orange juice and grated rind plus 1 teaspoon lemon juice for the vinegar in your regular recipe.

3. Shred raw peeled beets, cook in a skillet with butter; add salt and pepper plus either a snippet of fresh dill or a pinch of allspice. Simmer covered for about 20 minutes.

Broccoli

If stems are particularly thick, split into several lengthwise pieces. Cook in tall kettle only half full of boiling water. Salt the last 5 minutes of cooking; 15 minutes should be the total cooking time.

Although traditionally served with lemon butter or Hollandaise Sauce, try one of the following for variation.

1. ¹/₂ cup mayonnaise blended with 1 tablespoon lemon juice and 1 tablespoon prepared horseradish.

2. 1 cup medium white sauce to which has been added ¹/₄ cup grated Romano or Parmesan cheese and a sprinkling of dried minced onion.

3. Sour cream with a bit of crumbled dried tarragon.

See also Stir-Fry Vegetables.

Brussel Sprouts

Soak 15 minutes in salt water to drive out any possible insects; drain and rinse in fresh water. Cook 8 to 10 minutes in small amount of salted water; drain.

1. Combine with an equal amount of cooked chestnuts in a generous amount of butter; simmer over low heat for several minutes.

2. Dress with lemon butter and fresh dill.

3. Combine with sautéed mushrooms and a sprinkling of caraway seeds.

4. Top with buttered crumbs with a dash of lemon juice.

Cabbage

Cut each head into eighths or shred coarsely. Steam in tightly covered pan in ¹/₄-inch bouillon with a lump of butter and a sprinkling of caraway seeds, plus freshly ground black pepper. Maximum cooking time is 5 to 8 minutes. For variation:

1. Steam with sliced scallions and diced green pepper.

2. Steam in small amount of salted water; drain and dress with sour cream and bits of crisp bacon, or a rich cream sauce and grated cheddar cheese.

3. *German Style.* Fry 6 to 8 slices bacon in a skillet; remove, break into small pieces and return to pan; add 1 to 2 tablespoons apple cider vinegar (or herbed vinegar, such as tarragon) and ¹/₄ cup diced onion. Serve warm over steamed cabbage wedges.

Red Cabbage with Apple

1 head red cabbage, shredded coarsely
3 tart apples, peeled and chopped
½ cup brown sugar, firmly packed
2 allspice berries and 3 whole cloves
    tied together in cheesecloth
3 to 4 tablespoons butter
3 to 4 tablespoons vinegar

Cover first 5 ingredients with boiling, salted water and cook, loosely covered, 8 to 10 minutes, until just barely tender. Drain and toss with equal amounts of butter and vinegar.

For variation, follow same recipe as above, but cook tightly covered in 1½ cups red wine instead of water.

Carrots

1. Cut carrot and celery into julienne strips (or cut both into diagonal slices); steam in covered saucepan with butter and bouillon, salt and pepper, plus a pinch of either marjoram or fennel.

2. Bake small whole carrots and onions (cut an x in each end of onions) at 350° F. for about an hour in covered baking dish with a liberal amount of butter and a fresh grating of nutmeg.

3. Shred enough raw carrots to yield 4 cups. Place in buttered casserole, sprinkle with ½ cup sherry or white wine, add a dash of salt and nutmeg and dot with butter. Cover and bake at 350° F. for ½ hour.

Carrot Ring

4 cups carrots, sliced
2 tablespoons butter
Bouillon to cover
1 teaspoon onion, minced
Salt and pepper
3 eggs, well beaten

Cook carrots in butter with bouillon to cover until soft enough to mash. Put through ricer, season to taste, and add well-beaten eggs. Pour into well-buttered 6 cup ring mold; set in a pan of hot water and bake at 350° F. for 1 hour. Unmold on heated plate and fill center with fresh peas and scallions or green beans and water chestnuts.

Cauliflower

1. Steam whole over boiling water 25 to 30 minutes; drain. Serve as the center of attraction on a heated plate, with tiny whole carrots, green beans, cooked celery strips arranged in alternate groups around it. Lemon butter with a dash of paprika is all that is needed here.

Cauliflower (cont.)

2. Dress with buttered crumbs and a pinch of basil.

3. Top with cheese sauce, white mustard sauce or white sauce to which you have stirred in 2 teaspoons curry powder.

4. Garnish with toasted almonds sautéed in browned butter.

Celery

1. Excellent companion for other vegetables. Cook with peas, green beans, brussel sprouts, carrots, fresh lima beans.

2. Capable of standing alone in the finest company, especially when cooked in butter with a small amount of bouillon, salt and pepper and a bit of onion, until tender crisp.

3. Toss cooked celery with a light cream sauce and snipped parsley or chives.

Chestnuts

One pound provides 2 cups shelled nut meats and one of the most appropriate vegetables to accompany game.

To shell. Gash each chestnut with an X, using a sharp knife and place in boiling water for 15 minutes, then remove shell and inner brown skin. It is wise to do only a portion of the chestnuts at one time. If you prefer, you may bake the gashed nuts in a 450° F. oven for 20 minutes and then shell. *Or* if you have a microwave oven, microwave a few for a minute or two on high.

To cook. Cover shelled meats with boiling salted water and simmer until tender, about 15 to 20 minutes; drain; or steam. Serve with brussel sprouts as suggested before.

Or put through a ricer; beat fluffy with a bit of butter and cream, season to taste with salt and pepper; or use your food processor or blender to purée, then proceed as before. Reheat if necessary in a double boiler.

Corn

Fresh or frozen, cook only until milk has set, 5 to 6 minutes. Our favorite indoor method of cooking *corn-on-the-cob* is to place a layer of husks in the bottom of a large skillet, add only enough water to cover the bottom, place the ears on the husks and cover with another layer of husks. Cover tightly and steam. Serve with lots of butter, plain, or with snipped chives.

Frozen corn can be cooked briefly by the skillet method described above,

Corn (cont.)

adding a bit of chopped onion and green pepper or pimiento for color.

Combine cooked **corn niblets** with a savory cream sauce, fill small parboiled green peppers and heat briefly in the oven. Hollow out medium-sized ripe tomatoes; drain thoroughly. Fill with creamed corn and bake in a hot 400° F. oven for 15 minutes.

Corn Fritters, good with venison sausage patties and syrup for breakfast or to accompany a simple supper, can be whipped up real easy (*see* page 253).

Cucumbers

Delicate and delicious as a cooked vegetable. Peel, if young, cut into ½-inch slices; if quite mature, remove seeds and cut into large dice. Steam in covered skillet in small amount of water with butter, salt and pepper. To gild the lily, add heavy cream, a sprinkling of freshly grated nutmeg and heat thoroughly, but do not allow cream to boil.

Italian Vegetable Mélange

Olive oil
3 to 4 whole cloves garlic
**Young zucchini, unpared, scrubbed
    and thinly sliced**
**Frying peppers, sliced lengthwise,
    seeds removed**
Onion, sliced
Garlic powder
Freshly ground black pepper
**2 to 3 leaves fresh basil or ¼ teaspoon
    dried basil**
Oregano (optional)
**Romano cheese (preferably Locatelli or
    Pecorino), freshly grated**

Heat olive oil in a large skillet; in it brown garlic cloves, then remove. Sauté vegetables over low heat, moving about with wooden or slotted spoon. Add a whiff of garlic powder, a sprinkling of fresh pepper, the basil and oregano, if desired; return garlic to pan. Cover and steam for a few minutes until crisp tender. Stir in freshly grated cheese and heat through.

A variation on this would be to add peeled and coarsely chopped eggplant and a chopped fresh tomato or two.

Leeks

The delicate onion flavor of leeks is a rare treat. When I do find them in the market, I usually buy a large quantity and freeze them for later use, since they combine well with other vegetables.

Fresh leeks should be washed very well, as leaves are inclined to be full of grit and sand. Cut off root end and all but a few inches of green leaves. Boil 15 minutes in salted water, drain and serve

Leeks (cont.)

with lemon butter or a rich cream sauce.

Carrots and frozen leeks: In an 8-inch skillet, heat ¹/₂ cup bouillon and 1 tablespoon butter. Add 4 or 5 whole baby carrots per serving or the equivalent in mature carrots, sliced diagonally. Place frozen leeks on top of carrots, either whole or sliced diagonally to conform with carrots. Cover tightly and simmer over low heat until vegetables are just tender. Season with salt and pepper.

Mushrooms

The world of mushrooms is a remarkable one. These little fungi (and literally millions of them cover the Earth at any one time) come in all sizes, shapes, colors and flavors. Some are edible; some are not. Those that are edible—cultivated or wild—are treasured by connoisseurs everywhere, and much care should be given to their preparation and serving.

If you are among those cooks who wash, scrub and/or peel mushrooms, STOP. You are water-logging them and removing much of their flavor and goodness. Most of the mushrooms you will ever purchase at a green grocer or supermarket are cultivated ones, which are grown under quite sterile conditions. They require almost no, or very little, "cleaning." If they do, merely take a damp paper towel and gently wipe off any dirt.

If you buy fresh mushrooms under circumstances where you can select what you want (in other words, they're not prepackaged), choose only ones whose gills have not opened; if you can see the gills as you turn the mushroom cap over, it's past its prime. Also, handle mushrooms as sparingly as possible and only by the stem; the oils in your fingers will tend to darken them with even light touching. Do not store fresh mushrooms in plastic bags; place them in paper bags, white ones preferably, then chill them in the refrigerator. The moisture that beads in plastic bags will shorten their shelf-life considerably.

One last point. Most mushrooms require sparse cooking, so add them last to stews, casseroles and gravies in order to retain their full flavor and shape.

Wild Mushrooms. Many varieties of wild mushrooms are perfectly edible, exotic-tasting and go particularly well with game. Other types are look-alikes and are perfectly fatal. If you are curious about a fungus that's staring at you while you crouch below an oak tree waiting for that wild turkey, DON'T PICK IT and DON'T TASTE IT. Wild mushrooms are delicious, but only if you live to tell about them.

The woods stalker may run into certain edible varieties during the year: morels in the spring; chanterelles, meadow mushrooms and puffballs in the summer; and certain boletes (also known as cèpes or porcini) and hen of the woods in the fall. If you are acquainted with someone who KNOWS mushrooms, by all means ask to tag along on the next mushroom hunt. It's an unforgettable experience. But, I repeat, don't experiment unless you're sure. Stick to the dried varieties, which are becoming more available.

Mushrooms (cont.)

Dried Mushrooms. Here we are on safe ground. Many food specialty stores carry a number of different kinds of dried fungi. Imported from countries such as Italy, France and Poland, you can find morels, cèpes and chanterelles, and from China and Japan you will see black mushrooms, oyster mushrooms and perhaps a few others, depending on where you shop. These dried mushrooms should be reconstituted by soaking them in hot water for about 15 to 20 minutes, rarely longer. Any hard parts, such as the stem, will probably remain hard no matter how long they soak; cut them off. Remove mushrooms from the liquid and use that in whatever dish you are going to prepare; it will add extra flavor to a gravy, stew or mushroom filling.

Here are a few mushroom recipes, in addition to those that appear in other chapters of this book.

French-Fried Mushrooms

Select large mushrooms that have not opened to expose the gills. Wipe with a damp cloth, trim stem end and slice in half lengthwise. Dip in any fritter batter, then in crumbs. Allow coating to dry for 20 minutes. Deep fry at 375° F. until golden; serve with lemon wedges.

Mushroom Pie

2 tablespoons butter
Vegetable oil
1 cup onion, chopped
1¹/₂ pounds fresh mushrooms, sliced
Freshly ground black pepper
2 teaspoons Worcestershire Sauce
¹/₂ pound Swiss cheese, grated
1 egg, beaten
1 9-inch pie shell, partially baked
Fresh grating of nutmeg
3 tomato slices

In a large skillet, melt butter plus a little vegetable oil and lightly sauté chopped onion. Add sliced mushrooms and cook for about 5 minutes, stirring occasionally. Season with black pepper and Worcestershire Sauce; drain and cool slightly. Blend in grated Swiss cheese and beaten egg. Pour into partially baked pie shell. Sprinkle on a fresh grating of nutmeg and arrange tomato slices in the center. Bake in 350° F. oven about 45 to 60 minutes.

Sautéed Mushrooms

Sauté in butter with freshly ground black pepper for 5 to 10 minutes, depending on whether they are sliced or whole. Chopped parsley, minced onion, a bit of lemon juice or sherry may enhance the flavor.

Onions

Cut an x in each end to prevent them from separating; boil in salted water or steam until tender.

1. Serve with a rich cream sauce, with curry, Romano or Parmesan cheese, nutmeg or sherry.

2. Sour cream with caraway seeds or dill would be pleasant variations.

3. Boil small onions until nearly tender, then glaze in a skillet with butter and a bit of sugar until golden.

4. Tiny whole white onions (or scallions) may be cooked with green vegetables for a pleasing color and flavor combination.

Peas

Cook peas in small amount of salted water with butter and one of following:

1. Pinch of basil, chervil, marjoram; celery and/or scallions are also good companions in the pot.

2. Serve fresh peas with cream and chopped mint.

3. Toss fresh buttered peas with mushrooms, water chestnuts or slivered almonds.

See also Stir-Fry Vegetables.

Potatoes

Despite the fact that everyone knows how much the potato is part of the American diet, this tuber is usually dealt with unjustly. More often than not, it is overcooked, waterlogged and a generally mushy mess. To profit from the generous amount of vitamin C and iron they afford, potatoes should be thoroughly scrubbed and dried, and left unpeeled, if at all possible.

Broiled Potatoes. You may cut them into thick slices, drizzle a little oil over them and broil them on a low rung in your oven, turning after the top side is golden brown. They need not be cooked for as long as most people believe they should be.

Campfire Potatoes. If you're at camp and you happen to have white potatoes, wash, dry, wrap them in foil and prick with a fork. To cook, simply place them in the hot coals of your fire.

Home Fries. Wash, dry and slice or cut into large chunks unpared potatoes. Add them to a heavy skillet in which you have heated some oil. Add chopped onion and garlic and season with freshly ground black pepper and a sprinkling of Lawry's seasoned salt.

Rice

We prefer rice to potatoes, especially with game. Naturally, brown and wild rice head the list, but regular white long-grain rice can be prepared in many ways that are most delicious.

If you've had difficulty fixing rice so that each kernel is separate and fluffy, try this method, which my Mother-in-law taught me. It lends itself to many variations and is really foolproof. One pound of raw rice (2½ cups) will yield 8 cups of cooked rice, so figure your proportions accordingly. Always allow a bit extra, as leftover rice can be used in literally a million ways.

Place desired amount of rice in flameproof casserole that has a cover. (Use long-grain rice, preferably.) Rinse the rice six times in hot water, then six times in cold water. Despite what has been said recently about it not being necessary to rinse rice, you will be amazed at how much excess starch is eliminated in this way.

Cover the rice with fresh cold water, about ½-inch over the top of the rice, add salt, bay leaf or any other herb that will blend with the remainder of your dinner, and a generous lump of butter. Place over high heat and bring to a boil, stirring constantly until the water is bubbling and the butter melted and blended through the liquid.

Cover and place in a preheated oven, the temperature of which may vary from 350° F. to 400° F., depending on what is required for the other foods in the oven. (Convenient, isn't it?) After 20 to 35 minutes, test a grain of rice by rolling it between your fingers; if it needs additional cooking and the water has all been absorbed, add a bit more, cover and test after another 10 minutes. When the rice is tender, remove from the oven, set at the back of the stove, covered. It will wait until everything else is ready. Fluff with a fork before serving.

Variations.

1. Use chicken or beef bouillon (depending on the meat or fowl being served) in place of water; add diced raw celery and minced onion, plus snipped parsley before placing in oven.

2. Brown washed and dried rice in generous amount of butter in flameproof casserole. Add sliced onion, curry powder (1½ to 2 teaspoons), a pinch of cardamon or allspice. Stir constantly over low heat so that rice does not scorch, but browns evenly. Cover with water or stock and proceed as in basic rice recipe.

3. Fork in blanched raisins and slivered almonds sautéed in butter to the above curried rice for another variation.

4. Add ½ to 1 teaspoon crumbled saffron to boiling water or bouillon in basic recipe or variation 1. Stir until well blended before placing in oven.

5. For especially attractive service, butter a ring mold or individual custard cups. Pack in the cooked rice, cover with foil and keep hot in oven or in pan of hot water until ready to serve. Invert on a heated platter, fill rice ring with any colorful vegetable, or surround individual molds with an assortment of vegetables for buffet service.

6. Add grated orange rind and 1 tablespoon orange juice concentrate to the basic recipe, using a pinch of thyme as the herb.

Rice (cont.)

Brown Rice. White rice is nice, but brown rice is better. It is higher in fiber and essential nutrients and, once you taste it, you'll know there's a difference. It has somewhat of a nutty flavor and the only thing you need to do to dress it up is to add butter and chopped parsley. It's also good as the basis for fried rice (*see* below).

Since brown rice requires longer cooking time, plan accordingly. To prepare, rinse 1 cup raw brown rice and add to 2¼ cups boiling water; cover and simmer for at least 45 minutes. This will yield 3 to 4 cups cooked rice.

Fried Brown Rice. Heat 2 tablespoons peanut oil in a wok or large skillet; lightly sauté 3 chopped scallions, 1 chopped large stalk celery, 2 chopped cloves garlic; add a combination of 1½ to 2 cups vegetables, sliced or whole, depending on what they are—peas, broccoli, zucchini, mushrooms—and sauté. Add 2 cups cooked, *cold* brown rice and heat through. Season with 2 tablespoons soy sauce and freshly ground black pepper. You can make a meal out of this by simply adding cooked, diced game or fowl.

Wild Rice. This is always the cook's treat when we are having a special game dinner. It is expensive compared to white or brown rice, but worth every penny extra in flavor. Nowadays you can purchase packages of wild rice with pre-mixed herbs, the results of which are delicious, but here is the basic recipe I've used for years.

Rinse the rice well in several changes of water and cook as for regular rice, adding a bit more liquid and butter. Wild rice takes at least 45 to 60 minutes to cook. Add herbs to the cooking liquid—which should be game stock, if possible—and/or a bit of minced onion. When tender and all liquid is absorbed, combine with sautéed mushrooms or slivered almonds and butter. Snip some parsley over the top of the serving dish for garnish.

Creamed Spinach

Try this one with moose or elk tongue.

1 10-ounce package frozen spinach, chopped
1 cup medium white sauce (*see* page 166)
Dried onion flakes
Fresh grating of nutmeg

About an hour before serving, set out a package of frozen chopped spinach so it will thaw. Prepare medium white sauce, add a pinch of dried onion flakes and a grating of nutmeg. Add the thawed spinach, stir over low heat until spinach is well blended with the sauce and heated through. Check the seasoning and serve. In this way, the spinach is not drowned in water or overcooked.

Squash

Baked acorn squash is excellent with game, as is whipped squash. This is a nice variation of the latter, for a special occasion.

2¹/₂ cups squash, cooked and pureed
2 tablespoons butter, softened
2 tablespoons onion, grated
Salt and pepper to taste
1 tablespoon light brown sugar
4 eggs

In a large mixing bowl, combine pureed squash with softened butter, onion, seasonings and sugar (you can use a food processor or blender).

Beat eggs thoroughly, fold into squash mixture. Pour into liberally buttered ring mold. Bake in a pan of hot water for 1 hour at 350° F. Invert on heated platter, fill ring with any green vegetable.

Stir-Fry Vegetables

The beauty of this dish is that it is quick and requires only what you have at your fingertips (or in your refrigerator). And you can make it as colorful as your imagination will allow.

2 tablespoons peanut oil
Onion, chopped
2 cloves garlic, chopped
Vegetables of your choosing
Freshly ground black pepper
Oyster sauce and/or soy sauce

In a wok or large skillet, heat peanut oil; lightly sauté chopped onion and garlic, then add any combination of vegetables you desire—peas, zucchini, cauliflower, carrots, broccoli, green and/or red pepper, bamboo shoots, water chestnuts, green beans, chinese cabbage—all cut relatively the same size and shape. Stir to heat and cook through. Add mushrooms last, if you wish. For seasoning, you may add black pepper, oyster sauce or soy sauce, or whatever you think may blend.

Tomatoes

Baked Tomatoes. For a colorful service on the meat platter, or as an addition on a vegetable platter for a buffet, bake tomatoes as suggested under Corn. They may also be filled with peas and tiny onions with a snippet of fresh dill.

Broiled Tomatoes. A nice touch with venison steaks or a roast, as long as the fruit is fresh. Wash and dry tomatoes; slice them in half lengthwise. Sprinkle on garlic powder, freshly ground black pepper, basil, oregano or rosemary and drizzle a little olive oil over all. Place on a flat sheet and broil about 3 minutes until tomatoes are soft, but still firm.

Sweet Potatoes

High in vitamin A content, sweet potatoes are good with most game and fowl.

Candied Sweet Potatoes with Orange. Good with roast saddle of boar. Cook unpared sweet potatoes until nearly tender. Drain and peel. Prepare the following syrup in a large skillet: 1 cup brown sugar, packed; 1/4 cup butter; 1/2 cup orange juice. Simmer until sugar is melted and syrup is bubbling. Add sliced sweet potatoes and thick slices of unpeeled seedless oranges. Cook over very low heat, turning the potatoes and orange slices occasionally until they are well glazed and completely cooked. Baste once in a while with the syrup.

Sweet Potato Mash. Steam peeled and cut-up potatoes about 20 minutes, till soft. Mash with a conventional masher or place in a food processor with 3 to 4 tablespoons light brown sugar, 2 tablespoons butter and 1/4 teaspoon lemon extract (*not* fresh lemon); mash or process until well blended. 3 medium sweet potatoes will yield about 4 cups mashed.

HERBS

Herbs are a fascinating natural phenomenon. You can purchase them fresh or dried, crumbled, crushed or ground. They contain no extra salt, sugar or preservatives and, regardless of what form they're in, it is incredible how a pinch of this or a leaf of that can change the whole character of a dish. For anyone who wants to cook game successfully, herbs are a must. Here is a list of herbs I keep on hand at all times:

bay leaf	dill	parsley (flat and curly)
basil	garlic	rosemary
caraway seeds	horseradish	sage
chervil	juniper berries	summer savory
chives	marjoram	tarragon
coriander	oregano	thyme

Notice that I didn't say whether I keep them fresh or dried. I am of the old school—one of those cooks who likes food really fresh—and herbs are no exception. Nothing has annoyed me more in my lifetime than shopping for fresh herbs (when I hadn't planned ahead and had them at home) and finding wilted, sick-looking parsley or dill in the produce rack that supposedly arrived "fresh" on the morning truck run. Well, no more of that for me. I grow my own—and you should, too. It's so easy, and once you experience the difference between really fresh, "grocer fresh" and dried, you'll always prefer home-grown.

Most of the herbs listed above (except juniper berries) can easily be grown in a small plot of "kitchen garden" space among the marigolds (which, interestingly, can also be used in cooking for color), or in pots. Most herbs thrive in well-drained, nearly dry, sandy soil in full sun. Bay leaf, horseradish, marjoram, oregano, rosemary and tarragon are perennials that should come up every year, depending on the weather conditions; the others are easily sown (or transplanted) each year. Such herbs as parsley, for example, can be brought into the house in pots in the fall to be grown on a window sill all winter long. Not only will it enhance those hearty winter soups and stews, but it will add a bright spot of green to those long, dreary days.

Another reason to grow your own herbs is that they freeze extremely well. In fact, they taste virtually the same as fresh. So why buy dried, when fresh is best? Pick the leaves or sprigs before the plants "go to seed," that is, before the fall flowers and seed pods mature. The leaves are at their most aromatic at this point. Then gently wash them, being careful not to bruise any leaves (with basil this is especially important), shake them dry and place them in small freezer bags. Label with the contents and date, and remove whatever you need when the culinary occasion calls for it. Herbs will keep a long time this way (I've used chives and basil after being frozen for two years and they tasted perfectly fine; one year is a better limit, though). Bear in mind, though, that most herbs should be used once the plants are mature; don't wait until the fall to sample their flavors—pick them "along the way."

The only herbs I don't grow myself are garlic and juniper berries, which I purchase already dried. They keep just fine this way (besides, garlic requires drying even if you do grow it fresh). The only herb I garden, but don't freeze, is horseradish. This I wash, grate and store in a jar of vinegar in the refrigerator. You've never tasted more pungent horseradish than this.

So if you're looking for a new gastronomic experience, and have not fully experimented with herbs, do. They will add immeasurably to your game cooking—and your green thumb.

CHAPTER 15

BREADS AND OTHER FAVORITES

Nothing is more heart-warming than the aroma of freshly baked bread. And nothing is more soul-satisfying than to make it yourself—whether it's a simple type toasted over a campfire or a more complex one baked in your kitchen on a cold wintry day.

A good honest loaf of bread is not difficult to make and is infinitely superior to some found on grocery shelves. It seems more appropriate, too, to grace a game dinner with the kinds of breads our ancestors made.

The earliest breads consisted of nothing more than pulverized grain, salt and water, baked in flat cakes on a hot stone or griddle. This unleavened bread is still being made today in many parts of the world: in Mexico, the tortilla; in India, the chapati; in Scotland, the oat cake or bannock. In the U.S., the New England Jonny Cake had its origin as the Journey Cake, a simple bread of ground cornmeal and salt that the early traveler could do up as needed by adding water and baking over a fire in the wilderness.

With all the commercially prepared mixes available today, you can produce a bewildering array of breads and cakes by adding milk or water and following the directions on the box. However, the hunter or fisherman who is traveling in the wilds with all his supplies in a pack has no space or need for such things. With a few simple ingredients, he can satisfy his hunger and also his desire for variety in breadstuffs.

Very few men will want to take the time to prepare yeast breads when hunting and fishing are their primary reasons for being in camp. So let's start with the quick breads and see what can be achieved in the time it takes to get a fire going and the kettle boiling.

CAMP "QUICK" BREADS

 Bannock

Bannock is an unleavened cake of barley or oat meal, mixed to a stiff dough with water or milk, patted out less than an inch thick and baked on the hearth or on a griddle in much the same way as Journey Cake. Since it may be difficult to find stone ground oat or barley meal, I have found the following combination yields equally flavorful results.

$^1/_2$ cup whole wheat flour
$^1/_2$ cup quick-cooking oatmeal
$^1/_2$ teaspoon salt
$^1/_2$ cup milk or water

Combine the flour, cereal and salt and stir until they are well mixed. Add the liquid to form a stiff dough. Pat out into flat cakes about $^1/_2$- to $^3/_4$-inch thick.

Bake on lightly greased griddle or frying pan over a slow fire until brown on one side. Turn over and brown the other side. If you're really traveling light, you could bake the cakes on a hot rock or twist the dough around a peeled birch stick and bake over the coals. Use a splinter to be sure they're cooked through.

 Biscuits

There are so many things that can be made with a basic mix that it would be a wise idea to make up a large batch at home, so you won't have to spend so much time over culinary chores when you'd rather be hunting or fishing. I used to prepare this mix with white flour only, but nowadays whole wheat and graham flours can easily be found in local health food stores, often in better supermarkets. This mix is much more nutritious and has a delicious flavor, too. It keeps well in a covered container or heavy-duty plastic bag. The following proportions will make about 20 cups of mix. (If you want to use all white flour, just decrease the salt to 4 teaspoons.)

Basic Biscuit Mix:
8 cups unbleached all-purpose flour
8 cups whole wheat or graham flour
5 teaspoons salt
$^1/_2$ cup baking powder
3 cups vegetable shortening
2 cups dry milk powder

Sift dry ingredients together several times or mix very well with a spoon to be sure the baking powder and salt are evenly distributed. Cut in the shortening with two knives or a pastry blender until the mix looks like coarse cornmeal.

When you are ready to use the mix, spoon it lightly into your measuring cup—don't pack it down.
To make biscuits, keep these proportions in mind:

1 cup biscuit mix + $^1/_3$ cup water = 4 medium biscuits

Spoon biscuit mix into a bowl, add water and stir until the dough follows the fork around the bowl. Pat out with your floured hand on a clean surface about 1-inch thick. This amount will make 4 medium-size biscuits for a hungry man, so make up your dough accordingly. With a knife, divide into 4 portions per cup of mix used. Shape with your hands into round biscuits. There is enough shortening in this recipe that you need not grease the pan in which they are baked. Bake in a hot reflector oven 12 to 15 minutes.

Flavor variations.

1. Add ¼ cup grated cheese to each cup of biscuit mix, blend well with dry ingredients before adding water.

2. Add ½ teaspoon of parsley flakes, plus ½ teaspoon of one of the following: thyme, marjoram or oregano to dry mix.

3. For breakfast or dessert: pat or roll the dough out to ¼-inch thickness on a floured surface, cut 3-inch squares, put a spoon of jelly or jam in the middle of each square and then fold over into a triangle, pressing the edges together firmly.

4. Sweet rolls for breakfast: roll dough into an oblong ¼-inch thick, spread with butter and sprinkle with brown sugar and raisins. Roll up from the long side of the oblong, cut 1-inch slices and place close together in a greased tin. Bake in the reflector oven the same length of time, but watch a bit more closely because of the sugar.

5. For lunch on the run: bake extra biscuits, either plain or with herbs, split and fill with cheese and crisp bacon. Wrap in foil, reheat beside your lunchtime tea fire.

For other recipes using biscuit mix, *see* Camp Coffee Cake, Dessert Pancakes, Dumplings for Stew and Viennese Peas.

 ## Cornmeal Dumplings

This Roumanian recipe is the "plan-ahead" type. You might start this over the embers of your supper fire one evening, and then it's ready for last-minute frying the next.

1 cup cornmeal
4 cups cold water
1½ teaspoons salt
1 cup sharp cheese, grated
Cayenne or regular pepper

Combine cornmeal, water and salt and stir until smooth. Cook in double boiler or over a low fire on direct heat until very thick. Stir it once in a while as you're eating your supper, so it doesn't stick to the bottom of the pan. When the mush is thick, stir in the grated cheese and season highly with pepper. Spread out on a plate rinsed in cold water.

When the dough is cool enough to handle without burning your fingers, roll pieces of the dough into small balls and set aside in a cool place until ready to use the next day. Or rinse a loaf pan in cold water and pour the dough into that. When ready to use, slice the loaf. Brown in hot butter or drippings the next day and enjoy with kidney stew.

If you omit the cheese and pepper, and pour the plain mush into a loaf pan, you could have fried mush with syrup to go with the bacon the next morning.

Corn Muffins or Sticks

In camp, skillet corn bread goes mighty well with a big kettle of Brunswick stew. At home, you might like to be just a bit more fancy by using a corn stick pan that turns out little "ears" of corn bread.

3 slices of bacon, diced and fried until crisp, then drained
1 cup cornmeal
3/4 cup flour
4 teaspoons baking powder
1/2 teaspoon salt
1 tablespoon sugar
1 egg
1 cup milk
4 tablespoons drippings from bacon

Grease a cast iron corn stick pan and preheat it in a 400° F. oven.

Sift the dry ingredients together, beat the egg with the milk and the drippings. Add the liquid and the crisp bacon crumbles to the dry ingredients and stir just until blended. Spoon into preheated pan, filling each indentation 2/3 full. Bake at 400° F. for 20 to 25 minutes. If using a regular muffin tin, it is not necessary to preheat it.

 ## Journey Cakes or 'Pone

1 cup white or yellow cornmeal
1 teaspoon salt
1 tablespoon sugar, if desired
1 cup milk or water

While the skillet is heating over a slow part of the fire, mix the dry ingredients together thoroughly, then add the liquid and beat with a spoon until the mixture is smooth. When a drop of water dances

in the skillet, you're ready to start baking. Grease the skillet lightly, then drop the batter by the tablespoon into the skillet and flatten slightly with the back of the spoon. When the cakes are brown on one side, turn with a spatula and brown the other side. Good for breakfast with bacon and syrup or jam on the cakes. Good for lunch or supper with those freshly caught fish. 24 cakes.

 ## Hush Puppies

Originally, 'pone as made above were cooked after the fish fry and thrown to the hounds to quiet them—hence, the name. Some hungry soul discovered that they were too good to give to the dogs, so with the addition of two ingredients to the basic recipe, we come up with something slightly different in taste and texture.

Hush Puppies (cont.)

3 cups cornmeal
1 teaspoon salt
2 teaspoons baking powder
1½ cups water or milk
4 or 5 tablespoons bacon fat
2 teaspoons dried minced onion, if
    desired

Blend the dry ingredients together until they're well mixed. Add the liquid and the melted drippings and stir well. Let the mix stand for a few minutes, and then shape into small cakes with floured hands or just drop spoons of the dough into the hot fat with the frying fish, or after it, whichever you prefer. Fry until golden brown.

 Kentucky-Style Corn Fritters

2 cups corn kernels, uncooked (4 ears
    fresh corn or frozen or canned
    niblets, drained)
2 eggs
1 teaspoon sugar
¼ teaspoon baking powder
Pinch of salt
Sprinkling of freshly grated nutmeg
¼ to ½ cup all-purpose flour
Vegetable oil and/or bacon drippings
Butter and maple syrup or
    Confectioner's sugar

In a mixing bowl, beat the eggs and add the corn kernels, sugar, baking powder, salt and nutmeg; blend well. Starting with ¼ cup flour, add it to the corn mixture, stirring to blend it in to make the batter; keep adding flour until it is a thick mixture.

In a skillet, heat the oil and/or bacon drippings and drop the batter by tablespoonsful. Cook till golden brown on one side, then turn over and brown the other side. Serve with butter and maple syrup or sprinkled with confectioner's sugar.

This amount will yield about 16 fritters.

 Mushroom Spoon Bread

If you have a package of dehydrated mushroom soup in your grub box, this is a good supper dish in place of potatoes. The full recipe makes 6 servings, so cut the recipe in half for two people and use the rest of the soup for a mushroom sauce another day.

4 cups milk
1 package dehydrated mushroom soup
    mix
1 cup yellow cornmeal

2 tablespoons butter or drippings
3 or 4 eggs

Mushroom Spoon Bread (cont.)

Stir soup mix, cornmeal and milk together until smooth in top of double boiler (or set a pot into a skillet of hot water). Cook, stirring constantly, until thick. Cover and let the mixture steam another 5 minutes. Remove from heat and add the butter or drippings. Beat the eggs thoroughly in a small bowl and then add slowly to the hot mixture, stirring constantly. Grease a casserole and pour the spoon bread into it.

Bake in a hot reflector oven until golden brown—about 1 hour for the full recipe, less for only half the recipe. Test with a clean straw or splinter when the top is brown; if the straw comes out clean, it's time to dig in! If you wish to make this at home, the oven temperature is 400° to 425° F.

 Skillet Corn Bread

A reflector oven of the collapsible type is a handy gadget in camp, but a piece of aluminum foil will serve very nicely to reflect the heat onto the top of such breads as this, so they cook evenly top and bottom. Where every ounce of weight is important, heavy-duty foil can serve many useful purposes.

3 tablespoons bacon drippings
1 cup yellow cornmeal
1 cup white flour
2 tablespoons sugar
1/2 teaspoon salt
1 tablespoon baking powder
1 cup milk (or water and dry milk
**   powder)**
1 egg (fresh or dried and reconstituted
**   according to directions)**

Heat bacon drippings in a skillet until very hot—sputtering, but not smoking.

Measure and mix together the dry ingredients. Take another cup and beat the milk and egg together vigorously with a fork. Add milk and egg to dry ingredients and beat together just until blended. Pour in the hot drippings and beat very quickly and vigorously till they're well mixed. Pour the batter into the hot skillet and set in reflector oven near hot fire until done and golden brown, about 25 to 30 minutes. You can enjoy the same bread at home by baking it in a 425° F. oven.

HIGH-ENERGY TRAIL BREADS

Although the next recipes are not breads to be made in camp, they are old favorites which we have discovered to be good travelers on those weekend jaunts to the wilds. They're old family recipes which, prepared at home and wrapped in foil or plastic, will stay fresh and moist for days. The fruit and nuts also provide extra energy, so essential when tramping the woods and fields all day. In addition, they all freeze beautifully.

Date-Nut-Bran Bread

This bread is so delicious (and wholesome!) that I often bake it in a Bundt pan and serve it as a dessert, sprinkled with confectioner's sugar.

1 pound pitted dates, chopped
2 cups boiling water
1 teaspoon vanilla
1/2 teaspoon salt
2 large eggs
3/4 cup light brown sugar
1 1/2 cups whole wheat flour
1 teaspoon baking soda
2 teaspoons baking powder
2 cups unbleached all-purpose flour
1 cup whole bran
1 cup walnuts or pecans, chopped

Preheat oven to 350° F. and grease well and flour a 10-inch tube pan.

In a small bowl, pour the boiling water over the dates and allow to cool. When cool, stir in the vanilla and the salt.

In a large mixing bowl, beat the eggs until thick and very light, about 10 minutes with an electric beater. Gradually beat in the sugar until mixture is glossy and makes a rope when dropped from the beaters, much like the way you'd prepare a sponge cake.

Sift together the whole wheat flour, soda and baking powder. Add half of it to the egg mixture with half of the date mixture (and its liquid) and all of the white flour; stir until well blended. Then stir in the balance of the wheat flour and the date mixture. Fold in the whole bran and the nuts and pour into the prepared tube pan.

Bake about 1 hour or until done. Cool in pan 20 minutes, then remove to a wire rack to cool completely. (One time I made this and forgot to add the bran—it was just as good as with it!)

Orange-Raisin-Nut Bread

1 cup raisins, ground through medium blade of food chopper or processed in a food processor
1 teaspoon baking soda
1 cup hot water
Grated rind and juice of 1 orange
1 egg, well beaten
3/4 cup sugar
2 1/4 cups flour
1 teaspoon baking powder
Pinch of salt
1 teaspoon vanilla
1/2 cup nut meats, chopped

Sprinkle soda over the ground raisins; pour over the hot water. Add orange juice and rind and allow to cool. Add beaten egg and sugar, salt, flour and baking powder sifted together. Add vanilla and nut meats; blend well and pour into a greased loaf pan.

Bake for 1 hour at 325° F., increasing temperature to 350° the last 15 minutes.

Rhubarb-Raisin Bread

What to do with all that rhubarb from your early summer garden? Try this bread for a refreshing change. It travels well and, with the addition of the wheat germ and dry milk solids, makes a really high-energy trail food, packed with iron and B vitamins.

2 eggs
1 cup light brown sugar
½ cup light vegetable oil *plus* enough molasses to make ⅔ cup
1 cup sour milk (add 2 teaspoons white vinegar to cow's milk)
1 teaspoon vanilla
1 tablespoon orange peel, finely grated
1 tablespoon wheat germ
2 tablespoons dry milk solids
3 cups all-purpose flour, sifted
2 teaspoons baking soda
½ teaspoon baking powder
1 teaspoon ground cinnamon
½ teaspoon ground ginger
½ teaspoon ground nutmeg
2 cups rhubarb, finely chopped and drained, if necessary
1 cup raisins

Preheat oven to 350° F. and grease well 2 loaf pans (9" x 5").

In a large mixing bowl, lightly beat the eggs. Add the brown sugar, oil/molasses, sour milk and vanilla and lightly beat again. Stir in the orange peel, wheat germ and dry milk solids.

Sift together the flour, soda, baking powder, and spices and lightly beat into the egg mixture. Fold in the rhubarb and the raisins. If the rhubarb is moist, before adding it to the batter, stir into it 1 tablespoon flour so it will disperse evenly in the loaves; otherwise, it may sink to the bottom. Pour batter into loaf pans and bake 1 hour or so, until done. Cool in pans 10 minutes, then remove to wire racks to cool completely.

Vera's Date Bread

1 pound pitted dates, chopped
2 teaspoons baking soda
2 cups very hot water
4 tablespoons shortening
¾ teaspoon salt
1 cup granulated sugar
Grated rind and juice of ½ lemon
½ teaspoon vanilla
2 eggs, well beaten
3½ cups flour
½ teaspoon baking powder

Sprinkle soda over chopped dates in large mixing bowl, then pour the hot water over; add shortening, salt, sugar, lemon and vanilla. Stir to blend and let it cool. Add eggs and flour sifted with baking powder. The mixture is quite thin.

Bake in two greased loaf pans for 1 hour at 325° F. During the last 15 minutes, raise the oven temperature to 350° F. Turn out of pans and cool on wire rack. Allow to mellow for at least one day before slicing.

Zucchini-Nut Bread

A rich source of vitamin A and potassium, zucchini is another vegetable that makes up nicely into a wholesome bread.

3 eggs
1 cup light vegetable oil
1½ cups light brown sugar
2 teaspoons vanilla
2 cups zucchini squash, grated and well drained
1 tablespoon wheat germ
3 cups all-purpose flour, sifted
½ teaspoon baking powder
2 teaspoons baking soda
3 teaspoons cinnamon
¼ teaspoon salt
1 cup raisins (optional)
1 cup walnuts or pecans, chopped

Preheat oven to 350°–375° F. and grease well 2 loaf pans (9″ x 5″).

In a large mixing bowl, beat the eggs lightly. Add the oil, sugar and vanilla and lightly beat again. Fold in the zucchini and the wheat germ. Sift together the flour, baking powder, soda, cinnamon and salt, and add it to the egg mixture, stirring until well blended. Fold in the raisins, if desired, and the nuts. Pour into well-greased pans and bake for at least 1 hour, until done. Cool in pans 10 minutes, then cool on wire rack.

OLD-FASHIONED YEAST BREADS

Yeast breads are a lot easier to make than you might think. For the baker, it's really the initial mixing and kneading stage that requires the most time. The rest—the rising and baking—happen virtually by themselves. If you've never tried yeast breads, do; it's an "earthy," satisfying experience.

French Bread

1 package granulated yeast
2 cups warm water
1 tablespoon salt
5 to 5½ cups unbleached all-purpose flour
1 egg white, slightly beaten
1 tablespoon water

Soften yeast in ¼ cup warm water. Put remainder of warm water and salt in

large mixing bowl. Sift and blend in about half the flour, stirring until smooth. Add softened yeast, mix well and continue adding flour, beating well after each addition until you have a soft dough. Turn onto a floured surface and let the dough rest, covered, 5 to 10 minutes. Knead until smooth and elastic, place in greased bowl and turn to grease top surface. Cover and let stand

French Bread (cont.)

in a warm place until doubled in bulk, about 1½ to 2 hours.

A friend of mine taught me this trick for accelerating the rising time. Place the bowl on top of an electric warming tray and on the top of the bowl lay a heating pad set at its lowest setting. You'll be amazed at how much faster the dough will respond.

Punch down with fist and knead lightly for 2 minutes. Divide into 2 portions and let rest, covered, for 10 minutes. Roll each portion into an oblong and then roll up tightly into a long slender loaf, pinching the ends to seal and rolling gently back and forth with palms of hands to taper the loaf. Place each loaf diagonally on greased baking sheet. With a very sharp knife, cut diagonal gashes ¼-inch deep several inches apart along each loaf. Combine egg white and water, brush each loaf with part of the mixture, cover with damp towels and set aside in a warm place to double in bulk. Brush again with egg white when risen.

Preheat oven to 425° F., place a flat pan in the bottom of the oven and pour boiling water into it. Place the loaves in the oven and bake for 10 minutes. Reduce heat to 375° F., brush loaves again with egg white and bake 15 minutes more. Then brush once more with egg white and continue to bake until golden brown, about 20 to 25 minutes.

Hard Rolls

Follow the above recipe, but shape into round rolls about 2½ inches in diameter. Place on greased baking sheets and with very sharp knife, cut 3 gashes ¼-inch deep across each roll to form 6 pie-shaped segments. Brush with egg white, cover and let rise until nearly doubled in bulk. Brush again with egg white and sprinkle with poppy seeds. Bake in preheated 425° F. oven for about 20 minutes, with a pan of boiling water at the bottom of the oven.

Light Rye Bread

1 package granulated yeast
¼ cup warm water
1¾ cups milk, scalded
1 tablespoon salt
2 tablespoons butter
2 tablespoons caraway seeds
¼ cup dark molasses
3 cups rye flour
2½ to 3 cups unbleached white flour

Soften yeast in warm water. In a large mixing bowl, combine hot milk, salt, butter, caraway seeds and molasses. Stir to melt butter; allow to cool to lukewarm. Mix in the softened yeast, then gradually stir in the rye flour. Add sufficient white flour to form a stiff dough. Turn out on floured board and knead until smooth and satiny, about 10 minutes. Place in a

Light Rye Bread (cont.)

well-greased bowl, turning dough in the bowl so the top is greased. Cover and set in a warm place to rise until doubled in bulk—about 1 1/2 hours.

Punch dough down, turn over in bowl, cover again and let rise another 1/2 hour. Turn out onto floured board, divide into 2 portions and shape into round loaves. Place on greased baking sheets which have been sprinkled with cornmeal. Cover and let rise until light and nearly doubled in size, about 1 hour.

Bake at 375° F. for 45 to 50 minutes, or until loaves sound hollow when tapped. Cool on wire rack.

Limpa—Swedish Rye Bread

1 package granulated yeast
1/4 cup warm water
1 teaspoon granulated sugar
2 teaspoons caraway seeds
1 teaspoon anise seed
1 tablespoon salt
1/3 cup dark molasses
2 teaspoons grated orange rind (may be omitted, but we prefer to include it)
3 tablespoons shortening
1 3/4 cups milk, scalded
3 cups rye flour
3 cups unbleached white flour

Soften yeast in warm water to which the teaspoon of sugar has been added. Combine caraway, anise, salt, molasses, orange rind and shortening in large mixing bowl. Pour over scalded milk and stir until shortening is melted and ingredients are well blended; cool to lukewarm. Add softened yeast and mix well. Stir in rye flour thoroughly and add enough white flour to make a stiff dough. Mix thoroughly, then turn out onto a floured board and knead until smooth and elastic, about 10 minutes.

Place in a greased bowl, turn once to grease top surface, cover and let rise in a warm place until doubled in bulk, about 1 1/2 hours. Punch dough down, turn over in bowl and let rise again for 1/2 hour. Punch dough down, turn out onto floured board, divide into 2 portions, round up into balls, cover and let rest for 10 minutes.

Shape into round loaves, place on greased baking sheets, cover and let rise until nearly doubled in bulk. Bake at 375° F. 30 to 40 minutes. Cool.

Mimi's Herb Bread

1 package dry yeast
1/4 cup warm water
3/4 cup milk, scalded
2 tablespoons sugar
1 1/2 teaspoons salt
2 tablespoons shortening
1 egg, well beaten
1/2 teaspoon freshly grated nutmeg
1 teaspoon crumbled sage
2 teaspoons celery seed
3 1/2 cups flour

Mimi's Herb Bread (cont.)

Soften yeast in warm water. Combine scalded milk, sugar, salt and shortening and stir till shortening is melted; cool to lukewarm. Add yeast and mix well. Add egg, nutmeg, sage and celery seed, sift over 2 cups of flour and beat until smooth. Add enough of the remaining flour to make a moderately soft dough. Knead on lightly floured surface until smooth and elastic, about 5 to 8 minutes. Place in a greased bowl, turn once to grease top surface and let rise until doubled in bulk, about 1½ hours.

Punch down, let dough rest, covered, for 10 to 15 minutes. Shape into a round loaf, place in greased 8-inch pie pan. Cover and let rise until almost doubled in bulk again, 45 to 50 minutes. Bake in 400° F. oven for 35 to 45 minutes. Slide out onto wire rack immediately to cool.

New England Cornmeal Bread

½ cup yellow cornmeal
½ cup cold water
1½ cups boiling water
½ cup molasses
2 tablespoons butter
1½ teaspoons salt
1 package granulated yeast
½ cup warm water
6 cups unbleached white flour

Combine cornmeal with cold water and stir until smooth. Very gradually stir cornmeal mixture into boiling water, stirring constantly until well blended. Remove from heat, stir in molasses, butter and salt. Set aside until lukewarm.

Meanwhile, soften yeast in warm water for 10 minutes. Stir 1 cup of flour into the lukewarm cornmeal mixture and beat until smooth, add softened yeast and mix thoroughly. Gradually beat in enough of the remaining flour to make a soft dough. Turn out onto a floured board and let the dough rest for 10 minutes. Knead until smooth and satiny, place in a greased bowl and turn once to grease top surface. Cover and set in a warm place until doubled in bulk.

Punch down and turn onto floured board. Divide into 2 portions, shape into loaves and place in well-greased bread pans. Cover and let rise until nearly doubled, about 1 hour. Bake at 375° F. for 45 minutes, or until bread sounds hollow when tapped. Turn out onto wire racks immediately to cool. For a soft crust, brush tops of loaves with butter.

Never-Fail Roll Dough

After years of trial and error, I have finally worked out this recipe, which is literally foolproof for light yet rich dinner rolls and coffee cakes. It makes a large quantity of dough, but the lovely part of it is that you can make it all up in one big baking spree or spread the baking over several days.

Never-Fail Roll Dough (cont.)

2 packages granulated yeast
¹/₂ cup warm water
2 cups milk, scalded
¹/₂ cup sugar
1 tablespoon salt
³/₄ cup butter at room temperature
3 eggs
7 cups flour

Soften yeast in warm water for 5 minutes. In a large mixing bowl, combine scalded milk, sugar and salt. When cooled to lukewarm, sift about 2 cups flour into milk, beating constantly. When batter is smooth, beat in butter in small portions until thoroughly blended. Add yeast, another cup of flour and again beat until smooth. Add eggs, one at a time, beating vigorously after each addition until thoroughly blended. Add remaining flour and beat smooth.

Turn into liberally buttered bowl large enough for dough to double (or use 2 smaller bowls) and brush top of dough liberally with melted butter. Cover with waxed paper and towel, set in warm draft-free place until doubled. Punch down with spoon. Be sure top surface is completely buttered and refrigerate, covered, for at least 4 hours and up to 2 days.

This dough is very sticky to work with unless it has been thoroughly chilled. When ready to bake, punch dough down, turn out onto lightly floured board and knead gently for a minute or so. Cut off ¹/₄ of the dough, return the remainder to the refrigerator, covered. Shape rolls as desired— rosettes, crescents, bow knots, braids. Place on greased baking sheets, brush with melted butter, cover and let rise until almost doubled. Bake at 400° F. until golden brown, the time depending on the size of the rolls.

Sweet rolls and coffee cakes of all sorts may also be made with this dough, baking usually at 350° to 375° F.

Note: These baked goods freeze well. Cool completely, then wrap tightly in aluminum foil or in plastic bags, pushing out all possible air. Keep an extra coffee cake and at least a dozen dinner rolls in the freezer, plus a loaf of homemade bread. Then you can turn the most ordinary meal into something special when guests arrive unexpectedly.

Oatmeal Bread

1¹/₂ cups boiling water
1 cup quick-cooking oatmeal
6 tablespoons shortening
¹/₂ cup molasses
1 tablespoon salt
2 packages granulated yeast
¹/₂ cup lukewarm water
2 eggs, beaten
5¹/₂ cups unbleached flour

In a large mixing bowl, combine boiling water, oatmeal, shortening, molasses and salt; stir until shortening melts. Cool to lukewarm. Meanwhile, soften yeast in lukewarm water. Add softened yeast to oatmeal mixture; mix well, then stir in beaten eggs. Sift in flour, beating as you do so. Continue until dough is well blended. Place dough in greased

Oatmeal Bread (cont.)

bowl, brush top with melted butter, cover and place in refrigerator for at least 2 hours.

On floured board, shape dough into 2 loaves and place in greased 9" x 4" x 3" loaf pans and cover with a clean towel. Let rise in a warm place until doubled in bulk, about 2 hours. Bake in preheated 375° F. oven for 1 hour.

Whole Wheat Bread

1 package granulated yeast
1 cup warm water
¹/₂ cup honey or light molasses
1 tablespoon salt
3 tablespoons shortening (butter, preferably)
1 cup milk, scalded
4 cups whole wheat flour
2 cups unbleached white flour

Soften yeast in warm water. In a large mixing bowl, combine honey, salt, butter and scalded milk, stir to melt butter and cool to lukewarm. Add softened yeast and gradually stir in the flour to form a stiff dough. Turn out onto floured board and knead until smooth and satiny, about 10 minutes. Place in greased bowl, cover and let rise in a warm place until doubled in bulk, about 2 to 2¹/₂ hours.

Punch down and turn onto floured board, shape into two loaves and place in 9" x 5" x 3" pans which have been well greased. Cover and let rise in warm place until dough has doubled, about 2 to 2¹/₂ hours. Preheat oven to 350° F. and bake for about an hour until bread sounds hollow when tapped. Turn out of pans immediately and cool on wire racks.

CHAPTER 16

DESSERTS—
TART AND
SWEET

How often have you sat sipping your campfire coffee and wished for something "just a little sweet" to go with it? Or when you served your last sauerbraten, perhaps you wondered what dessert would best complement the meal? This chapter is devoted to the final touch at your game table—whether it's the simplest outdoor fixings or the fanciest oven roast.

If you are planning a short hunting trip, or day trips, that will eliminate camp cooking, why not pack what I call "Take-Alongs For Short Hunting Trips," such as butterscotch brownies or fruit-filled oatmeal squares. Baked at home, they provide an energy boost and satisfy that brief craving for something sweet.

When you're in the woods for an extended time, the inventive cook can come up with a number of easy-to-prepare desserts. I know, for I've done it. Pick some apples from the orchard you've been stalking for deer or grouse and bake them, or whip up an apple crisp using the biscuit mix (*see* page 250) I recommend that you bring on all long hunting trips. It has many wonderful uses. What about wild blueberries or cranberries? They make a great camp coffee cake that, when served warm, is delicious.

For those elegant at-home occasions when something more elaborate is called for, I have included "Great Endings For Game Dinners." Some are Old-World favorites that have been handed down through the years in my family; others are more simple, tart desserts, which I usually prefer, such as Cranberry Bavarian Cream and Lemon Velvet. All in all, here are a variety of desserts to choose from that will complete whatever type of game meal you are preparing.

TAKE-ALONGS FOR SHORT HUNTING TRIPS

Butterscotch Brownies

1¾ cups flour
½ teaspoon baking powder
¾ teaspoon salt
¾ cup butter
1½ cups light brown sugar, firmly
   packed
3 eggs
1 teaspoon vanilla
2 cups pecans, chopped

Preheat oven to 350° F.

Sift dry ingredients together. Cream butter and sugar, then add eggs, one at a time, beating well after each addition. Add vanilla, then sifted dry ingredients. Mix thoroughly, then blend in nuts. Spread in waxed paper-lined jelly roll pan and bake for 25 minutes. Cool, package and freeze as for fudge brownies, below.

Fudge Brownies

This, as I recall, was my first "substitute" recipe. I had started to prepare a double batch of brownies when I discovered that I was short of the necessary amount of white sugar. With my fingers crossed, I substituted brown sugar for 1 cup of the white sugar and have been making them that way ever since. The brown sugar adds flavor and also keeps them from drying out too fast.

½ pound butter
4 ounces (squares) bitter chocolate
3 eggs
1 cup granulated sugar
1 cup light brown sugar, firmly packed
2 teaspoons vanilla
1½ cups flour
1 teaspoon baking powder
1 teaspoon salt
½ pound walnuts, coarsely broken

Preheat oven to 350° F.

Melt chocolate and butter together over hot water, then set aside to cool. Or melt in a glass (or non-metal) bowl in your microwave oven. Beat eggs until thick, add sugars and vanilla, beating until well blended. Continue to beat while adding chocolate. Sift dry ingredients together and mix in thoroughly. Add walnuts and stir in.

Spread into jelly roll pan 10″ x 14″ which has been lined with waxed paper. Bake for 30 minutes, turning pan around in the oven after 20 minutes.

Cool, turn out of pan, peel off waxed paper and cut into 4 large squares. Wrap each section in foil and freeze. I prefer not to cut any pan cookies of this type until they are to be eaten; there is less chance of them drying out.

Serving suggestions. Frost with chocolate butter frosting, cut into 1½-inch squares. *Or* cut into large squares, top with scoop of coffee ice cream and chocolate sauce.

Fruit Bars

These were originally concocted to use up candied fruit left over from the Christmas baking. They have since been accepted with almost as much enthusiasm as brownies. They are excellent for hunting trips, since they travel well, stay moist and are high in energy.

1/2 **pound butter**
2 **cups light brown sugar, firmly packed**
2 **eggs**
1 1/2 **teaspoons vanilla**
3 **cups flour**
1 **teaspoon soda**
1 **teaspoon cinnamon**
1/4 **cup milk**
3/4 **cup mixed candied fruit**
1/2 **cup nuts, coarsely chopped**

Cream butter and sugar together, add eggs and beat well. Blend in vanilla. Sift dry ingredients together and add alternately with milk. Blend in fruit and nuts. Spread in waxed paper-lined jelly roll pan and bake at 350° F. for 1/2 hour, turning pan in the oven after 20 minutes. Cool, package and freeze in the same way as brownies.

Fruit-Filled Oatmeal Squares

These, too, stay moist and are high in energy. The choice of jams, jellies and preserves as fillings is endless, but I have mentioned a few fillings we especially like.

3/4 **cup butter**
1 **cup brown sugar, firmly packed**
1 3/4 **cups flour**
1/2 **teaspoon salt**
1 **teaspoon soda**
2 **cups quick-cooking oatmeal**

Cream butter and sugar together thoroughly, add dry ingredients which have been sifted together. Mix in oatmeal until the dough is well blended and very crumbly. Line a jelly roll pan with waxed paper and pat 1/2 of the oatmeal mixture evenly and firmly into the pan. Spread with the fruit filling of your choice, add the remainder of the crumbs and pat down. Bake at 350° F. for 25 to 30 minutes.

Cook any of the following combinations to the consistency of thick jam. Cool, then use as filling.

Apricot: 3 cups chopped dried apricots, 1/2 cup water; 1/2 cup orange juice; 1 cup sugar. Add 3/4 cup chopped walnuts after cooling the fruit mixture.

Date: 1 pound dates, pitted and cut up; 3/4 cup white sugar; 1/2 cup water; 1/2 cup orange juice; 1 tablespoon lemon juice; coarsely shredded rind of 1 orange.

Fig: 2 to 3 cups fresh figs, chopped; 4 tablespoons butter; 1/2 cup brown sugar; 1/4 cup almond paste; 1 teaspoon cinnamon; 1/4 teaspoon nutmeg. Cook until somewhat thick, then put in a blender to puree. It will thicken more as it cools.

Raisin: 2 1/2 cups raisins; 1/2 cup sugar mixed with 2 tablespoons cornstarch; 3/4 cup water; 1/4 cup lemon juice.

Rangers

These good travelers have ranged far and wide in this country. Mother always included them in packages of "goodies" mailed to us when we were away at school.

1 cup vegetable shortening
1 cup granulated sugar
1 cup light brown sugar, firmly packed
1 tablespoon milk
2 eggs
1 teaspoon vanilla
2 cups flour
1 teaspoon soda
1/2 teaspoon baking powder
1/2 teaspoon salt
2 cups quick-cooking oats
1 cup coconut
2 cups corn flakes
1/2 cup walnuts, coarsely broken

Cream shortening and sugars together, continue to beat as you add milk, eggs and vanilla. Sift dry ingredients together and beat in until well blended. Stir in oats, coconut, corn flakes and nuts. Mix thoroughly. Drop by spoonsful on greased baking sheets and bake at 350° F.

for 9 to 10 minutes, reversing the pans after 5 or 6 minutes in the oven, so all the cookies brown evenly.

Plan-ahead hint: Prepare a double batch while you have the ingredients out. Bake some of the cookies right away, drop the remainder of the dough by the spoonful on waxed paper covered pans very close together. Freeze, uncovered, until the cookies are hard, then store unbaked in plastic bags for emergency use. For freshly baked cookies in 15 minutes, preheat oven while you grease a baking sheet. Place the individually frozen cookies on it and into the oven. It will take only a minute or so longer than the normal baking time. You may, of course, freeze the cookies baked, but my own preference has always been for cookies fresh from the oven.

CAMPFIRE DESSERTS

These desserts may be made at home as well, but their simplicity makes them ideal for camp cooking.

 ## Dried Fruit

Although the modern processing makes dried fruit tender enough to eat as is for a quick energy snack, it is somehow more appealing for dessert when it has been cooked for a time. This is our favorite method.

Dried fruit
Water
Sugar

Cinnamon
Whole cloves
Lemon, sliced *very* thinly

Dried Fruit (cont.)

Barely cover the fruit with water and set over a slow fire to simmer gently (unless you prefer fruit mush). Add a dash of cinnamon or a piece of stick cinnamon and a few whole cloves. If you have it, slice a lemon into *very* thin slices and simmer it along with the fruit. There is also a dried grated lemon peel that makes a mighty good substitute. Most people seem to like fruit very sweet; I don't, so sugar to your own taste, preferably after the fruit is cooked and removed. Then boil down the remaining syrup and pour over the fruit.

 ## Apple Crisp

If the apples you have are not perfect enough for baking whole, this is a good dessert to make, using only the good parts of the apples.

Apple pieces
2 tablespoons lemon juice
Lemon rind, grated

Topping:
¹/₄ cup flour *or* Biscuit Mix
³/₄ cup firmly packed brown sugar
Dash nutmeg *or* cinnamon
4 tablespoons butter
³/₄ cup dry cereal (corn flakes, rice crispies, etc.)

Butter a baking dish, peel and slice into it enough apples to equal 6 or 7 whole ones. Sprinkle the apples with lemon juice and some grated rind if you have it. Top with the following mixed together until crumbly: flour or biscuit mix, brown sugar, a dash of nutmeg or cinnamon, butter and dry cereal. Pat this firmly atop the apples and bake in a moderate reflector oven for 45 minutes. (350° F. if you want to make it at home.) Serve warm with cream or as is.

 ## Baked Apples

In deer and ruffed grouse country, you're quite likely to stumble upon an abandoned orchard; as a matter of fact, you probably had it spotted long before the season opened. You can find some pretty good apples in these old orchards. Here's what to do with them.

Apples
Cinnamon
White sugar
Brown sugar
Raisins
Dried mincemeat
Butter

Core the apples and cut through the skin around the middle of the apple; that will keep it from bursting as it cooks. Place each apple on a double square of foil; fill the centers with cinnamon and sugar, brown sugar and raisins, dried mincemeat reconstituted according to

Baked Apples (cont.)

package directions. Add a bit of butter to each package, fold over securely with the drugstore wrap.

Place beside the coals of your dinner fire, turn once in a while to ensure even cooking. Depending on the size of the apples and the heat of the fire, they should be ready in less than an hour.

 Blueberry Roll

Wild blueberries are available through mid-October in the North country. If you find some in your travels, pick a hat full! Better yet, go back with a pail!

2 cups blueberries
2 cups Biscuit Mix (*see* page 250)
½ cup sugar
1½ tablespoons lemon juice *or*
**   reconstituted lemon crystals**
Lemon Dessert Sauce (*see* page 270)

Wash the blueberries and drain while you prepare the dough. Add an extra tablespoon of sugar if you wish to the biscuit mix, but it isn't really necessary. Mix it just as you would for regular biscuits and roll or pat it out on a clean floured surface to ½-inch thickness in an oblong shape. Mix the blueberries with the sugar and sprinkle over the lemon juice or reconstituted lemon crystals. Distribute the fruit over the dough, leaving an inch on the short side of the oblong uncovered. Roll up, starting at the opposite short side. Place seam down on greased pan and bake in hot reflector oven for 25 to 30 minutes. Cut in crosswise slices and serve with Lemon Dessert Sauce.

You could also use any dried and stewed fruit, mashed to a pulp with a fork and spread over the dough. Wild cranberries would also be a treat this way, but add a bit more sugar, since they are considerably more tart.

 Camp Coffee Cake

2 cups Biscuit Mix (*see* page 250)
2 tablespoons sugar
1 egg
¾ cup water

Crumb Topping:
½ cup sugar (white or brown)
½ cup Biscuit Mix

3 or 4 tablespoons butter
Pinch cinnamon

Add sugar to the dry mix; stir in water and egg which have been beaten together. Spread evenly into greased 8- or 9-inch pan. If you've found any wild blueberries in the vicinity, sprinkle a

Camp Coffee Cake (cont.)

cup or so on top of the batter.

Top with the crumb mixture. Blend sugar, biscuit mix, butter and cinnamon together with a knife until you have a coarse crumbly mixture. Sprinkle on top of the batter, and bake in a hot reflector oven at a slightly lower heat than for biscuits for about ½ hour. With or without blueberries, it's darn good!

 Dessert Pancakes

2 cups Biscuit Mix (*see* page 250)
1½ cups water
2 eggs
**2 to 3 tablespoons melted butter or
    drippings**
1 cup blueberries, washed and drained

Beat eggs and water together; add all at once to mix with butter or drippings; beat thoroughly with fork, then stir in berries. Skillet is hot enough when a drop of water will dance on the surface. Drop the batter by the spoonful into the skillet, flip over when bubbles appear on the uncooked surface.

Eat with butter and brown sugar, wild honey or Lemon Dessert Sauce. If you're a chocolate fiend, you could use chocolate chips, but be sure the pan is well greased. Raisins or chopped apricots could also be used.

 Fruit Cobbler

To my way of thinking, there is no better camper's dessert than the old New England cobbler, for any fruit, fresh or dried, can be used. For several hungry hunters, use 4 cups fresh fruit such as blueberries, sliced apples, a combination of apples and wild cranberries.

4 cups fresh fruit
1 cup sugar
2 to 3 tablespoons flour
**1 to 2 tablespoons orange *or* lemon
    juice**
2 cups Biscuit Mix (*see* page 250)

Mix the fruit with the sugar blended with flour. Add orange or lemon juice and place in the bottom of a greased baking dish. Top with biscuit dough, mixed with a bit more liquid than for regular biscuits. Your aim is a softer dough. Drop this by the spoonful on top of the fruit, leaving spaces between the drop biscuits. Bake in a hot reflector

Fruit Cobblers (cont.)

oven until the biscuits are browned and the fruit is bubbling, about ½ hour.

Dried apricots, peaches, dried apples stewed as above and then turned into the baking dish are excellent when fresh fruit is not available. For a zesty change, try combining stewed apples with reconstituted mincemeat—it's delicious!

 Lemon Dessert Sauce

1 tablespoon cornstarch *or*
2 tablespoons flour
2 tablespoons plus ¾ cup cold water
Pinch salt
¼ cup sugar
3 to 4 tablespoons lemon juice or reconstituted crystals
1 tablespoon butter

Moisten the cornstarch *or* flour with 2 tablespoons cold water and stir until all the lumps are out. Cornstarch will give you a clear sauce, but if flour is all you have, who cares, as long as it tastes good? Now, in a small pan mix the ¾ cup water, salt, sugar and lemon juice (if you don't have lemon, use orange or grapefruit). Bring to a boil, add cornstarch or flour mixture and stir over low heat until thick and smooth. Simmer 5 minutes, remove from the fire and stir in the butter.

This sauce is good on blueberry or cranberry rolls, dessert pancakes, etc.

GREAT ENDINGS FOR GAME DINNERS

A game dinner served at home is usually a special event. And you may wonder what type of dessert best suits a venison roast, Doves en Casserole or Rabbit Fricassee. My preference is for light, tart desserts, many of which appear below. However, there are times when you want to show off "just a little," so I've included a few elaborate, rich desserts for those gala evenings.

Applesauce Cake

This old-fashioned favorite is so appropriate for a country-style supper with stew as the main dish. I usually double the recipe and bake one part in two loaf pans. Frosted, frozen unwrapped, and then wrapped in foil, they travel well to picnics and such and are defrosted by the time you're ready to eat.

Applesauce Cake (cont.)

½ cup butter
½ cup light brown sugar, firmly packed
1 cup white sugar
2 eggs
1 cup thick unsweetened applesauce
2 cups flour
¼ teaspoon salt
1 teaspoon baking powder
½ teaspoon baking soda
1 teaspoon cinnamon
½ teaspoon cloves
½ teaspoon allspice
1 cup raisins
¾ cup walnuts

Preheat oven to 350° F.

Cream butter and sugars together, add eggs and beat well. Add applesauce and continue to beat until blended. Sift together all dry ingredients, including spices, then add gradually to the batter. Fold in raisins and walnuts.

Turn into well-greased 8- or 9-inch square pan and bake for 50 to 60 minutes. Cake is done when top, touched lightly, springs back. Frost with lemon butter frosting.

Austrian Dessert Pancakes (Palatschinken)

1 cup flour
¼ teaspoon salt
3 eggs
¼ cup sugar
1 cup milk
2 tablespoons butter, melted
Jam or preserves
Confectioner's sugar

Sift flour and salt together. In a large mixing bowl, beat eggs until very thick, add sugar, milk and melted butter, continuing to beat until well blended. Add sifted dry ingredients and beat until smooth.

Lightly butter a 5- or 6-inch skillet and warm over medium heat. Ladle into the skillet just enough batter to cover the bottom of the pan, tilting it back and forth to spread the batter thin. Cook until pancake bottom is light brown and top is firm to the touch. Turn over with a spatula and lightly brown the other side. Transfer to a hot platter and keep warm in the oven as you cook the other pancakes one at a time. Because of the melted butter in the batter, it should be unnecessary to grease the skillet after making each pancake (a Teflon or Silver Stone lined skillet works well).

To serve, fill with a tablespoon or so of your favorite jam or preserves, roll up and sprinkle with confectioner's sugar.

Or you can prepare an even more Austrian dish by tearing the pancakes into bite-sized pieces with two forks and mixing them into hot **Kaiserschmarren Sauce:** blend well and heat ¾ cup melted butter, ½ cup raisins, ½ cup chopped nuts, 1 teaspoon cinnamon, 1 cup sugar.

This recipe yields 18 pancakes.

Blackberry Pie

Who can resist a fresh berry pie for dessert? Not me, and certainly not blackberry. These berries abound in summer, growing virtually wild in many deciduous forests of the U.S. I usually pick lots of them and freeze them for use in the winter—for sauces, jellies and jams, too.

Pastry for double-crust pie
4 to 5 cups fresh blackberries, washed
1 cup sugar
3 tablespoons quick-cooking tapioca
2 tablespoons cornstarch
1 tablespoon lemon juice
1 tablespoon butter
Pinch ground cinnamon
1 egg
Confectioner's sugar
Vanilla ice cream (optional)

Preheat oven to 450° F. and prepare your pie crust. Place 1 shell in a 9-inch glass pie plate and reserve the other for the lattice top.

In a large mixing bowl, place the washed berries and sprinkle over them the sugar, tapioca and cornstarch; let stand for 15 minutes. This may seem like a lot of thickening agent, but I find that blackberries are *very* juicy and require it to make a handsome pie. Drizzle over the lemon juice and gently pour the berry mixture into the pie crust. By this time you'll see that a lot of berry juice has collected in the bottom of your bowl; don't add it to the pie. Top with dots of butter and a sprinkling of cinnamon.

Cut the reserved pastry into strips, using a pastry cutter or a knife; place on top of filling in a woven lattice pattern. Seal and crimp the edges. Beat the egg and brush the crust with it. Bake at 450° F. for 10 to 15 minutes; reduce heat to 350° F. and continue baking for another hour. You may want to put a piece of aluminum foil or a baking sheet on the rack below the pie to catch the berry drippings.

Serve at room temperature, garnished with confectioner's sugar and a dollop of vanilla ice cream.

Black Walnut Pound Cake

Black walnuts are a natural phenomenon you may unknowingly stumble upon during your autumn walks through the woods. They appear as small, greenish spheres, a little smaller than a tennis ball, and are usually strewn below the trees of the same name. Don't pass them by, for inside are one of the forest's treasures—delicious to eat as is, or baked into a scrumptious batter, such as the one below. This classic recipe is from the files of the Editor's grandmother, Agnes Steuber, who was a baker.

1 pound butter, unsalted
1 pound sugar (2 cups)
1 pound fresh eggs (9)
1 pound flour (4 cups)

1/2 teaspoon baking powder
1 teaspoon almond extract
1 cup black walnuts, chopped, and
    mixed with a little flour

Black Walnut Pound Cake (cont.)

Preheat oven to 350° F. Grease, wax paper and grease again a 10-inch tube pan.

In a large mixing bowl, cream butter and sugar well. Beat eggs into mixture one at a time, beating well after each addition. Sift together flour and baking powder; fold into egg mixture. Blend in the almond extract and finally fold in the nuts.

Bake for 1 hour. Cool slightly in pan, then remove to wire rack to cool completely after carefully peeling off wax paper. Serve sprinkled with confectioner's sugar.

Cheese Cake

Crust:
2 cups zwieback crumbs
¹/₂ cup sugar
1 teaspoon cinnamon
¹/₂ cup butter, melted

Filling:
4 eggs
1 cup sugar
¹/₈ teaspoon salt
1¹/₂ tablespoons fresh lemon juice
1 cup cream
8 ounces cream cheese
1 pound cottage cheese
4 tablespoons flour
1¹/₂ teaspoons lemon rind

Combine crust ingredients and pack into bottom and up the sides of a 9-inch spring form pan. If you are making plain cheese cake, reserve ³/₄ cup of the crumb mixture for topping. If you plan to top with glazed berries, use all of the crumbs in the crust.

Preheat oven to 350° F.

Beat eggs with sugar thoroughly until light. Add remaining ingredients in order given with the exception of the lemon rind. Beat until well blended, then force through food mill. Stir in lemon rind and pour into crust. If serving plain, mix reserved crumbs with ¹/₄ cup chopped walnuts and sprinkle over the top.

Bake for 1 hour, turn off oven and open the door. Let the cheese cake cool slowly for another hour this way. Remove to a wire rack to finish cooling, then refrigerate overnight in the pan. To serve, remove the sides of the pan—it is not necessary to remove the bottom— and serve at room temperature.

Cranberry Glaze. Cook 2 cups cranberries, ³/₄ cup water and 1 cup sugar together until skins pop. Soften 1¹/₂ teaspoons unflavored gelatine in 2 tablespoons water for 5 minutes, then stir into hot cranberry mixture until the gelatine is dissolved. Refrigerate until the glaze begins to thicken, then spread over the cheese cake from which the sides have been removed. Chill several hours before serving.

Strawberry Glaze. Wash, hull and drain 1 quart fresh strawberries, reserving perfect ones for the top of the cheese cake. Crush one cup of the less perfect berries, add 1 tablespoon lemon juice, ¹/₂ cup sugar and 1 tablespoon cornstarch. Cook over low heat, stirring constantly until the glaze is thick and clear. Press immediately through a fine sieve to remove pulp and seeds. Set aside to cool.

When whole berries are thoroughly dry, gently mix with glaze, then remove each glazed berry with a spoon and set on the cheese cake. Drizzle any remaining glaze over the berries. Chill for an hour or so before serving.

Cranberry-Mincemeat Pie

1 9-inch pastry shell, unbaked
2 cups fresh cranberries
1/2 cup water
1/2 to 1 cup sugar
2 cups mincemeat
1/4 cup white rum
4 tablespoons butter
1/2 cup flour
1/2 cup confectioner's sugar
1/3 cup pecans, chopped

Prepare pastry shell and place in a 9-inch pie plate. Preheat oven to 450° F.

Cook cranberries in water and sugar to taste, until skins pop; drain the berries and cool. Combine with the mincemeat, add the white rum and fill the pie shell.

Prepare topping by melting butter in a small saucepan, then off the heat add the flour and confectioner's sugar all at once, stirring until crumbs form; stir in pecans and sprinkle over pie.

Bake at 450° F. for 10 minutes; reduce oven heat to 350° F. and continue baking another 50 minutes or so. Serve at room temperature sprinkled with confectioner's sugar.

Cranberry Bavarian Cream

2 tablespoons unflavored gelatine
3/4 cup water
4 cups cranberries
1/2 cup orange juice
2 cups sugar
Pinch salt
1/4 cup lemon juice
4 egg whites
1 cup heavy cream, whipped

In a small bowl, sprinkle gelatine into 1/4 cup water and let soften 5 minutes.

Cook cranberries in 1/2 cup water and orange juice until skins pop. Stir in 1 cup sugar; cook 5 minutes on low heat. Remove from heat, add salt and gelatine; stir until dissolved and add lemon juice. Chill until mixture starts to jell.

Beat egg whites until soft peaks begin to form, then gradually add the remaining cup of sugar and beat until very stiff. Fold egg whites and whipped cream into cranberry mixture.

Here is another of my plan-ahead

Cranberry Bavarian Cream (cont.)

schemes. This amount will provide enough for two 1-quart fluted molds, each one serving 6 portions. I rinse each mold with cold water and shake, then pour in the Bavarian. When the mixture is frozen, I turn it out onto serving plates and a few hours before serving, decorate with whipped cream and a few whole berries from the spiced cranberry sauce. It will keep well in the refrigerator. In summer, I often serve it frozen.

Cranberry Sherbet

We enjoy this particularly in the summer season. That's one reason I always freeze cranberries.

1 quart cranberries
2½ cups water
2 cups sugar
2 *teaspoons* unflavored gelatine (less than 1 envelope)
½ cup orange juice
½ cup lemon juice

Cook cranberries in water until the skins pop. Put through a food mill, add sugar and gelatine softened in orange juice about 5 minutes. Stir over low heat until sugar and gelatine are dissolved. Cool slightly and add lemon juice. Freeze firm, then break into chunks and beat in large, well-chilled mixing bowl until smooth and fluffy. Work quickly, so the mixture doesn't melt. Pack into chilled plastic containers and freeze. 8 to 10 servings.

Glazed Strawberry Pie

1 baked 9-inch pie shell (graham cracker crust goes well)
5 cups fresh strawberries
1 cup water
1 cup sugar
3 tablespoons cornstarch
1 cup heavy cream
Sugar to taste

Wash and drain the berries well, leaving them whole. Arrange 3 cups of the berries in the baked pie shell.

In a saucepan, combine ⅔ cup water and the sugar and heat until the sugar dissolves; add the remaining 2 cups berries. Dissolve the cornstarch in the ⅓ cup water remaining and add to the berries with syrup. Stir constantly until mixture thickens; cool.

Pour berry glaze over berries in pie shell and refrigerate until glaze is set (I usually prepare this the night before I'm going to serve it). Top with sweetened whipped cream.

Königsküchen

The perfect cake to serve with Viennese coffee—strong black coffee topped with a spoon of sweetened whipped cream

¹/₂ pound butter
1²/₃ cups sugar
9 egg yolks
3 tablespoons lemon juice
2¹/₂ cups flour
³/₄ cup blanched slivered almonds
³/₄ cup chopped citron and lemon peel
²/₃ cup currants
³/₄ cup golden raisins
9 egg whites, stiffly beaten

Preheat oven to 350° F. and thoroughly grease a 10-inch tube pan or turkshead mold of equal capacity; dust with flour.

Cream butter and sugar together, add egg yolks one at a time, beating well after each addition; then add lemon juice. Mix in flour gradually, then fold in nuts and fruit, stirring until well distributed through the batter. Fold in stiffly beaten egg whites, folding only enough to blend.

Spoon the batter into pan and bake for about 2 hours or until a cake tester comes out clean. Allow to cool for a few minutes on a wire rack, then invert on the rack and remove from the pan. This cake improves with standing and should not be served until the next day. Dust, if desired, with powdered sugar.

Lemon Cake Pudding

One of my childhood favorites, proved by Mother's comment when she wrote out the recipe for me, "Serves 4—3, the way you like to eat it!"

2 eggs, separated
1 cup sugar
1 tablespoon flour
Pinch of salt
Grated rind and juice of 1 lemon
2 tablespoons butter, melted
1 cup milk

Preheat oven to 350° F.

In a large mixing bowl, beat the egg yolks well. Blend sugar, flour and salt and add to egg yolks. Then add lemon juice, rind, butter and milk; beat well. Beat egg whites until stiff, then fold into batter. Bake in buttered baking dish set in a pan of hot water for 40 minutes. Serve warm or chilled. This cake has a very delicate sponge on top, with a lemon sauce beneath, after it is baked.

Lemon Velvet

An especially good ending for fish or a spaghetti dinner.

2 eggs
¹/₂ cup sugar
¹/₂ cup white corn syrup
2 cups light cream
¹/₄ cup lemon juice

Lemon Velvet (cont.)

Beat eggs until very thick; continue beating as you add sugar gradually. Beat until lemon colored and light, then add corn syrup, light cream and lemon juice and mix thoroughly. Freeze firm in refrigerator tray.

Set large mixing bowl in freezer to chill thoroughly. Break up the frozen mixture into chunks, turn into chilled bowl and beat until smooth and fluffy with electric beater. Pack quickly into chilled tray or freezer carton and freeze firm. Serve with fresh blueberries or strawberries in season or garnish each serving with one or two frozen strawberries for winter service.

A delicious variation can be made by substituting lime for lemon, adding a bit of grated lime rind and tinting a delicate green with a drop or two of food coloring.

Ricotta-Rice Pie

I like this pie because it is light, packed with vitamins and minerals and needs no separate crust.

3 large eggs
³/₄ cup sugar
1 teaspoon vanilla
1¹/₃ cups milk
1 pound ricotta cheese
2¹/₂ cups cooked rice
¹/₂ teaspoon cinnamon
Freshly grated nutmeg

Preheat oven to 350° F. and butter a 10-inch glass pie plate.

In a large mixing bowl, beat the eggs; gradually beat in the sugar and blend in the remaining ingredients, except nutmeg. Pour into pie plate and sprinkle top with a fresh grating of nutmeg.

Bake for 1 hour, or until knife inserted comes out clean. Serve at room temperature. (If you have any of the filling left after you've poured it into the pie dish, butter 1 or 2 custard cups and fill them; bake them along with the pie, checking after 30 minutes.)

Southern Sweet Potato Pie

This is somewhat of a sweet dessert, but I never feel guilty eating it because the sweet potatoes are chock-full of vitamin A.

1 9-inch pie crust, unbaked
2 eggs
¹/₂ cup light brown sugar, firmly packed
1³/₄ cups milk
1 teaspoon ground cinnamon
¹/₂ teaspoon ginger
Pinch salt
2 cups sweet potatoes, steamed and mashed
2 tablespoons unsalted butter, melted
Fresh grating nutmeg

Southern Sweet Potato Pie (cont.)

Preheat oven to 450° F. and line a 9-inch pie plate with any crust; crimp the edges.

In a large mixing bowl, beat the eggs, then beat in the sugar. Stir in the milk, cinnamon, ginger and salt; fold in the mashed potatoes with the melted butter. Pour into prepared pie shell and sprinkle with a fresh grating of nutmeg.

Bake at 450° F. for 10 minutes; reduce heat to 350° F. and continue baking another 50 to 60 minutes, until set.

Viennese Nüsstorte

2 cups walnuts, finely ground
1 cup unblanched almonds, finely ground
1 tablespoon ground coffee
Vegetable shortening
Dry bread crumbs
6 egg yolks
1 tablespoon lemon juice
1⁷/₈ cups powdered sugar
6 egg whites, stiffly beaten with a pinch of salt
Tart orange marmalade
1 pint heavy cream
Perfect walnut halves for garnish

Preheat oven to 350° F. Using a rotary-type grater or food processor, grate or grind the nuts and lightly spoon into a cup to measure. Blend in the coffee and set aside.

Prepare two 8-inch layer pans by greasing first with vegetable shortening, then fitting in waxed paper rounds to cover the bottoms of the pans. Cut strips of waxed paper to fit around the sides of the pans. Grease the waxed paper linings lightly but completely, then dust with fine dry bread crumbs so the entire inside of the pans is coated. Actually, this is the most work in the entire cake, but there are no successful shortcuts. I know, for I've tried.

Beat egg yolks with lemon juice and sugar until very thick and lemon colored. In a separate bowl, beat egg whites until stiff. Place the egg whites atop the egg yolk mixture, sprinkle ¹/₃ of the ground nuts on top and begin to fold the whites into the yolks with a few folding strokes. Repeat with another portion of the ground nuts, continuing to fold gently. Do the same with the remainder of the nuts and continue to fold *only* until the batter is blended. Gently turn or spoon batter into the prepared pans.

Bake about ¹/₂ hour. When the top springs back when touched lightly, the torte layers are done. Cool on wire racks for a minute or so, then invert and remove from pans. Carefully peel off waxed paper so as not to disturb crumb crust. I usually do this much preparation several days before a party and freeze the carefully wrapped layers until an hour or so before my guests are to arrive.

To finish the cake, place the bottom layer on your prettiest cake plate, spread with tart orange marmalade (English, if you can find it), then swirl on whipped cream slightly sweetened with sugar and vanilla. Place the second layer on top and frost the entire cake with whipped cream. Decorate the top with perfect walnut halves and chill in the refrigerator until ready to serve.

Wine Jelly with Grapes

1 envelope unflavored gelatine
¹/₄ cup cold water
¹/₂ cup boiling water
¹/₂ cup sugar
¹/₄ cup orange juice
1 tablespoon lemon juice
³/₄ cup sherry, port or Madeira wine

Soften gelatine in cold water, dissolve in boiling water. Add sugar and stir until dissolved. Add remaining ingredients, mix well and pour into wet molds. Chill until set.

Garnish with small bunches of grapes "frosted" by brushing with slightly beaten egg white and sprinkled with fine granulated sugar and set to dry thoroughly.

INDEX